▸▸▸▸▸▸▸▸▸▸▸▸▸▸

"I started this [...] **finished at 6 A.M. (she ruined my day!) But she's High Speed Janice, spirit triumphant."**
LAUREN HUTTON

During the 1970s, lush-lipped, long-stemmed, dark-eyed brunette Janice Dickinson broke the long chain of all-American blondes to become the world's first "supermodel"—a phrase she herself coined—gracing the cover of every major magazine from *Vogue* to *Cosmopolitan*.

In this unadulterated memoir, she tells her incredible story, filled with dizzying highs and lows—from the cruelty and abuse of her childhood to the money, power, and fame of her stardom; from her glory days with Gia Carangi and Christie Brinkley to nights with Warren Beatty, Jack Nicholson, and Sylvester Stallone; from a dizzying drug-and-alcohol habit to three failed marriages; from cavorting around the globe to struggling to make it in Los Angeles as a working mom.

Following her precarious ascent to stardom, her notorious fall from grace, and her triumphant journey to recovery, this captivating and cautionary tale reveals the smart, passionate woman beneath the glossy photos—and strips bare the business that made her a legend.

"Janice Dickinson is a funny and fluid narrator . . .
what makes [her book] interesting
is her scathing inventory
of everyone's desperate behavior, including
her own . . . She's like all forces of nature—
you take them on their own terms."
New York Observer

"Dickinson has managed to take what life has offered
and work it . . . what keeps the book from
becoming too tawdry is Dickinson's sense of humor."
Women's Wear Daily

"She's a brilliant model, the best ever, I think. She will
be talked about for as long as modeling exists."
Tara Shannon, model

"Entirely real . . . it is the honesty with which
it is written that may drive you from
beginning to end in a single sitting."
The Independent

"I love Janice. She is crazy, unbearable, flamboyant,
excessive—but she is true. There must be a reason
she's been able to survive all her excesses:
some kind of guardian angel who was moved by
her difficult trials, her profound generosity,
her truthful speech, and her lack of arrogance."
Jean-Jacques Naudet

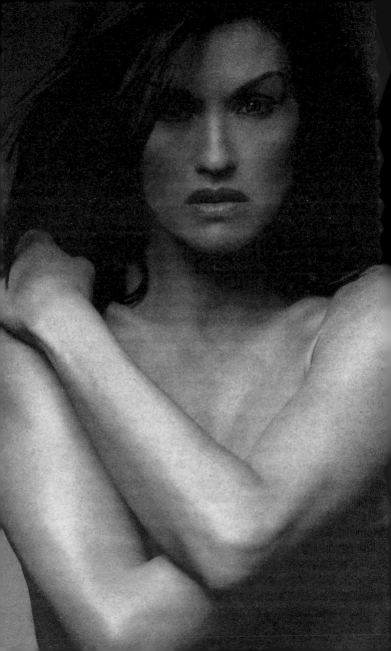

NO LIFEGUARD

THE ACCIDENTAL LIFE OF THE
WORLD'S FIRST SUPERMODEL

ON DUTY

JANICE DICKINSON

ReganBooks
HarperEntertainment
An Imprint of HarperCollinsPublishers

All photographs are courtesy of Janice Dickinson except: **Cover:** Front cover photo by Arthur Elgort; **Insert:** Photographs on pages 1, 2, 3 (bottom, first and second photographs from left) by Mike Reinhardt; photograph on page 3 (bottom, third from left) by Francesco Scavullo; photograph on page 3 (bottom, fourth from left) by Hiro; photograph on page 4 by Arthur Elgort; photograph on page 5 by Stan Malinowski; photograph on page 4 by Peter Beard.

Text: Photograph on page iv by Davis Factor; photographs on pages viii, 119, 121, 145 by Mike Reinhardt; photograph on page 302 by Antoine Verglas.

HARPERENTERTAINMENT
An Imprint of HarperCollins*Publishers*
10 East 53rd Street
New York, New York 10022-5299

ISBN: 0-06-056617-5

HarperCollins®, ®, and HarperEntertainment™ are trademarks of HarperCollins Publishers Inc.

First HarperEntertainment paperback printing: October 2003
First HarperCollins hardcover printing: September 2002

Printed in the United States of America

Visit HarperEntertainment on the World Wide Web at
www.harpercollins.com

10 9 8 7 6 5 4 3

ATTENTION: ORGANIZATIONS AND CORPORATIONS
Most HarperEntertainment paperbacks are available at special quantity discounts for bulk purchases for sales promotion, premiums, or fundraising. For information, please call or write:

Special Markets Department, HarperCollins Publishers, Inc.,
10 East 53rd Street, New York, N.Y. 10022-5299.
Telephone: (212) 207-7528. Fax: (212) 207-7222.

For my children, Nathan and Savvy,
whose unflagging zest for life and humor
are a wonder and inspiration to me.
With love forever, your mom.

And
to my glorious sisters, Alexis and Debbie,
for showing me the way.

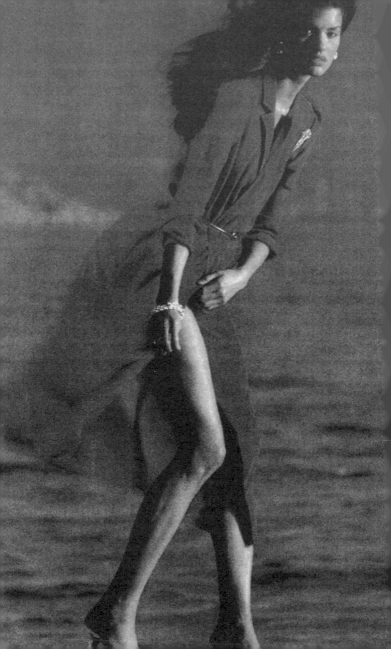

CONTENTS

ACKNOWLEDGMENTS

To:

Mr. Simon Fields and his devoted wife, the talented Melanie Apple. Thank you, Simon, for the greatest boy that ever lived.

Mr. Michael Birnbaum and family. Michael, thank *you* for the most precious jewel in the entire universe.

Christian Straub, for inspiration, whimsical genius, and all the love in this and the next life.

Mr. Thomas O'Sullivan, the Rock of Gibraltar.

Mr. Liam for structuring my words on computer.

Mr. John Pearson for continuously bailing me out of trouble.

For:

Cal Morgan, my undying gratitude forever for polish and sparkle and keeping it real. Thank you. Yo! P.Lo, the artist of artists, the real writer, that goes without saying. You're the Lord. Thank you. The entire staff at Regan-Books, especially Paul Olsewski, Cassie, Carl, Kurt, Joyce, Conor, Liz, Dan, Tom, and Evan. Last and first, to Judith Regan, the one and only. This book happened a long time ago and without your insight and vision it wouldn't have been possible. You were there all along. Thank you.

Thanks to (in complete random order):

Mike Cestari, the greatest screenwriter. Period. Odet Bahat for just being cool. Page Jenkins for his guidance and knowledge throughout the years. Michael and Randolyn Foster. The Thacker family, especially Susan for her guidance. Ted Field. My longest and dearest friend, Eric Salter. Lionel George, The Great. Barbara Malone and Reed. Djody Situan. Aida Thiabant. Suzanne Hughes. Ron Galotti. Tony Peck, for always being there. The Naudet family, especially Jean Jacques. Peter Knapp and Odile at *Elle*. Kodgi Toyoda for the most amazing hair in the world. Period. Leslie Kawamura. Yuki, Goro, and Chin. My friend Chad, who also does the raddest hair in the universe.

Dr. Jon Perlman. Dr. Steven Hoeflin. Dr. John Joseph for incredible Botox. Dr. Frank Ryan, surgeon to the stars and the Bony Pony Ranch. Dr. Uzzi Reiss and his lovely wife, Yael, for the delivery of both my children. Without you I would have been nothing, except a dead racehorse. My gynecologist's son, Jacob Reiss. Dr. Ed Kantor and Joe and Odette Sugarman. Dr. Mark Saginor; Dr. James Grotstein; Dr. Josh Trabulous; Dr. Cohen.

Howard Stern and Robin for keeping me going every morning since you've been on the air.

The Beverly Glen Pharmacy, especially Sue and Mark. The Beverly Glen Cleaners. The Beverly Glen Deli, especially George and Karen. Thanks for not spitting in the food. In loving memory of Rita from the Smile Skin Care Salon. Thanks for your warmth and kindness. Mr. Chris Smith at Sierra Leasing, thank you. Book Soup, especially Glen and Andrea. Robert at Solarium. L.A. Cellular phone; Alex and his spirited brother.

Azzedine Alaia. Donatella Versace. Paul Beck. Angelo. Valentino. Calvin Klein. Carlos deSouza. Diane Von Furstenerg. Michael Kors. Thierry Mugler. Jean Paul Gaulthier. Kenzo. Issey Miyake. Karl Lagerfeld. Chanel Chanel Chanel. Manolo Blahnik for my entire life's shoe fetish.

Richard Avedon and Justin White. Stan Schaefer. Stan Malinowski. Phillip Dixon. Veronique Vial. Albert Watson. Norma Stevens. Arthur Elgort and Marianne. Paul at Fleshtone Labs and his lovely Isabel Snyder. The Great Davis Factor. Mr. Gille Ben-Simon. Peter Beard and Najma. Bill King and Janet McClelland. Francesco Scavullo and Sean Byrnes. Hiro and Pieta at Hiro Studio. Patrick DeMarchelier. Michael Reinhardt for all your photography guidance and help with this book.

Lauren Hutton. Christine Peters. Jon Peters. Brooke Shields. Warren Beatty. Mick Jagger. Matthew Modine. Michael Fuchs. Steve Bing. He put the "R" in RICH. Mark Abell of Critical Mass. David Giler. Iman. Patti Hansen. Rosie Vela. Esme. Beverly Johnson. Cheryl Tiegs. Kevin Barry. Rene Russo. Jack Osbourne for his advice and the only Ozzfest tickets for Nathan.

Rod Stewart, thank you for Maggie May.

Muddy Waters. Way Bandy, the most incredible make-up guru ever. Suga, may you be wedging in heaven forever. Gia Carangi—a true light angel, not a dark angel as she has been depicted. John Belushi. Frank Zappa. Perry Ellis. Barry McKinley. Billy Tsutsos. Joe MacDonald. Paul Gobel. Gianni Versace, may you forever rule. Ariella. May you all rest in peace.

Harry King. Sandy Linter. George Pipisick and Santa Monica Bodybuilding. Thank you for keeping my ass off the back of my kneecaps. The Pain Management Clinic, especially Dr. Tom Marinaro. Judy Townsend. Wendy Gralnick. Monique Pillard, for her years of service. Patrice Casanova. Jacques Malignon. Guy. Dominique and Jacques Silverstein. Lorraine Bracco. Ron Levy. Jeanne Damon-Levy. Al Gersten. Jon Sahag.

Russ, Cynthia, and Shannon Berri. The Haskell Family. Grace and Matthew Morton. Linda Wells. Suzanne

Schwartz at *Glamour*. Diana Vreeland. Grace Coddington. Anna Wintour. Andre Leon Talley. Myrna Blyth and Alanna. Phillipe from Ford Models. Lois Joy Johnson and Thea. The Elite Agency, N.Y. and L.A. Katie Herrera for not stealing my underwear. Mr. Ish Moran at Maha Yoga. Rita of Rita Flora. Pepe and Clarissa Moreno and family. Freddy Leiba. Maury Hopson. Ben Dickinson. Alec Sorkin. Adam Glassman.

Jimmy Rip, who got me sober, thank you with all my heart and life. Rick O'Shea (aka Mark Abramson) for being the most fabulous PR guru in the universe. Mr. Edward Tricomi. Steve and Michel Kerner. Mr. Harry Sloan. Miss Morgan Brown and Will. My entire Polish family. Daniella and Fabio Belotti. Dr. Francesco Colombo. Edwardo and Hilde Poli. Bill Bloch. Francesco Gamero and Eli Rivera at You-Wash Doggy. Lydia Umano. Marie Scoedeller. Chris Royer. Jon Fawcett and the guys at 76th Station. Anne Kelly for skin. Kevin Barry. Chad, for taking over where Way Bandy and Kevin Aucoin left off. Suzy Weiss. Tracy Tweed. Bruno and Winston. Dave and Raphael. David Giler. Deborah Wachine.

Thank you to Vicky Felmar, Liza Sperling, and the Warner Star Program for keeping my daughter truly balanced. Thank you to all of the aftercare at the school, the Warner Avenue teachers, and the Warner Avenue School. The Curtis School. Mont Clare Prep School. Mrs. Terada. Lori Saunders. And Mrs. Kirshner. The Ungers, Mulberry Street Pizza, and Mr. Richie Palmer for the best slice this side of the Mississippi River. Broadway gym for lending expertise and gymnastics knowledge and support to Savvy and all the kids on Saturday mornings.

Thanks to AA and everyone who ever walks through the door for allowing me the true support (notwithstanding the *Wonderbra*), solution, encouragement, and hope.

I want to salute every gay man that I tried to seduce. Thank you for letting me down easy. I want to thank lesbians everywhere. May the LAP LAP 500 club continue to reign.

Last but not least, to Lina Perl, the sexiest bitch of all.

Due to the loss of brain cells left somewhere in a jar, if I've forgotten anyone, thank you to you.

P.S. I can't wait for book #2! Read on . . .

PROLOGUE

Tried to run, Tried to hide
Break on through to the other side

Hollywood, Florida. February 28, 1969. I am going out of my head. It is ten o'clock at night and I am lying in bed and I hear my father's footfalls on the stairs. They are getting louder, more distinct. He reaches the landing and approaches and pauses outside my door. I hold my breath. He opens the door. I pretend to be asleep. I can picture him standing there, silhouetted against the dim light in the hallway. He hates me. The hatred comes off him in waves.

He closes the door. Moves down the hallway, to Debbie's room. He opens her door. I can hear the squeaky hinges. I hold my breath, praying he won't go inside. *Please God, please please please.* A moment later, he closes her door. He comes

**WALKING MY FIRST RUNWAY.
HOLLYWOOD, FLORIDA, 1957.**

back down the corridor and moves past my door again, toward his own room. I am so relieved I begin to shake. Then I hear him slow down. Stop. I break into a sweat and clench my fists to try to bring the shaking under control. He's outside now. At the door. He opens it. Takes a few moments . . .

"I know you're awake," he whispers, addressing the darkness. "I know everything." I don't move. I don't breathe. He closes the door, cackling to himself, and moves off. I wait for his footfalls to fade before I take a breath. I lie there trembling. I am fourteen years old and I am going out of my fucking head.

I'm up at eight o'clock the next morning, a Saturday. I am in the kitchen making breakfast for my father. He's upstairs, getting ready for the day ahead. My mother is still asleep. She's on the night shift at the hospital and generally doesn't get home before seven A.M. I prepare everything just so. His plate is perfectly centered. The utensils are laid out with military precision.

At 8:45 sharp, his eggs are ready. I wait, but not for long. I hear the door to the master bedroom opening and I set the eggs on his plate and rush back to the sink and drop the frying pan into the suds. He's on the stairs now, on his way down. I grab my stuff and rush through the living room and I'm out the front door before he reaches the kitchen.

I make my way down our street, already baking in the early morning sun. I have a ballet class to go to, then a long shift at the Orange Bowl, a local pizza parlor.

I look at the houses around me and think: One day I'll go home to the wrong house and pretend I live there. And nobody will say anything. They might be a little surprised at first, but they'll be nice people, and they'll understand why I'm there. They will make room for me at the dinner table. We will have a very pleasant time over dinner, making conversation and such, and after dinner one of them will show me to my room. I will brush my teeth and slip under the covers of my new bed and sleep like I haven't slept in years and years. In the morning, I will wake refreshed and happy, a new Janice. And after a few days it'll be like I've always lived there.

Before my ballet class I stop at a pay phone and call Bobby McCarthy. He is a senior at Nova High and has promised to try to score a pair of tickets to the Doors concert. The concert is tonight. I am in love with Jim Morrison.

Bobby McCarthy doesn't answer the phone. I feel like crying.

I make it through ballet class and hurry out to catch the bus and take it across town to west Hollywood. I am anxious. I am always anxious. I should change my name to Anxiety Dickinson. I am anxious about my little sister. My big sister. My mother. Myself. Life. I am anxious about what to wear, what to eat, what to say, how to breathe.

I get off the bus two blocks from the Orange Bowl and walk through the minimall and I'm there. I change in back, in the storage room. I can see the owner trying to get a peek at my ass as I slip my uniform over my head. I don't say anything. I go out front. It's early yet, but in Florida people like their pizza at all hours. You wouldn't think so, with the heat and all. But they do.

During a lull, I try calling Bobby again. I am on anxiety overdrive. If he doesn't get those tickets, I'll die. I know it. I have been thinking about this concert for eleven weeks. I've been living for this concert. It occurs to me that I don't have much to live for. Then I remind myself that I'm fourteen years old and that things might change. They probably won't, but they might. And it's all about *hope*, right?

Bobby is still not answering the phone. If he doesn't get the tickets, I'll kill him.

At four o'clock, my shift ends. Bobby hasn't called, and we have a long way to go if we're going—all the way to the Dinner Key Auditorium, in Coconut Grove—so I figure it's not happening. My life sucks worse than ever.

Then suddenly, *vrooooom*! The windows are rattling like crazy. Everyone turns toward the parking lot. Bobby's pulling up on his Harley. I can see him through the plate glass, which is thick with grease. He's looking dead at me, but I can't read his expression. He's giving me nothing. He's Mr. Poker Face. Then he smiles and flashes a thumbs-up.

I run to the storage room, grinning like an alligator, and put on my miniskirt and platform shoes; suede, with thick, cork soles. I look six feet tall. I am mostly legs, spindly legs and no tits. I'm in a red tube top—not that anyone would notice—and my hair's parted down the middle, just like Cher's. I look in the storage room mirror and I'm happy, *idiotically* happy. I am so happy I'm grinning *and* crying. I stop crying long enough to put silver glitter on my eyelids and then take another long hard look at myself and I tell my reflection, *You rock, babe.*

I rush outside and climb onto the back of Bobby's chopper and off we go. He drives like a fucking maniac. I don't care if we die. Just let it be after the concert.

The minute we get inside the auditorium, I lose him in the crush of bodies. I look around for a while, but I don't see him. I don't care. I am here. Then the lights flicker and the curtains part and some local band is up on stage and the lead singer asks us, "Can you feel the love in the room?" And everyone roars back in unison. Yeah! And then the band is rocking, warming us up, and people are passing joints around and taking off their clothes and communing with God or the Devil (depending on what kind of acid they're dropping).

And I'm working my way through the crush of bodies, toward the stage. Floating, effortless, as if it were my destiny. And then there I am and there he is: Jim Morrison. Right in front of me. So close I can see the sweat on his brow, the veins on his arms. And I don't know what happens, but suddenly everything around me goes black and deathly still. It's as if the entire universe has fallen into some bottomless abyss, gone forever—every living creature wiped off the face of the earth, except for Jim Morrison and me. He is just so stunningly beautiful. That shoulder-length hair, that square jaw. He looks like an angel. He's bathed in this angelic light, singing to me, looking at me, loving *only me*.

And suddenly I remember something I once read in a book, how there's supposed to be this moment in childhood when a door opens and lets the future in. And I think: *This is it. This is my moment. That's what I want.* No, not Jim Morrison. I want to be up there, on stage, bathed in that otherworldly light, looking like an angel. I want to be adored the way Jim Morrison is adored.

And then they're playing "Break On Through" and I lose it. Tears just streaming down my cheeks. And I'm thinking: *Please God. Help me break on through. I can't take it anymore. I can't take another day of this.*

MEET THE PARENTS

My father was a tall, slim, handsome man with a thick head of silver hair, buzzed flat, and gunmetal gray eyes. People liked Ray. He had an easy smile. A pleasant laugh. He was a good storyteller, a good listener, popular with the neighbors.

But I didn't often see that easy smile. Or hear that pleasant laugh. I saw, instead, the way his eyes changed color when he got angry, the whites glowing red. Or the way he balled up his big, freckled fists when he came after me, like a bull in heat. I hated him. I hated his eyes; his hair; that acrid breath; the wife-beater, Fruit of the Loom T-shirts. I hated him with every fiber of my being.

I hated my mother, too; hated her because she was numbed into oblivion with the pills she'd been prescribed for an old back injury. She would come home at the end of the day, *floating,* and she stayed aloft with the help of those lovely pills. She would glide through the house on a cushion of air, in slow motion, unaware, unseeing, her voice soft, her mind elsewhere, always smiling this benign Hare Krishna smile—like she was At One With God or something; which she was, I guess, at least chemically.

Those were my parents. So I ask you: My two sisters and I—what fucking chance did we have?

* * *

They met, appropriately enough, in a bar. My mother, Jennie Marie Pietrzykoski, was the eldest of nine children. Her Polish-born father owned a little pub in Plymouth, Pennsylvania, right next to the railroad tracks, and I guess she felt comfortable around booze. She went to nursing school in Manhattan, and at night she'd hit the elegant nightclubs with her fellow nurses.

One night, at a Midtown watering hole, some asshole came by to harass Mom and her fellow nurses. Ray Dickinson intervened, decking the guy and tossing him into the street. My mother and her friends were so grateful they asked him to join them. He looked good in his Navy uniform. He was a radioman. Mom couldn't stop staring at those gray eyes. Three days later they went down to City Hall and got married.

The following week they ran into the "asshole" from the bar. Turns out he was a friend of Ray's; they'd set the whole thing up to make my father look like a regular hero. My mother thought it was funny. I would have had the marriage annulled.

They got an apartment in Brooklyn, and I guess those first few months were pretty hot. My mother was a looker. She wore stylish pumps and blood-red lipstick—not particularly original, true, but it worked. She loved the camera and the camera loved her back.

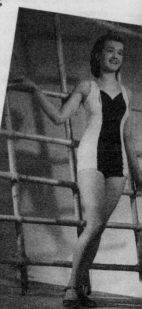

MY MOM,
JENNIE MARIE PIETRZYKOSKI.
WHAT A SET OF PINS!

Alexis came along a year later. She *didn't* love the camera. There's a picture of her I'll never forget: She's about five years old and sitting stiffly on my father's lap, and she has a look in her eyes that's a caught-on-film cry for help. He was already into her. I guess five was old enough. I don't know where that picture is today, but I've got it imbedded in my brain. I wish I could erase it.

I came along five years later. My mother was working as a nurse in Manhattan, already dabbling with prescription drugs, and my father was grumbling about his nowhere career with the Navy.

Now there was more bad news: another daughter. Ray was devastated. He'd been hoping for a boy and made no secret about it. I swear to God, I remember him hating me when I was barely a few weeks old. I know that seems unbelievable—I was way too young to be forming memories—but his hatred was the air I breathed from birth.

When I was just eighteen months old, in 1957, the family moved from Brooklyn to Florida. "Ray dear"—as my mother called him—had been tossed out of the Navy for assaulting an officer. He was going to start again, in sunny South Florida. Become Captain of His Own Goddamn Ship.

Only it never quite happened for him. He got a gig with the Coast Guard, but he didn't think much of those "pussies," so he ended up with the U.S. Merchant Marine.

He hated taking orders, but he loved the sea. And he loved the long trips he got to take. So did we. Life was different when he wasn't around. At night I'd kneel next to my bed and pray that the Seaman's Union would call in the morning and drag him off to some remote hellhole, where he'd fall overboard in a storm and get eaten by a shark. Alas, all my prayers went unanswered. Ray always returned to the family. He couldn't get enough of his family. Ray dear had a problem, see. He liked to be serviced. And with four women in the house, he felt entitled.

I was nine years old when he came to my room one night and told me we were going to play the *lollipop* game, a special game for a father and a favorite daughter. And— *We have a winner!*—I was that favorite daughter.

"This is the way it works," he said, his voice low, excited. "You see this? This is Daddy's dick. You rub it like this. You see how it's getting all rubbery and big? Watch. Go ahead. Touch it. You see how hard it's getting?" I was afraid to touch it, but I was more afraid of what would happen if I didn't touch it. So I touched it. It didn't feel like much. He came closer. "Now open your mouth," he said. He came closer and closer. I refused to open my mouth. "Are you going to disobey your daddy?" he asked. His voice wasn't low anymore. It was taut, strained to bursting. He pumped his cock, an inch from my face. "Didn't you hear what I said?" he asked through clenched teeth. "I said, *Open your mouth.*"

"I won't," I said. His left hand shot out with such speed and force that it knocked me clear off the bed. I opened my mouth this time—to scream—but he put me in a headlock and began to squeeze. I couldn't breathe. I thought I was going to die. I could feel his hot breath on the back of my neck. He put his lips close to my ear. "You ungrateful little punk," he whispered. "You're nothing to me, you know that? *Less* than nothing. You're trash. *You'll never amount to anything.* Some day you'll be on your knees begging guys to suck them off for a few bucks." He flung me across the room and I lay in a crumpled heap in the corner, afraid to turn around and look at him. I took a deep breath, and then another and another. My lungs ached. My cheeks grew damp with tears. I bit my lip to keep from crying out. I was afraid to make a sound, but my heart was pounding so loud in my ears that I was sure he could hear it, too. He was still behind me; I could feel him hovering there, staring at my back, wild with anger.

"Look at me," he said finally. I was afraid to disobey him. I turned around, slowly, my whole body trembling. His eyes were red, his features twisted in fury. "You ever say a word about this, I'll kill you."

That's a father's love for you.

On the surface, we looked like every other family in the neighborhood. Those Wonderful Dickinsons. Three adorable girls: Alexis, the bright, bookish one, with her fair complexion, reddish hair, and green-gray eyes; me, Janice, olive-skinned and exotic-looking, just like her mother; and little Debbie, the junior gymnast, blond and blue-eyed and always smiling. Such lucky girls, too. That devoted, hardworking mother. And that wonderful father—so deeply in love with his daughters. And so protective, too! God help any man who even looked at them funny.

Of course, most of the surrounding families had their own demons. Don't get me wrong; it was a nice neighborhood, block after block of Mediterranean-style homes with well-tended yards and terra-cotta entryways. Some with pools even. But this was back in the days when eighteen thousand dollars would get you the Ponderosa, and all sorts of people came up with the money—from drug dealers to horny single mothers to your basic Stepford families.

In short, it was a typical American neighborhood, with its fair share of typical American horror stories. And for a time I was convinced that the horror in our home wasn't all that horrible. How could it be? We had a beautifully manicured lawn, bougainvillea bushes, Spanish tile on the roof. Maybe there were worse things going on next door, right? And how bad was it, really? I had fought my father off and won.

One afternoon, though, I learned different. We'd just come home from school. Debbie was in the den, parked in front of the TV, watching *Gilligan's Island*—dreaming a little girl's dreams of escape. I was walking upstairs to dump my books and wash up and help Alexis get dinner started, when I heard something that sounded like an injured animal, crying for help. But we didn't have a pet.

I crept down the hall, toward my parents' bedroom. The door was open a crack. I held my breath and took a step closer. I could see my father next to the bed, and—as I moved in for a better look—Alexis, kneeling on the mattress, facing him. She was crying; whimpering. But I couldn't quite see what they were up to. I crept toward them, still holding my breath. One more tiny step—the floorboards creaked—and my heart all but stopped. My father was . . . I can't even go there. It was unspeakable, horrible. Alexis must have

ME AT THREE. NOTE THE
DIANA VREELAND DO.
➤➤➤➤➤➤➤➤➤➤➤➤➤➤➤

sensed my presence. She turned her eyes a fraction of an inch and saw me. Her eyes flashed: She was telling me to run.

I stumbled back to my room and puked my guts out, then lay on the cold bathroom tile, numb with shock. That's what I did. *Nothing*. Absolutely nothing. You can hate me for that if you want to. But you'll never hate me as much as I hated myself. I know, I know. I was only nine. And Alexis was fourteen. But I should have done something. Anything.

Still in shock, I washed my face and hands and went downstairs to get dinner started. Alexis appeared a few moments later. She wouldn't look at me. She began setting the table, ignoring my third-degree stare. I didn't know what to say. Her lower lip was torn.

"Your lip is bleeding," I said.

And she said: "If you ever say anything about this, he'll kill us all."

"Alexis—"

"Don't you get it, Janice?" she snapped, barely able to contain herself. It was scary: When she got angry like that, she looked like my father. "He's been at it since I was five."

I couldn't answer. For a moment, I couldn't *breathe*. What the hell was going on here? My father was already having his way with one daughter. What, then, had he wanted with me? Variety? A new flavor? What was he, a fucking *connoisseur*?

A few minutes later he came downstairs and walked past us, into the den. He sat on the couch and put his arm around Debbie, and, as easy as that, the two of them sat there watching TV together. Alexis and I got the meat loaf in the oven, made a salad, finished setting the table.

Alexis took a beer from the fridge and poured it into a chilled mug. She walked into the den with it, and he took it from her with a smile—a smile like a shark. "Thanks, kitten," he said. "You're the best." I looked down at my hands. They were shaking.

Half an hour later, just in time for dinner, Mom came home in her crisp little nurse's uniform, smelling faintly medicinal, like the ward, floating on her cushion of air.

And then there we were, the five of us, sitting around the dinner table, our heads bowed, saying grace, being grateful and thankful for the Good Lord's wonderful bounty and for His Great and Infinite Love.

And then we were eating. Father first, of course. The Goddamn Emperor. And almost immediately he would launch into his nightly litany: "Those porch monkeys! We ought to ship every last one of them back to Africa." Or: "Those rich kikes with their gaudy yachts! You know why they have such big noses? Because the air is free!"

Mother would just nod and smile, oblivious, and get up from time to time to go into the kitchen and dip into her not-so-secret stash. Anything to keep reality at bay. Alexis never said a word. Debbie would feel compelled to share with us every detail of the day's television experience. Gilligan did such and such. And wasn't Ginger just amazingly beautiful?

Me? I did nothing. I said nothing. I just looked at Alexis, my heart breaking. And at my father, wanting to kill him. I was nine years old. I could hear myself screaming at the top of my voice, but I was screaming only in my head. And when my father said pass the bread, I passed the bread. The dutiful, spineless daughter.

Saturday afternoons Ray would pile us into the car and drive us to Fort Lauderdale to look at yachts. We lived midway between the ocean, to the east, and the alligator swamps to the west. En route to the marina, there would always be an incident. Someone wouldn't be driving fast enough. Or too erratically. Or Ray imagined that they had cut him off—*deliberately.* And invariably this led to a confrontation. He would maneuver his way ahead of the offending car and pin it to the curb, then leap into the street and scream and gesticulate wildly, thoroughly terrorizing some poor, innocent person. But he was careful: His victims were always old and feeble and nonthreatening (no shortage of those in Florida). Because, hey—Ray wasn't exactly the courageous type. He would have fallen apart if one of them actually stood up to him.

We three girls would sit there side by side in the back of the car, humiliated, watching him let off steam. It was as if he *needed* it; without the outlet for his rage, he would have exploded. He was the ultimate rageaholic.

"Isn't he something?" Mother would say from the front seat, smiling and nodding and looking for all the world as if she'd been lobotomized. "Isn't he funny?" And I would think: *This can't really be happening to us. This can't be my real life.*

Sundays we went to church, hair neatly combed, clean behind the ears, dressed in our Sunday finest. Those Wonderful Dickinsons, all in a neat row in their regular pew, glowing, putting the long years of enforced Bible study to good use, the Lord's Light Shining Brightly From Within. Yeah, sure! I would kneel and beg God to please please please change things, to please please make our lives the way they were meant to be. But was He listening?

It had been almost a year now since I'd found out about Ray and Alexis, and for all that time I'd been desperate to tell someone about it. Mother would have been the obvious choice, but there was no lifeguard on duty.

There weren't any neighbors I could talk to, either. And no one at school. Plus I kept thinking about Alexis's warning: "If you say anything about this, he'll kill us all." What if she was right? What if I told someone and Ray went on a murderous rampage? With my luck, I'd survive, probably in a coma, and I'd lie in a hospital bed for the rest of my life, hooked up to all sorts of blipping, bleating monitoring devices, knowing I'd been responsible for the murders of my entire family.

Whenever I tried to talk to Alexis about it, thinking that maybe together we could figure out how to get help, she would turn on me, furious. She seemed to have inherited my father's propensity for rage—though of course *she* had the better claim to anger.

Once we were all tucked in bed, though, her rage gave way to pain. She cried every night. Long and contagiously.

One Sunday—an Easter Sunday, big day for Jesus and His pals—I heard her whimpering in her bed, trying to stifle her cries with her pillow. I got up and crawled under the covers next to her and held her close and tight. The ceiling fan was squeaking like a motherfucker. "I'm sorry," I said, whispering. I was overwhelmed with guilt. Guilt, terror, pain—these were words I understood. Love? Not a fucking clue.

Alexis stopped crying. Dried her tears with the back of her hands. Turned to look at me in the darkness.

"Do you believe in God?" she asked me.

"I don't know," I said. "I guess so." It was an odd question coming from her. She was five years older than me. Surely she knew better.

"I don't believe that bullshit anymore," she said. "If there was a God, why would he do this to me? What did I ever do to deserve this?"

It was a good question. And it made me wonder: *If there was a God, why didn't he give me the courage to stop my father?* Guilt guilt guilt.

Sundays after church we'd come home and get out of

our nice clothes and hit the mops and buckets. It was cleaning day. The girls and Mom and I ran around like a bunch of Cinderellas, making sure everything was spotless; Ray tended to the manly tasks—the leaky faucets, the squeaky hinges, the lawn. There he stood, gloating in his manhood, pausing now and then to step outside and wave and smile at a passing Stepford neighbor. *Look at me. Ray Dickinson. Hell of a guy, huh?*

Late in the day he would come around to inspect our work. "Is this dust here?" "There are streaks in the mirror." "I dropped a quarter on the bed and it hardly bounced at all."

He would pace, seething. He would look at each of us in turn, shaking his head, trying to impress upon us the depth of his disappointment. "When I ask you to do something, I expect you to do it right," he'd bark. "Shape up or ship out."

And we'd go back and do it again. And again. And again. Scrubbing the floors, dusting, washing and rewashing windows so that to this day I jump when I hear the squeak of newspaper against glass. "You're not finished here, girl," he'd say. "I'm seeing streaks." Grinning at me, that evil, lopsided grin. Daring me to say a word. Looking at me like he *wanted* me to sass him so he could beat my sorry ass.

And I'd turn around and try again and think, *Is this life?* It couldn't be.

And then I'd think, *God helps those who help themselves.* And I wondered what that meant. What did God want from me?

There *was* life outside the house, of course. And sometimes it actually felt normal; sometimes it actually felt *good*.

I don't know how I managed it; it wasn't until years later that I heard about something called *compartmentalizing*— the ability to close one part of life off into a separate part of the brain, a compartment, to avoid having to live with it. And I'm pretty sure that's what I did. I put the horror of home in a compartment and went out and tried to live a normal life. Apparently, it's quite common among murderers.

For obvious reasons, I spent as much time as possible away from the house. My best friend from the age of ten was Eric Salter. He lived a few blocks away, in a big place with a pool. He had very laid-back parents, stoned most of the time, and they let us neighborhood kids drift in and out of their home throughout the day. It's not like you could talk to Eric's parents, though; they were pretty self-absorbed, being high all the time. But they were decent and good-hearted. And they'd *smile* when they saw me. I couldn't believe it.

In 1966, not long after I turned eleven, Alexis ran away from home. She was only seventeen, but she'd fallen in love with a GI and decided to move to Monterey to live with him.

The day before she left, she took Debbie and me to the beach—Debbie, who was still so young—and sat us down and told us to stay away from Ray. "He's evil," she said. "An evil, terrible man. Don't let him near you, understand?" She wanted to say more, but the words caught in her throat and she began to cry. "I'll be right back," she said, her lower lip quivering. She stood and walked off down the beach, trying to pull herself together, getting smaller and smaller. I looked over at little Debbie. She hadn't understood a word. "Do you have money for ice cream?" she asked.

The next day, Alexis was gone. I was crushed. Ray missed her, too, of course. He wasn't getting serviced anymore. And the man loved his blow jobs.

At night, as I lay in bed reading or trying to sleep, I would listen for his step. I heard it now. The Monster was on his way to bed. I heard him reach the landing, heard him turning toward the master bedroom, heard him stop.

My heart beat like a motherfucker. He turned and made his way down the hall, approaching. His footfalls stopped outside my door. I couldn't breathe.

The door opened and I looked dead at him. He stood there staring at me. He smiled. He was trying to make it look like a warm, friendly smile.

"What?" I said.

"Why are you so hostile?" he said.

I didn't say anything. We stared at each other. He knew I'd kill him if he tried anything. Or die trying.

"You are an ungrateful, ugly little animal," he said.

I didn't say anything.

"You'll never amount to anything."

He took another moment, staring, actively hating me, then shut the door and moved off, toward the master bedroom.

You'll never amount to anything. That's a father's love for you.

The next day, when I came home from school, he was lying in wait. He sucker punched me the moment I walked through the door and kicked me when I fell to the floor. "How's the rabid dog?" he said. "Feeling any friendlier?"

He was standing over me. A giant. His freckled fists looked as big as baseballs.

"No," I said. So he stood on my stomach till I peed myself.

It didn't end there. This went on for weeks and months and years. I never knew what to expect when I came through the door, and the uncertainty was crippling. He knew it, too. For him, it was entertainment.

One afternoon, after a particularly vicious bout, Ray disappeared into his room and came back with his favorite gun:

a .357 Magnum. In a way, I was praying he would use it. Instead, he told me we were going hunting.

We drove out to the Everglades. Just the two of us. En route, he did most of the talking, and it was mostly about Alexis. "What do you think that little whore does with her boyfriend?" he asked, his lips curling with disgust. "You think she takes it up the ass? You think she's a backdoor girl?"

I was eleven years old. I didn't know what to say. I didn't know what he meant.

When we got out to the Everglades, I told him I didn't want to hunt. That was fine with him. He made me climb into the trunk of the car and locked me in. I lay there in the dark and peed myself again. It was getting hot, and I had trouble breathing, and at some point I passed out.

When I regained consciousness, hours later, I found myself on the ground, next to the car, his big face hovering over mine—full of concern. It was the first time I'd seen him worried over my welfare. And the reason was obvious.

"Jesus Christ," he said. "I thought you'd gone and died on me!" He slapped me. "You crazy little punk. You ever do that again, I'll kill you." I am not making this up.

Not to put too fine a point on it, but I was a fucking mess. I'd go over to Eric's house and get stoned. When we were bored, we'd go to the music stores in town. I was a great little shoplifter. Eric would wait outside, trying not to panic; then we'd run home with the stolen LPs and drink and get high and crank up the volume and dance.

Eric was a great dancer. He was gay and knew it by the time he was thirteen. Nova Junior High, in Fort Lauderdale, was crawling with cute boys, and Eric loved pointing out the ones he liked. "I'd do him," he'd say with false bravado. He didn't even know what "doing" someone meant. Neither did I, really. Well, okay—we had a fair idea, but we were both virgins.

I liked this boy called John Burnett. He was always smiling, like he didn't have a care in the world. I look back on it now and realize it was all about self-confidence—something I could have used in spades. Whenever I saw him, in the hallway, between classes, or in line at the cafeteria, I'd hide. I know it sounds corny, but I felt such intense longing for him that it would bring tears to my eyes. I was starving for affection. I had *heard* all about love—it was out there somewhere—and I wanted it pretty bad.

Unfortunately, I was pathologically shy. Or maybe—having seen what I'd seen at home—I was terrified. Every time John came over to talk to me, I'd run off in a panic. He finally gave up, of course. I was crushed, in a funk for weeks. I thought I was worth fighting for. To this day, John

AT SIXTEEN WITH TWIN BOYS WHOM I LOVED THEN BUT CAN'T REMEMBER NOW.

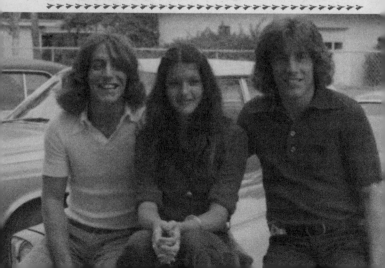

has no idea how much he hurt me. But of course it wasn't him; it was me.

The following year, at the ripe old age of fourteen, Eric finally entered the world of sex. All of a sudden, he was doing all these cute guys, and every last one of them was straight. He *loved* straight guys. He once told me that one of the great tragedies of being a gay man is that you aren't really attracted to other gay men. "It's *real* men you're after," he explained. "And if you keep after them, they'll fuck you. But they won't stick around."

Eric loved sex. He claimed to give the best head south of the Mason-Dixon, and he enjoyed describing his technique in detail: This is how you hold the shaft. This is how you flick your tongue. This is how you keep things nice and wet.

I would get hot just listening to him. But I was confused. I'd seen that done in my own home, and it didn't look like fun.

One afternoon, both of us stoned and lying half-naked by his pool, I almost told Eric about my father. But I was afraid—more for him than for myself. Eric was oddly brave. He didn't take shit from anybody. And he was very fair-minded, as if he understood morality at a very early age. He always knew the right thing to do. Which is exactly what frightened me: I could imagine him picking up a gun and going back to my house and shooting my father dead. Talk about confrontation! Suddenly, I really wanted to tell him. "Eric . . . " I said.

"What?" he said.

I looked at him for a beat. "Nothing," I said. "I'm glad you're my friend."

My two best girlfriends in high school were Maria Romano and Jill Jensen. We would drive up and down the Florida coast, hanging out at the lesser-known surfing beaches, listening to Hendrix, the Stones, the Doors, and going through endless packs of Kools. I dropped my first Quaalude with those two, and I was hooked instantly. I liked 'ludes a lot better than pot. I liked the way they took the edge off life, mellowed you out. Life became bearable under their influence, and I always felt a little blue when the effects began to wear off. I also did a couple of half-hits of acid with them, but I was wary. We'd all heard stories about kids who thought they could fly, or thought they were turning into orange juice, and—bad as things were—I wasn't ready to check out.

Still, one afternoon, sitting on the beach with Maria and Jill, the three of us nursing beers, watching the surfers go by, waiting for our LSD to kick in, a strange thing happened. As I brought the beer to my lips, I saw my reflection in the can. Only it wasn't me staring back at me. It was my mother. I know it was just the drugs, but still . . .

That's when I decided I had to buy a car. Behind the wheel, I could put a lot of miles between me and the rat bastard. He'd never find me. I could drive clear across the country, maybe go to Monterey and hook up with Alexis and her boyfriend. I'd stop now and then to wait tables for gas money and sleep in my car if I had to. It wouldn't be so bad. I could get to work early and wash up before my shift. There were Laundromats everywhere. I knew I could make it. I'd be free! I'd be safe!

I got work, locally, the following week. I lied about my age—I used Alexis's ID—and got a gig making pizza at the Orange Bowl. It didn't take long to figure out Rule #1 of the food-service industry: the shorter the skirt, the better the tips. Needless to say, I made out like a bandit. Men! When a guy thinks he might get lucky, he'll put his pay-check on the table.

Eric used to come in with this friend of his, Vinny Mangione. He was a poor man's Jim Morrison. He had that swagger, that coolness. One night, when the boss was out running errands, Vinny bet me twenty bucks that I wouldn't get up on the counter and dance. He lost. All the guys in the place started cheering and throwing money. I cranked up the music. One fat guy started yelling, "Take it off! Take it off!" And the others took up the chant. I've gotta tell you, I was tempted. But then I looked over at Eric. He shook his head from side to side, almost imperceptibly.

Bobby McCarthy used to come in a lot, too. He was eighteen and had just graduated from high school, and he had his heart set on becoming an FBI agent. Don't ask me why. He was smart and wonderful and had beautiful blue eyes, and I think he was in love with me. He was a good kisser. We would kiss for hours, but that's as far as it went. Sometimes he'd try to force my hand toward his crotch, but I refused to touch him there. (I couldn't even say the word *penis* in those days!) He'd get pretty pissed, but that didn't change things. He wasn't going to get lucky. Not just yet, anyway. I wasn't giving it up at fourteen. I wasn't thinking about sex in those days, anyway. At least not with any joy.

What I was thinking about most, to be honest, was getting the hell out of Florida. I was miserable and Bobby knew it—though of course he didn't know why. And I couldn't tell him. I couldn't tell anyone. At one point I remember thinking that maybe the Dickinsons were normal; that this went on up and down the streets of Every City, U.S.A.; that all fathers were *entitled*.

It was right around this time that we heard the rumor about Jim Morrison. He was coming to South Florida. By the time I had scraped enough money together for a ticket, they were sold out. I was crushed.

A few nights later, Bobby came by on his motorcycle and gave me a ride home. I was so depressed I didn't even feel like necking. I told him I'd had my heart set on seeing Jim Morrison, and I began to cry. I know, I know. It sounds pathetic. But of course it wasn't really about Jim Morrison, but about what he represented.

So Bobby came through for me and we went to the concert and I had my weird out-of-body experience or whatever the hell it was, where Jim and I were the last surviving beings on Planet Earth. And I remember thinking, *The only thing standing between Jim and me are his leather pants.* And then I emerged from my altered state to find that things had taken a nasty turn. Morrison was drunk and getting drunker. He became increasingly antagonistic. He started shouting obscenities at *us,* his fans. The people who loved him.

Then the fans began shouting back and he got *really* pissed. He pulled those leather pants down and exposed himself. Next thing I knew, the cops were on stage, dragging him away in handcuffs.

It was so fucking confusing. This was my hero? This crazy hostile motherfucker represented *hope*?

CROSSTOWN TRAFFIC

❦❦❦❦❦❦❦❦❦❦❦❦❦❦❦❦❦❦❦❦❦❦❦❦❦❦❦❦❦❦❦❦❦❦❦

I spent most of that summer on a float in Eric's pool, with the music cranked to the max. I loved loud music. Loud music drowned out all the voices in my head. It kept the demons at bay.

Mangione would come over in jeans so tight you could read Braille through them. Yeah, it was pathetic, but I kind of liked him. He was an incorrigible flirt. He was always telling me how much he wanted me. And he said he'd wait because I was worth waiting for. Girls like to hear that kind of shit. Especially if they're as fucked up as I was.

That was the summer I met Pam Adams, who possessed all the security I lacked. I think she was related to John Quincy Adams. She had milky white skin and freckles and the most gorgeous hazel eyes, and I found her irresistibly beautiful. So did most of the guys at Nova Junior High. And she knew it; she'd slept with plenty of them. She did everything I wouldn't do. "I wish you had a cock, Janice," she told me once. "You'd make a great boyfriend."

She met Mangione and liked him. And one afternoon, at Eric's place, with the sun hot and high in a clear sky, and the place crowded with neighborhood kids, and my courage fueled, in part, by Pam's approval, I asked Eric what *he* thought of Mangione. Eric looked over at Mangione, who was lying in the shade, stoned. We had a head-on view of his prominent crotch. I was dead curious about that thing. I was curious about what it would feel like inside me.

"I would love to wrap my lips around that big cock," Eric said. He'd been trying for years, apparently, but it wasn't happening. He knew why, though. Or so he thought. His theory was that guys who know they're gay are always too afraid to get it on with other guys, because they realize there's no going back. "Once you've had me," Eric liked to say, "you're hooked."

By sundown, only Mangione, Eric, and I were left by the pool. Most of the other kids must have had real families. I didn't feel like going home. My father was away at sea again, and Mom was working the night shift.

Darkness fell, but the heat just wouldn't quit. Still, it was a sexy kind of heat, the kind of heat you see in movies: you know, the whirring fan, white curtains billowing in the breeze, the blue-green Caribbean visible beyond the deck. *Languorous* heat, I'd guess you'd call it. I know that's how I was feeling. Languorous. And I guess Mangione was feeling it, too. Only he'd probably call it *horny*.

When Eric went into the house, Mangione turned to look at me. "You have the sweetest, tightest little ass I've ever seen," he said.

My Little Flower tingled. I called it my Little Flower because that was the name of the Sunday school I'd been packed off to when I was still too young to protest. They talked about God being inside you. I wondered how He got there. I used to think maybe He crawled in between my legs. So I'd put my little hand between my little legs and hold it there, tight against my damp Little Flower. And it felt good: God-like.

"That's right," I said. "And it's *my* ass."

Mangione just smiled.

Eric emerged from the house. He'd been watching us flirt for years and years and he must have thought we were pretty pathetic. But at that moment our unrequited passion was the last thing on his mind.

"What?" I asked.

He held up three tabs of windowpane acid. "Look what I found in my mother's stash," he said. We looked at each other. It was one of those moments. *Do we go for it?* And we did. (Parents, please note: Take your kids to the movies once in a while, especially on Saturdays. Most girls lose their virginity on a Saturday. And don't leave your fucking drugs where your kids can find it.)

The next thing I know, dawn is about to break, Jimi Hendrix is wailing on the stereo—"Crosstown Traffic," I think—and Mangione is wailing on me. On *top* of me. *Inside* me.

And let me tell you, it was *not* fun. Getting your cherry popped while peaking on acid is definitely *not* the ticket, girls. Trust me. I felt like my insides were being hacked apart with a machete. I was screaming, all right. But not for joy.

Mangione didn't quite get it, though. He thought he was giving me the time of my life. He was up there pumping, beaming, proud. *Take it all, bitch!* He thought he was taking me places I'd never dreamed of going. And he was right, but they were the wrong places.

You'd think the experience would have soured me on sex, but I knew sex couldn't be that bad. So from time to time, almost reluctantly, I tried again—usually with guys who looked a little like Jim Morrison. Things improved, sure— there was less pain, for starters—but where was the magic?

One night, the latest Morrison wanna-be took me down to the Hotel Diplomat to a B. B. King concert. I loved B. B. King. I had every album he'd ever made. I loved plenty of other musicians—the Doors, Otis Redding, Aretha, the Allman Brothers, Michael Jackson—even some of that nyaa nyaa nyaa music, but B. B. King ruled. It was an awesome show, made that much more electric by the piano player. He was this intense guy, the only white guy in the band, and the way he played turned me on something awful. *That's it,* I thought to myself. *That right there is what I call passion.*

We went backstage after the concert. My friend didn't want to but I got all pouty and manipulative and used my considerable charms to get past the security guard. In a heartbeat, I was introducing myself to the piano player. His name was Ron Levy, and he looked a little like Morrison, a Jewish Jim Morrison. Okay, call me crazy. But it's the truth. He looked more like Morrison than the guy I'd come with—and he looked a *lot* like Morrison.

Ron Levy shook my hand and wouldn't let go. I went all ga-ga. That fair skin, the baby fuzz on his chin, the Kool dangling from those moist, kissable lips. "Hey," he said. He looked me in the eye when he talked. And his voice was gentle and tender. "I'm glad you enjoyed the show," he said. "What'd you say your name was? *Janice*—I love that name. You from around here, Janice? You have time for a drink, Janice?"

There was nothing I wanted more than to run off with Ron Levy and have a drink and listen to his dulcet voice and fall into his bottomless green eyes. But I wasn't that trashy. I couldn't do that to my date. So I went back to Hollywood with my friend and pretended he was Ron Levy. It was nice, but I still didn't know squat about the Elusive Female Orgasm.

* * *

Back on the home front, it didn't take long for Ray to figure out that I was getting laid. The thing is, I *wanted* him to know—wanted to taunt him with it. You know the old joke: *What's the difference between a slut and a cunt? A slut puts out for everyone. A cunt puts out for everyone except you.* So, yeah—I wanted Ray to know that I was out there doing things that he couldn't even begin to imagine.

It pissed him off. And the violence escalated.

One night I got home after curfew; I was supposed to be there at 10:30, but it was storming like crazy and I could barely see to drive home.

"You're late," he barked. It was a few minutes after eleven.

"Look out the window," I said, unable to bite my lip. "That sound you hear is thunder."

Wham! He hit me in the face and broke my lip. He'd always been smart about that—no visible marks, no blood. But he got a little carried away, and suddenly there was that locked-in-the-trunk fear in his eyes again. He moved toward me and began to stammer.

"Get the fuck away from me," I said, snarling. "I'll go to the police."

He backed off. He was terrified.

By the time Mother came home my lip had started to swell. She couldn't help but notice, and all at once she began playing nurse. She took me upstairs and sat me on the edge of the tub and dabbed at the cut till it was clean. Tears were streaming down my face, but they had nothing to do with the torn lip. And she knew it. I mean, Christ— you'd think a normal mother would ask what happened. But she didn't ask. Because she didn't want to know; because she already knew.

After she finished what she was doing, we sat there in

the bathroom, face-to-face, quiet, saying nothing for the longest time. Finally she broke the silence. "I never noticed how amazingly beautiful you are," she said. "You are much more beautiful than any of those girls in the magazines you're always looking at."

It was the nicest thing she had ever said to me. And I just fell apart.

Those girls in the magazines. Okay, I admit it. I had my share of crazy childhood fantasies. I wanted to be discovered. I thought, you know, I'd be out at the mall and an elegant older woman would come up to me and say, "Hello, my name is Eileen Ford. I think you have what it takes to be a model. Here's my card. Please call me as soon as you can, and I'll send you a first-class ticket to New York."

Or I'd be working at the Orange Bowl, and Richard Avedon would come in with Lauren Hutton for a slice of pizza. I'd act real cool, like I didn't know who they were, and mosey on over to take their order. And Lauren Hutton would look up at me, and her jaw would drop, and she'd say, "My God! Richard! *Look* at her! Look at those gorgeous lips! This is it! This girl is the Next Big Thing!"

Yes, it's true. When I was sixteen, Lauren Hutton was my hero. I loved the way she sailed across the pages of *Vogue.* I mean, to use an expression of the day, she was *bomb-diggedy.* This was a girl who had survived her childhood in Florida and made it in the big leagues. I loved her face. I loved the gap between her teeth. I loved that mischievous look in her eyes. I loved her because she gave me hope.

And Richard Avedon, well—he was The Master. I think back on it, and of course I was only just beginning to appreciate his art. But there was something bright and clean about the images; the way he lit his girls; the way you felt they were literally staring back at you, smiling at you, telling you—*me,* in this case—that you were one of them.

"Do you really think I'm as beautiful as they are?" I asked my mother. We were still in the bathroom, facing each other. She reached across and wiped away my tears. I felt so fucking ugly my whole life. I was too thin and I had no tits and I didn't see them coming in any time soon.

"More beautiful," she said.

And I believed her. I *wanted* to believe her. By the time I was fourteen, I had probably spent a thousand afternoons on the cold linoleum floor of the local Publix supermarket, poring over the fashion magazines as they arrived. *Glamour, Mademoiselle, Vogue.* I was a fixture there. Me, little Janice, lost in those pages, my long spindly legs blocking the aisle. The magazines seemed thicker in those days, more substantial, like little phone books, and I studied them as if I were preparing for finals. All those amazing women! Cheryl Tiegs. Rene Russo. Apollonia. Gunilla Lindblad. Lauren Hutton. Yes, especially Lauren Hutton. She was paper thin, and not classically beautiful—like Grace Kelly, say. And even when she was standing still, she looked as if she were flying. And I would think, *I can fly, too. And I'm not Grace Kelly, either. And I'm as thin as she is.* I figured that I, too, could stand on the snowy slopes behind the Suvretta-Haus resort in Saint Moritz, in my fluffy beaver cap, my gloved hands resting on my ski poles, looking radiant and beautiful and happy.

I'd turn the page and see Catherine Deneuve in a St. Laurent tuxedo; turn it again and see Marisa Berenson in a billowy Bill Blass gown. *I can do that, too,* I told myself. I'd look good in a tweed suit by Coco Chanel. Or anything by Halston: I loved the way Halston layered fabrics; he could layer me anytime at all.

The thing is, I *had* to believe. I had nothing else. Modeling was going to be the way out for me. Without my crazy fantasy life, I was lost.

"The new *Vogue*'s in, Janice!" It was Doris, with her raspy voice. She was in her late fifties and had leathery skin and platinum, bubble-teased hair. She put in forty hours a week as a checker, and Friday nights she went off to play bingo with her friends. This was her life. "What is it with you and these magazines?" she asked. "You're like a drug addict." And I thought, *Doris, you don't know how right you are.*

The week after my mother told me I was beautiful, she took a morning off from work and said she had a surprise for me.

"What's the surprise?" I asked.

"It wouldn't be a surprise if I told you, now, would it?"

She told me to dress nice and helped me with my makeup, but she refused to tell me where we were going. I put on a form-fitting silk shirt with high-waisted bolero pants and platform shoes; *always* the platform shoes.

We got in the car, and I kept pestering her, and she'd just laugh and smile and say, "You'll see!" For a moment there I thought, *She's almost like a normal mother.*

And then we pulled off the freeway and she parked in front of a squat little building with a small sign out front that read, *John Robert Powers/School of Modeling.* I couldn't believe it. She really did think I was beautiful.

And we went inside and met the woman who ran the place, Dawn Doyle, a perfect little specimen, all poise and polish. She looked me up and down with obvious displeasure, like this was some kind of joke or something. But then suddenly—*ka-ching!*—"We have another paying client, people!" So she changed her tune. Smiled. Became pleasant and wonderful. Circled me two or three times. "Yes. Hmmm. I think wc can work with Janet."

"Janice," I said.

She smiled at me, a tight and venomous smile. She turned me around and indicated my reflection in the mirror. She tried hard to look pensive, to convey that she was thinking about how she was going to transform me. And I looked at my reflection, too. My hard little body. Bone thin. Visibly undernourished. Those raisin breasts. My huge lips. It was obvious she thought I didn't have it. And I hated her for it.

"Well, we have our work cut out for us, but I see a lot of potential here," she said brightly.

You don't know how right you are, bitch.

So, yes, I pursued the dream—as they say. Really threw myself into it. This is how you walk the John Powers Walk. This is how you apply makeup the John Powers Way. This is how you smile—from the inside, *deep* inside, even if you have to fake it.

The other girls in my class were about the biggest dullards I'd ever met in my life, but we all shared the same, immediate goal: to make it to the annual National John Robert Powers Modeling Contest, to be held later that year in New York's Waldorf-Astoria Hotel.

"You're going to win," Pam Adams told me. She wasn't at all interested in modeling—she wanted to be a writer—but she thought I was beautiful, and she knew I saw the fashion business as my way out. "You're perfect," she said. "Look at you. You've got long thin legs and beautiful stick-thin arms—you look like a plate of spaghetti. Plus you've got no tits. None of these girls have tits." It was true. *Haute couture* was made for girls who looked like young boys. "And you know what the best part is?" Pam added. "Once you make it, you can have any man you want." She was right about that, too.

I loved her for believing in me. I loved her friendship. I loved hanging out at her place and stealing prescription pills from her mother's medicine cabinet and getting high and singing along to James Taylor and talking about guys and where we saw ourselves in ten years. I saw myself in Manhattan, of course. Walking past a billboard of myself: a hugely famous model. Pam had different aspirations. "I see myself on a sailboat in the Caribbean, bronzed gold by the sun, stoned out of my fucking head, getting laid."

My mother had promised to buy me a ticket to New York when the time came for the contest, and for a few weeks she even remembered that fateful first morning at John Powers. "Someday you'll look back and remember that I'm the one who launched your modeling career," she said, smiling like a regular June Cleaver. But eventually the pills got the better of her, yet again, and she was gone, beyond my reach.

But not me. I was serious about modeling now. Now it wasn't just the girls I looked at; I looked to see who took the pictures. Avedon. Horst P. Horst. Guy Bourdin. Helmut Newton. Bill King. Scavullo. Irving Penn. Sometimes they even had little blurbs about the photographers. I was fascinated. I couldn't wait to meet Avedon. And I was sure he couldn't wait to meet me. I told myself that he might show up at the modeling contest.

"I'm going to need that ticket to New York," I told my mother one night.

She looked across the table at me as if she was trying to figure out who I was. "What?" she said. She always sounded like she was under water.

"That ticket to New York," I repeated. "The contest is at the end of the month."

"New York?" she repeated, the synapses misfiring. And then it hit her: "Of course. The ticket to New York! Absolutely. Anything you want, dear."

Later that week we drove to a travel agency on Las Olas Boulevard, and she paid cash for the ticket. "I thought you'd quit modeling," she said as we left the agency. I was clutching the ticket as if it were a lifeline. "You never talk about it." Of course I never talk about it, you bitch. You never *ask*.

"Could you drop me at the mall?" I said.

"Sure," she said. She didn't pursue it. That was my mother. She was relieved. She really didn't want to know. She was just making conversation, trying to get through the day. Life for her was about distance; she was happiest when she was disengaged.

I spent the rest of the day at the mall, looking for a dress. I had seen this little silk number in *Vogue,* and I wanted something like it. I found an outfit at Burdine's that was reasonably close. It had this little wraparound motif, with bold blotchy flowers, and it made me look a little Hispanic. I liked the effect. I knew I didn't look like most of those wholesome all-American girls in the magazine ads, but I also knew that no amount of trying was going to turn a little Polish mutt into a blue-eyed blond. And I didn't want to be a blue-eyed blond anyway. Nyaa, nyaa, nyaa.

Okay. I'm a goddamn liar. If someone had asked me then what I wanted to be when I grew up, I would have probably said: "A blue-eyed blond." I had a vision of myself, on stage at the Waldorf in midcontest, telling the judges and the assembled guests: "When I grow up, I want to be Cheryl Tiegs."

I knew I was going to love New York while we were still circling La Guardia. It was immense. Endless. A girl could get lost in New York. Lost so she'd never be found again.

I loved everything about it. I loved the noise in the terminal. The strange twanging voices. I loved the energy—the snap and crackle all around you even when you were standing still, with your mouth open, which I guess I was. I even loved waiting for my bags at the conveyor belt.

I loved the crush of bodies when we got outside. I loved looking for a cab that was big enough for Dawn Doyle and the three other girls who had flown up with us. I loved the ride into the city. I couldn't breathe. I couldn't talk. I loved my first glimpse of the Manhattan skyline, all aglitter in the afternoon sun.

"Why are you crying?" one of the girls asked me.

I noticed a huge billboard just ahead. A blond, all-American girl, twenty feet tall, smiling down at me, clutching some blond all-American soap in her blond all-American hand. I hated her. She looked like every other whitewashed Wonder Bread girl on every billboard in every city in the country.

"Because I'm going to win," I said.

We stayed at the Waldorf and I got lucky and ended up with a room of my own. I thought it was a sign, the beginning of great good things.

The next morning, after breakfast, a tour bus came for us. I piled aboard with dozens of other contestants. We were driven through Greenwich Village and SoHo. We had lunch at some Italian place that was crowded with Japanese tourists. We took the elevator to the top of the Empire State Building. We went to a ballet. Toured the Metropolitan Museum of Art. Visited the Whitney. Some of the girls were too cool for all this "culture," but not me. I loved every minute of it. I was on sensory overload. I thought I was tripping.

Right then and there I decided that I was going to move to New York as soon as I could. I even thought about never going back to Florida, but I didn't know how I'd swing it. So I concentrated on the contest.

I was so fucking nervous, but so were the other girls. We were just kids, after all. And we thought this was the Big Time. So we went through our paces, which involved mostly changing in and out of clothes and going out front and smiling and strutting our stuff for the crowd. "Next we have Susy Murgatroyd!" the MC would say, like he was announcing the Second Coming. Everyone would clap, including the judges, and Susy Murgatroyd would do her thing and hurry back and another girl in another little number would go out and do her best to sell herself and the dress she rode in on.

When it was my turn, I was shaking like a rosebush in a hurricane. But when I got out there, something happened. Those judges looked like a bunch of dirty old men. Telly Savalas was one of them. He had that Kojak grin going. I half-expected to see a lollipop in his mouth. What a schmuck! He looked like he was drooling.

So, yeah, I went out there and walked up and down the runway and just looked eminently fuckable. That was it. Simple as that. And I was good at it, too. Knew how to work it. I could *hear* the judges getting hard. Even the one female judge was getting hard.

Sure enough, I won the contest, but to this day I don't know what the fuck I won. *Miss High Fashion Model?* Explain that! They gave me this cheap little trophy with what looked like a brass penis on top. The judges hovered round, congratulating me, trying to get me alone so they could talk me into dinner, followed perhaps by a pleasant round of fellatio. I smiled a lot. From deep *inside*. And the next thing I knew I was back on the plane to Florida.

My father would come home and rib me mercilessly. "Hey, Cheryl, how you doin' today?" This was a reference to Cheryl Tiegs, the only model whose name he knew. "Where's your tits? Who stole your tits?" Or he'd say, "How many judges did you have to blow to win that Mickey Mouse contest?" God, I hated him.

I hadn't been back a week when he came home one afternoon with a black eye. He was in a hellacious mood. He went and got the phone book and looked through the Yellow Pages and called some fly-by-night lawyer. I could hear him raving about how he was going to put that "fucking nigger" in jail. Somewhere not too far into the conversation, the lawyer at the other end must have hung up on him. Even an ambulance chaser knew better than to deal with a lunatic like Ray.

He walked into the kitchen, steaming. I was setting the table.

WINNING *MISS HIGH FASHION MODEL.*

I looked up at him. He was staring at me like he wanted to kill me. "What the hell are you looking at, *Cheryl*?"

"I never noticed what nice eyes you have," I said, focusing on his shiner. I couldn't believe I'd said it out loud. But I couldn't help myself. His hatred was contagious.

He fucking pounced. The sonofabitch started hitting me and at the same time yanking at my pants like he was going to rape me. I was screaming at the top of my voice, fighting back for all I was worth. I kept swinging for his injured eye; I whacked him a couple of good ones, even knocked the bridge out of his mouth. But he kept coming. He was relentless.

"You perverted motherfucker," I shouted, swinging blindly. "I know why Alexis left home!" This really got to him. He grabbed my hair and pinned my arm behind my back and I thought for the life of me he was going to snap it at the elbow.

"You little tramp," he wheezed. "No more Mr. Nice Guy."

He wanted to kill me, and I wanted to kill him. But just then my mother got home and joined the fray.

Ray threw her across the room, and her head slammed against the coffee table and cracked open. Everything went still for a moment. Panicked, my father went over to see if he could do anything. She slapped his hand away.

I ran into the kitchen and hurried back with a roll of paper towels, but the blood just seeped through. I grabbed a handful of linen napkins and helped her to the car. Ray looked genuinely scared, just the way he had out in the Everglades.

I drove Mom to the hospital where she worked, Hollywood Memorial. It was the closest hospital to our house. She was holding a third linen napkin to her head, and it was already soaked with blood.

"How long has this been going on?" she asked me.

"It's not me, Mom," I said. But I knew she knew. "I never let him get near me. It was Alexis from the start."

My mother began to cry, but her sorrow was lost on me. Was it my job to comfort her? What I felt like saying to her was, "Where the fuck have you been all my life?" Instead, I didn't say a word.

A handsome young doctor stitched Mom up. He knew her from the hospital, of course, and treated us especially well. He said head wounds had a tendency to bleed like a motherfucker, though I believe he used the word *profusely*. My mother didn't say anything. This was her own hospital; this is where she had worked for a decade; these were her *friends*. But she couldn't bring herself to tell any of them the truth. She told the doctor she'd slipped and fallen. I stormed out in disgust. What hope was there?

I cooled my heels in the waiting room for half an hour. When she reappeared, she looked at me and said, "You don't have to worry about your father anymore."

I didn't know what she meant. I didn't say anything. I didn't believe her. I just got up and walked toward the exit and she followed me to the car. We drove home in silence. It was only when we reached the driveway and I cut the engine that she finally spoke. "I know I haven't been much of a mother," she said. I swear to God—if she had started crying, I would have strangled her then and there. To put that kind of shit on a kid. But she didn't cry. And we got out of the car and I said, "You're right. You haven't been much of a mother."

Still, something happened that night. I don't know what exactly, and I don't understand it to this day. But clearly she said something to Ray; maybe she had something on him, some evidence, something concrete. Maybe she even threatened to go to the police. I really don't know. All I know is that he pretty much stayed out of my way for the rest of the year.

And that's how I got through my senior year in high school. I told myself I was going to make it. I decided to believe that Real Life would start as soon as I graduated. And Real Life meant modeling, of course. Getting the hell out of Florida. And away from *him*.

I was still a fixture at Publix, still gleaning what I could from the magazines. Though of course now I'd added *Rolling Stone* to my reading. After all, models and rock stars—that was a hard combo to beat. So I'd sit there on the cold floor, whiling away the hours, dreaming, lost in those fantasy pages. The management didn't seem to mind; they knew me by name. Even the blue-haired Jewish ladies came over with their shopping carts and stopped to chat. "Hello, Janice," they'd say in their New York twangs. "How are you, dear? What's new? What's cookin'? Who's hot this month?"

Then I'd go home and preen in front of the mirror. "Yes, Mr. Avedon," I'd say. "I'm almost ready, Mr. Avedon." I'd sigh a lot, and suffer gracefully through my shoot—I was wonderful, almost painfully beautiful, a delight to work with—and as the day grew long I would have to beg off. "You'll have to hurry, Mr. Avedon," I'd say. "Hendrix is waiting for me at the Plaza."

Then I'd snap out of it and realize that it really *was* late and that the only thing waiting for me was my homework. And I'd buckle down and do it. Because I had to graduate. Nothing could stop me. I couldn't afford a single *F*.

That's when Wendy Gralnick came into the picture. She was this real smart Jewish girl with a pear-shaped butt and beautiful hazel eyes and the longest lashes I'd ever seen in my life. "So how ya doin'?" she said to me one day in front of the school lockers. "Me?" I said, pointing at myself. I couldn't understand why this brainiac would even bother with me. "Yeah," she said. *"You."* Suddenly we were studying together. And liking each other more and more. And of course I loved her for loving me and thinking I was smart, too.

I began spending less time with Pam Adams and less time with Eric and men in general—all that sweating and grunting, what was the point?—and more time at Wendy's house. It was a goddamn mansion, near the water. She was from a really rich family. Or *half* a family, anyway. Her father had been a hugely successful dentist who died and left them a small fortune. But Edna, her mother, was going through the money awfully fast—she had no self-control— and for years now her accountant had been begging her to slow down. Unfortunately, she couldn't help herself. And now they were in trouble. They were going to sell the house, Wendy told me. It was already on the market. And they were going to take the money and move to New York, where—thanks to rich kids with bad teeth—they had a huge co-op on the Upper East Side. I was so jealous I could've died.

I went home that night in a funk. Debbie and I got dinner ready and washed up afterward and watched TV till bedtime. Debbie knew something was bothering me. She kept asking me why I was so sad. I told her I wasn't sad, I was just tired. But just looking at her, at her perfect little body curled up on the couch next to me, made me even sadder. She was not yet a teenager, and already turning into a real beauty. I wondered how much longer my father would be able to resist.

The next day, after school, I was back at Wendy's house, studying for finals, when the phone rang. It was the realtor, calling for Edna. They had an offer on the house, a *good* offer. We could hear Edna in the other room, discussing it with the realtor. After a few minutes she hung up and came into the dining room. We had our school books spread out in front of us on the mahogany dining table.

"I guess we just sold this dump," Edna announced. "We're leaving this backwater as soon as school's out. We're going to New York."

I got tears in my eyes. I couldn't help it.

"What's wrong, Janice?" Edna asked.

"Nothing," I said. But she insisted on knowing and I broke down. The tears came in earnest now. Buckets of tears, rivers of tears. "You and Wendy are so lucky," I said. "I love New York. I wish I could move to New York, too." Hell, I would have stowed away on the Apollo moon rocket to escape the rat bastard.

"So come with us!" Edna said. Everything she said ended in an exclamation point.

"You mean it?" I said. I thought I was dreaming. I was prone to out-of-body experiences, after all.

"Why not? The place has five bedrooms. We used to be rich!"

And that's how I got to New York.

FREEDOM

We drove to New York in Edna Gralnick's big silver Cadillac. It was a Saturday, in mid-August. She pulled up outside at noon, right on time. Though of course I'd been waiting by the open front door since eight A.M., hoping she'd be early.

"Mom," I said, "they're here."

My mother floated out of the kitchen; she looked out the open door and waved at Edna and Wendy, then turned to face me. Debbie was at gymnastics class; my father had gone fishing. I hadn't said good-bye to either of them, not properly, anyway. I don't think Debbie wanted to believe that I was really leaving. And my father—he didn't give a shit.

"Oh, honey," my mother said, and tears welled in her eyes.

"Please don't cry, Mom. Everything's going to be fine."

"Promise me you'll be a good girl," she said, hugging me. "Promise me you'll go to church every Sunday."

"I promise," I said, and I grabbed my suitcase and ran down the driveway toward the waiting Cadillac.

Edna was a terrible driver, but she wouldn't give up the wheel. She didn't trust either Wendy or me. We entertained ourselves with silly road games, stopped at all the worst fast-food places, and spent two nights in motels. Edna taught me how to play poker. I only had fourteen dollars to my name, so I played aggressively. I won four bucks the first night, three the next. And I needed every last penny of it, believe you me.

And then there we were, in New York City. Lexington and 63rd. A regular goddamn palace! Five bedrooms. Marble bathrooms. How could I *not* make it, living in a place like this?

I kept thanking Edna and Wendy for being so good to me. I couldn't believe I was really in New York. What's more, it felt like home. I'd wake up in the morning thinking, *Here I am, where I belong.*

So, okay, it took a little getting used to. There were the garbage trucks that roared through the alley every other day at the crack of dawn; the crush of humanity on the streets; the honking horns and the squealing brakes and the lumbering buses that seemed determined to mow me down at every turn . . .

I walked everywhere. Me and my pathetic "portfolio"— four cheesy photographs of little Janice in the most amateurish poses imaginable. I walked like a speeding bullet, hyperaware, hyperanxious, hypertense. I loved the city but I was afraid of it, too. I would jump like a frightened thoroughbred when men hissed at me on the street, jump when construction workers whistled, jump if a man so much as smiled at me on the bus.

I carried my keys in my hand, with the sharpest one wedged between my fingers like a weapon. I'd read in one of the magazines that the streets were full of predators, and that one should always go for the eyes. And that's what I was going to do. Any man who fucked with me would regret it for the rest of his life.

Eventually, the fear began giving way to desperation. I had knocked on the doors of every agency in town, but nobody gave a shit. I was invisible. You had to be blond and blue-eyed and all-American to get any attention at all. And me? I was a Polish mutt.

"You're not what we're looking for," I was told.

"What are you looking for?" I once asked.

"Well, we'll know it when we see it—but you're definitely not it."

This does something to you. *Duh.* Beyond making me feel like crying, or beheading the fucking messenger, it fueled my insecurities—and they didn't need fueling. I was still that lost, cripplingly self-conscious kid from South Florida. People had no idea how hard I worked at appearing *normal.* I swear to God, I would wake up mornings and have to talk myself out of bed. *You're great, Janice. You're wonderful. You're smart. No, really. It's true.* And sometimes I even believed it. Sometimes I went *overboard.* Sometimes I'd swagger into the noisy streets of Manhattan, convinced I was the hottest thing in town. But not often. Not often enough. Mostly I felt like a goddamn pinball, caroming between emotional extremes—up, down, sideways, down the fucking drain—with absolutely no control at all. So, yeah—I was crazy. But I knew one thing for certain: I had a great body.

So one day I took that great body to a place on 7th Avenue that was advertising for a fitting model. The ad had been placed by a middle-aged Russian couple who were building up a little sportswear line. They had me out of my clothes within five minutes, and I spent the next two hours modeling those tacky little "casuals" you find in cheap stores in all the worst malls in the country. The husband loved pinning me, and he spent plenty of time in and around my crotch. Tucking, marking, straightening, *sniffing*. But hey, I was making seventy-five bucks an hour, a fortune in those days. They could only afford me for a few hours a week—and they worked me like a demon when they had me—but it was well worth it.

The rest of the time I concentrated on becoming a model.

People tell you to do your homework if you want to be a model. You're supposed to look at the magazines and how you might fit in and get to know your strengths and play to them. I'd already looked at the magazines; I had them goddamn *memorized*. I thought I was nothing but *strengths*; I thought I could do anything. There wasn't anyone who looked even remotely like me. I mean, there was Ginger on *Gilligan's Island*, if you were looking for nonblonds on TV. And I'd seen Bianca Jagger in *Rolling Stone*. She was pretty damn exotic. But even so, I was different. That's what made me special. I was an original. Then I got this horrible, sinking feeling that maybe the business didn't want an original, wasn't interested in what I had to sell. I was a breed apart, and maybe this breed was destined to *remain* apart.

It was driving me crazy. I had to fight that kind of defeatist thinking. I kept telling myself I was going to make it. Surely someone would see what I'd been working so hard at believing: that I was a fucking star, greatness personified. So I took a closer look at the magazines. At the fine print. At the names and addresses. And I bypassed the agencies and went directly to the photo studios.

"I'm sorry, dear. You'll have to go through proper channels. You'll have to get an agent first." No one was even vaguely impressed.

I was crushed. I tried to remind myself that it was just a business. That I shouldn't take it personally. That they weren't rejecting *me,* the real Janice. But I didn't even know who the real Janice was. And it *was* personal. Still is. Rejection hurts like hell. I began to think this was a pretty odd career choice for someone as deeply damaged as myself.

Of course, there were plenty of people who pretended to be interested the minute I walked through their doors. *Too* interested. Some of them would ask for money up front, which was a dead giveaway. Even *I* knew that was seriously fucked up.

The so-called model conventions were another big scam. Everyone had a convention coming up next week, out at a Holiday Inn in Long Island, say. There would be agents from all the name houses there, you were told, and plenty of famous photographers from all corners of the world. And *you* could be there, mingling with all those powerful people—for a mere two hundred and fifty dollars. I was tempted, but I'd heard that only the lowest of the low ever showed up at these things, and that anyone with a real foothold in the business wouldn't be caught dead within a mile.

I was getting pretty depressed. I was also hungry all the time. I ate the worst kind of junk. A lot of candy. Candy gave me energy. And yogurt for the protein.

Wendy, meanwhile, took a job waiting tables at a Greek restaurant. It was owned by an old friend of the family. We were both nineteen, but all she wanted to do was meet a guy and get married and never work again. And there were plenty of handsome single guys to meet at the restaurant.

Edna approved. "I don't understand girls nowadays," she said. "All this fuss about careers. It's so much easier to find a rich man to take care of you." Clearly, Wendy had had this idea drummed into her head since puberty. She was looking for a knight in shining armor. She wanted to be saved. Was that so wrong? I didn't know anymore. I just knew I was getting tired of pounding the rock-hard pavements of Manhattan. I was beginning to lose confidence in myself—and I didn't have that much to begin with. But was I ready to give up on the fantasy?

"Mom?" It was late one Sunday afternoon. I was beyond depressed. I'd called collect.

"Oh, hi, honey. How are you?" She sounded far away. She must have been trying some potent new drugs.

"Oh, I don't know," I said. And then the dam broke. I told her how frightened I was. How alone I felt. I told her about the miles and miles I'd logged on the crowded city streets, about feeling friendless and unimportant and completely anonymous. And I told her it was hard being broke all the time.

"Well, Janice," she said in her Hare Krishna voice. "I have to get dinner ready for your father. Be a good girl and go to church."

That's a mother's love for you.

But hey, terror is a great motivator. I was going to keep trying till I made it. I *had* to make it. And since I had nothing to lose, I decided to aim high.

Irving Penn's studio was on lower Fifth Avenue, in the

same building as legendary photographers like Bob Richardson and Bill King. One day I put on my sensible shoes, my less sensible *crepe de chine* top, and my red miniskirt, then hopped on the downtown bus. I walked right up to Penn's studio, knocked on the door, and asked to see the man himself. Alas, I was told—a shade less than politely—to make myself scarce.

I went outside and watched the world go by for a few minutes. I wondered when I'd start becoming a joke. I didn't think I could take much more of this. A person needs a reason to get out of bed in the morning, and marching from one end of Manhattan to another just to have doors slammed in your face is not a very good reason.

There was a big white limo parked at the curb. The driver smiled at me. He looked cool and comfortable. I was sweating and my feet hurt. My top was so wet by this point you could see the lace on my push-up bra. Maybe that's why the driver was smiling.

I was about to ask him if he minded giving me a ride— it was only sixty blocks to my temporary home—when he leapt out of his seat and got the door. I turned around just as Lauren Hutton emerged from the building. I couldn't believe it. She'd been upstairs with Penn, I figured, or one of the others, looking beautiful for the camera and making oodles of money. She smiled at me—that electric gap-toothed smile—and climbed into the limo. The driver jumped behind the wheel and pulled away.

I watched them till they were out of sight, kicking myself for missing an opportunity. I should have said something to Lauren Hutton. Then again, I probably would have stuck my foot in my mouth. *I'm glad you didn't get that gap fixed, Lauren. Smart move.*

I was so hot I thought I was melting. Some day, I told myself, I'd have an air-conditioned limo of my own. So

I'm shallow. Fuck you. I was tired and my feet hurt and I was this close to admitting defeat.

I didn't quit, though. My dogs were barking, but I kept walking. Uptown, to Richard Avedon's place, back down to see Penn again, with stops at all the photographers in between: Art Kane. Patrick Demarchelier. Stan Schaefer. John Stember. Bill Cunningham. Oliviero Toscani. Pierre Houles. Bob Richardson. Jean-Paul Goude. Scavullo. Jean Pagliuso (one of the few female photographers in the business).

But they were all out of reach. Their doors were closed—to me, anyway. I finally cried. I sat on a bench in Central Park and the tears just poured out of me. They were the size of walnuts. I could have drowned in those tears.

I wondered if I was approaching it wrong. Maybe what I needed was to *lower* my sights. I'd heard about a half-decent photographer who had a studio downtown, His name was Christopher Robinson, and he was listed in the white pages. I made my way over without so much as a phone call. It was a sixth-floor walk-up. I was winded by the time I got upstairs. I made a mental note to think about cutting back on cigarettes. The door was open. It was one of those heavy steel doors. I knocked and let myself in. It was a dump. No, it was *worse* than a dump. It was one of those places that intelligent people don't poke around in because it looks like a Hollywood set for a grisly murder. Me? I went in. I'm a genius, but I'm not always real bright about basic, mundane things. And I was a kid, for God's sake. A *desperate* kid.

Christopher Robinson was sitting on a couch, watching TV. He looked over at me and told me I was late. His assistant, Art, came out from the bowels of the apartment, scowling, then *he* told me I was late. And he was nasty about it.

My first impulse was to tell them both they were assholes, but I knew a lucky break when I saw one. So I apologized for being late and promised it wouldn't happen again. See? I told you I was a genius.

The assistant went off to set up the lights and Christopher cranked up the volume on the stereo. It was fucking deafening. I went behind a curtain and changed into the little outfit I'd bought for the modeling contest—that wraparound number with the blotchy flowers, one of the few decent things I owned—and came out and stood there in front of the lights and tried to smile. I didn't know what I was supposed to do. I didn't even know how to fake it.

"Well?" Christopher said. He had to shout to make himself heard above the Rolling Stones. I was frozen. "Would you fucking do something!" he shouted.

I posed. I *fucking* jumped. I looked like a frightened idiot. He snapped away and I kept posing and jumping, trying hard not to look as terrified and lost as I felt. Then all of a sudden a succession of crazy images began flooding my brain, images from my days on the cold linoleum floor at Publix, images from the magazines that had been such a significant part of my life. Models, modeling. Looking beautiful and regal and confident. Lauren Hutton, floating. *Not* looking terrified. And I tried to jump the way she'd jumped, and smile the way she'd smiled, and float the way she'd floated. And it goddamn worked!

"What the fuck is that!?" Christopher shouted over the din.

Well, what can I say? I *thought* it was working.

With no bus fare to my name, I walked all the way back to Lexington and 63rd. Edna was out and Wendy was working at the club, and for a moment I thought about showering and hustling on down to meet her for a drink and some companionship. But I didn't do it. I was bone tired; plus I was beginning to feel that I was wearing out my welcome at the Gralnicks. They hadn't said anything, of course. But these days when I'd come home after another fruitless trek through the city they seemed to look at me funny, like they felt sorry for me or something. I didn't want anyone feeling sorry for me. I could do that on my own, thank you very much.

There was an open bottle of wine in the fridge. I poured myself a glass and sat down on the couch and picked up the phone and dialed home. The rat bastard answered.

"It's me," I said. "Is Debbie there?"

"Is that any way to say hello to your daddy?" His voice was full of venom. How'd he dredge it up so fast?

"Dad, please. I'm tired. Would you put Debbie on?"

"What's wrong? Doesn't my Nile Princess have a minute for her loving father?"

Nile Princess. It had been a decade since he'd called me that. When I was a little girl, it was a term of endearment—a reference to my exotic looks and dark coloring. Now it was a nasty dig, another joke about this ridiculous attempt at modeling. He was laughing at me. He was asking, *Who the hell are you to think you can compete with all those gorgeous, blue-eyed blonds?*

"I have nothing to say to you," I told him. I was determined not to let him get to me. "Nothing nice, anyway."

"How's the big modeling career coming?"

"Great," I said. "Richard Avedon thinks I'm the Next Big Thing."

"I told you you'd never amount to anything," he said, then put the phone down and hollered for Debbie. I cupped my hand over the receiver and took a few deep, bracing breaths—the rat bastard knew how to hurt me—and Debbie got on the line a moment later. We chatted about school and gymnastics, and she told me all about a cute guy in her class. I listened for clues. I knew Debbie so well that I was confident I'd catch even the smallest hint of trouble in her voice. But she seemed to be doing fine. Then she had to go—there was something on TV—and she told me she loved me and hung up.

I finished my wine and sat there in the growing darkness for the longest time, listening to the muted roar of the city. When I'd left for New York six months earlier, my biggest concern was leaving Debbie in Florida with the rat bastard. But I didn't have a choice. Well, I *did,* I guess; life is all about choices. So I had to rationalize it. And this is what I came up with: Ray had *never* molested Debbie. She'd always been his favorite. Why would he start now, when she was a teenager?

It was dark already. I forgot about Debbie and my thoughts turned once again to me. Ah, the miracle of self-absorption. All these weeks and months in New York, and what did they amount to? Sure, I'd been lucky that afternoon. A mediocre photographer had wasted a few rolls on me. *By accident.* But how good would they be? He wasn't exactly Irving Penn. And what would happen when I went by his studio to pick up the prints?

I'm a loser. I'm not going to make it.

I had another glass of wine, popped a 'lude, and crawled into bed.

When I went back for the pictures two days later, Christopher wasn't happy. Eventually he'd realized his

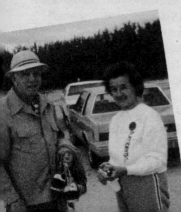

MY PARENTS,
RAY AND JENNIE DICKINSON.

mistake, of course, but he also knew it wouldn't make much sense to keep the pictures from me. After all, if I ever happened to get lucky, it would help his career, too.

"You owe me," he reminded me as I was leaving. Art showed up as I reached the door. "You owe me, too," he said. What did they expect? Blow jobs?

So off I went with my new, improved portfolio—the all-important tool of the modeling trade—and tried the agencies yet again. First stop: Eileen Ford. I'd been there half a dozen times already, but I figured if I made a pest of myself someone would cave and give me a break. There was also a slim chance that someone might *recognize* me and mistake me for a ravishing creature they'd seen in a magazine. That is, a *real* model.

Eileen and her husband had launched the agency in 1946, out of their home, and had gone on to create the most recognized name in the business. Eileen was known as a strict disciplinarian, a control freak. Jerry was quieter but very sharp. It was Jerry who negotiated the first big-money contract in fashion, way back in 1974, for my hero, Lauren Hutton. I was hoping he'd scale new heights with me.

A dowdy assistant took me back to a tiny office and started paging through the new photographs. They were pretty good, actually, and she seemed impressed. She took me over to see Monique Pillard, one of the bookers. Monique was very friendly. She was a little overweight and had a very thick French accent. She told me she liked what she saw, and it was clear she meant it. She also had the power to do something about it. I thought I would burst with hope. Just then, the far door opened and Eileen Ford walked into the room. In the flesh.

"Who's this?" she said, looking me up and down with obvious displeasure.

"Janice Dickinson," I volunteered. I offered her my hand, but she didn't take it.

"I'm sorry, dear. You're much too ethnic. You'll never work." She let herself out through another door, but she wasn't done with me yet. Before the door closed, I heard her say to no one in particular: "My God, did you see those *lips*?"

I swear to God, I almost died. I was just a *kid,* for Christ's sake. Did she get a kick out of humiliating me? What kind of sick people was I dealing with?

I took a few deep breaths. Once again, pain curdled into anger. *Too ethnic?* Wasn't Beverly fucking Johnson on the cover of American *Vogue*? Who the hell did Eileen Ford think she was? Sure, there were some narrow-minded assholes out there who thought a black cover girl meant the Great Exotic Apocalypse. But not Eileen Ford. Surely she had enough sense to see that the business was changing. This endless bullshit about the all-American look—it had to end sooner or later. And didn't they get it? Blond? Blue-eyed? That's not American, you idiots. It's *Scandinavian.*

I had to fight the urge to run after her and push her out the window. Then it hit me. *What if she's right?* I suddenly imagined myself back at the Orange Bowl, waiting tables—at age fifty. It happens. To lots of people. Was I going to be one of them?

I ducked into the bathroom and looked at my face. Yes, my lips were big. And my hair was a little on the frizzy side. And those brows could use some serious tweezing. And I didn't have much in the way of cheekbones. And— and and and and and . . . I bit my lips together to make them look smaller. I could hold that pose. I looked good all of a sudden. Well, okay, not really; now I looked like a *thin-lipped* Polish mutt. I left the bathroom and found Monique waiting for me in the corridor.

"I am so sorry," she said in her thick accent. "But I have a feeling our paths will cross again."

"What should I do?" I asked her. I was falling apart. I was not going to cry. *Not not not.*

She looked around to make sure we were alone, then whispered: "Wilhelmina."

I went out into the street. I was upset and angry. Being upset never did shit for anyone. Being angry, on the other hand—that could work wonders. If you used it right.

I walked to Wilhelmina's, at 37th and Madison. I was going to make it. Nothing was going to stand in my way. I was getting angrier by the second. *Fuck you, Eileen Ford. You'll be sorry.* It wasn't my first time at Wilhelmina's, either. The receptionist smiled that familiar smile: *You again.* She let someone know I was there. Didn't exactly jump to it, either.

I sat down to wait and tried to look pleasant and charming. But I was burning up inside. *Did you see those lips?* Twenty minutes later, a young Hispanic gay guy came out to greet me. Dealing with walk-ins wasn't exactly a task the top brass fought over. He smiled his most professional smile and took me back to his cubicle. The poor bastard didn't even rate an office. We squeezed into it. There was barely enough room for two chairs. Our knees touched. He looked at my book, which didn't take long. He shut it, handed it back to me.

Do not fucking thank me and send me on my way! I am not a loser.

"These pictures aren't great," he said. There was a "but" in there somewhere. I knew it was coming, but it took an eternity. "But I'm intrigued. I kind of like you. I like your energy. I like the fact that you're, well, not ordinary. There's a certain *je ne sais quoi* about you."

Of course there is, you wonderful little homosexual

you! I smiled demurely. "Thank you," I said. I could hardly breathe.

"I'll talk to Willie."

Willie! He was going to talk to Willie herself!

"Good," I said. I was so poised. So unruffled. So la-di-da not-really-interested-thanks. "Let me know."

I smiled and waved ta-ta and sashayed my way back to the lobby, hoping I wouldn't faint.

I met Wilhelmina the following week. She had a neck that wouldn't quit, and her long hair was piled on top of her head in a huge, messy tower. There was something wonderfully classy about her. I wanted to like her. I wanted her to like me. I told her my hard-luck story. She listened attentively, chain-smoking all the while. When I was done talking, she lit another cigarette and blew a cloud of smoke and studied me for a long time. "I think you're interesting," she said finally. She had a pronounced Dutch accent. "You have an unusual look." *Interesting?* An *unusual* look? For a moment there, I went into a panic. I thought she was going to smile politely and send me on my way. But she didn't. She said she would sign me—start me on the "testing board"—and see how it went. I didn't know what the "testing board" was, but she was good enough to explain: Photographers often needed junior models to help them test their lights, say, or pose for a new type of film, or work with a revolutionary fish-eye lens, that kind of thing. "It's not much," she said with a pleasant smile. "But it's a start."

Not much? You must be fucking kidding me. I was walking on air. If I'd been wearing a cap, I would have tossed it, Mary Tyler Moore–style. But I didn't. I contained myself. *Barely.* "Sounds really interesting," I said, sounding—to my insecure self, anyway—like a complete moron.

Wilhelmina reached for her buzzer, and a moment later

an elderly secretary came in and introduced herself and took me on a brief tour of the premises. "The bookers are your lifeblood," she said in a dull, sad monotone. I wondered if she, too, had dreamed of being a model many years ago. We walked into a large room. The phones were ringing off the hook. Three bookers were sitting in front of what looked like a giant lazy Susan that spun like a roulette wheel.

"No, she's not available."

"She's in Milan. She'll be back Friday."

"She won't model in sunlight. She doesn't like what it does to her skin."

"You can't afford her. Sorry."

"No, no lions this week. She's having her period."

I could see slots for each model, but they sped by so quickly that I couldn't make out any of the names. I tried, though. I wanted to see some famous names. The secretary reached over and plucked a clipboard from one of the slots. It had the name of the model across the top: Deirdre Nobody, with all her vital statistics in a neat row below that. Further along, I could see that her day was broken down into hours, starting at seven in the morning and going through till eleven at night. At any given moment, at a glance, you could see where Deirdre was or what she was doing next. "Deirdre is a tester," the secretary explained in her dull monotone. "Testers don't get paid. If she does well, though, she'll move up a notch, to the Big Board, and start in editorial. Those are the photographs that run with the fashion articles. If *Cosmo* decides that pink is suddenly the hot color, for example, they'll run a piece on, say, 'New York Pink,' accompanied by shots of a beautiful model dressed in pink from head to toe. Editorial doesn't pay particularly well, maybe a hundred a day, but if you're noticed and you're lucky it might lead to advertising. Of course, you won't be starting with Revlon."

A hundred a day? Not much? Are you kidding me? Give me fifty dollars and I'll work for a month!

"Then it gets exciting," the secretary droned on, her voice betraying no excitement whatsoever. "Giant billboards, your face all over the subway station, runway shows, television, maybe movies even. Who knows?"

Who knows indeed!

I walked back to the apartment, floating. I was in love with Wilhelmina. She represented hope. And that bitch Eileen Ford—well, who gave a shit? I'd show her soon enough. *I am it, baby.* Different? You bet your skinny ass I'm different; I'm *better.* So, hey—I'm beyond crazy. I'm manic, okay? I go from the pits of despair to the peaks of elation. In the space of a day, of an hour, of a *look.* Doesn't everyone?

Edna was out, trolling for rich older men with a weakness for middle-aged Jewish women. Wendy was in the shower, getting ready for work. When she got out, I told her I'd just been signed by Wilhelmina. She jumped up and down, screaming and giggling. She was genuinely happy for me. I didn't tell her I was just a tester or that "signed" was a pretty broad definition for what had actually happened. It wasn't as if Willie had put a contract in front of me and told me that she absolutely positively had to have me. But hey, I was happening, right?

I went down to the club with Wendy and sat at the bar. Two businessmen were sitting nearby, checking me out. They were talking about some big deal that had gone down in their Wall Street office that afternoon, trying to sound important and rich for my benefit, and when they were done talking business one of them said something about getting tickets for B. B. King. My ears perked up. It turned out B. B. King was at Carnegie Hall at that very moment. I finished my drink and got my too-ethnic ass over to Carnegie Hall.

I waited by the back door. When one of the grunts came out for some fresh New York air and a cigarette, I slipped inside. I was stopped by a security guard who wasn't going to be easy to charm. He must have been seventy years old, and—from the way he cocked his head and squinted—half-blind.

"Excuse me, miss. You're not allowed in here."

"You don't understand," I told him. "Ron asked me to meet him."

"Ron?"

"Ron Levy," I explained. "The piano player. The white guy."

There was some hemming and hawing, but just then the musicians took a break and he sent someone to get word to Ron Levy. A few minutes later, I was told that Ron was waiting for me in the dressing room.

I went in. Ron came over and hugged me. "Janice! Jesus, it's nice to see you, girl!" I wondered if he was bull-shitting me. "I guess you're back for that drink I offered you in Florida!" He *wasn't* bullshitting me! He remembered me!

I stayed for the last set and then Ron and his intense green eyes and I went over to the Plaza for drinks. He was gorgeous—my Jewish Jim Morrison. We closed the place down and he took me back to his hotel, where there was some coke. I'd never done coke. I was just a kid. I couldn't have afforded it. But I didn't want to look naïve, so I just leaned over and—toot—took one line in each nostril. I looked up and smiled ear to ear. I felt powerful. I felt invincible.

Ron made love to me, and I had an orgasm you could hear all the way to Poughkeepsie.

My God—is life good or what? Signed and stoned and properly laid, all in one day! Yowza!

When you're in love, you want the whole world to know it. And I did my part. I told the waitress at the coffee shop. The nearsighted girl at the checkout stand. My bank teller. Cabdrivers. Strangers on the subway. Any fool who made eye contact with me had to hear it: "Hey, look at me! I am in love, goddamn it!" I felt like Mary Tyler Moore again, only happier and much better looking, and without that stupid fucking beret.

When I ran out of people to tell, I phoned Alexis. Her marriage had fallen apart. Mr. Hubby had developed a nasty drug habit and fried his brain. I mean, to hear Alexis tell it, the man was a fucking vegetable. So she left and moved to Santa Cruz and was trying to start over with some flower-children commune types. Sheesh!

So, yeah, I kept it short and simple. *Met a guy. He's okay.* I couldn't go on and on about how happy I was, could I? It would only make her feel worse. But the thing is, I *was* happy. I couldn't get enough of my Jewish Jim Morrison. I hated it when he had to go to work. He'd leave and I'd try not to pout and I'd go back to the Gralnick apartment and pull myself together and call the agency, pushing for work of my own.

Alexis was very sweet about it. "That's so great," she said. "I can't wait to meet him." I could hear tears in her voice. I asked her if there was anything I could do for her. She said she was fine, thanked me for calling, and hung up.

Eventually, Wilhelmina began sending me out. It was pretty much what I'd been told it was going to be—a lot of test shots. It didn't pay, of course, but it was work, and it felt real. "Some day you'll make it to the Big Board," one of the girls told me. She said it like nothing could be further from the truth. Still, I knew I would; I knew my big break would come when one of the photographers cleared the fog off his lens and started paying attention to me.

Patrice Casanova was one of the first to really notice me. He wasn't narrow-minded about beauty, and came right out and told me he thought I had "international" appeal. He was also a perfect gentlemen, which I hadn't expected; I had heard countless horror stories about the French Mafia, the group of Parisian photographers who were very hot at the time. They thought of themselves as "street" guys. They were into their 35-millimeter cameras and liked shooting outdoors with minimum fuss, kamikaze-style. They liked movement, action, acting. They didn't like mannequins. They prided themselves on being the exact opposite of the Irving Penns and Helmut Newtons and Richard Avedons of the world. And they all had major attitude about it.

But not Patrice. Of course, as it turned out, Patrice was from the *south* of France—which explained it. Parisians in general are real snobs, and Parisian men are the pits. Trust me. I also discovered that I wasn't Patrice's type. His type was Jessica Lange, who happened to be his girlfriend at the time.

Patrice was incredibly good to me. And his photographs were little gems of discovery. They went beyond the surface shit—beyond lips, legs, and crotch to my *energy*. The shots we took together found a prominent place in my growing portfolio. Later, they would change the course of my life.

One night, Patrice invited me to join him and Jessica Lange for dinner. Jessica wasn't just a top model; she'd already made a name for herself in *King Kong*. She was a sweetheart, and he was crazy in love with her. He called her *cherie* all night. Made sure she had enough to eat and drink. Made her feel loved. Every few minutes he'd take her hand and kiss her under the wrist, as if he were Gomez, from the Addams Family, and she his very own Morticia.

I told them all about Ron, who was in New Jersey with the band. We all agreed that love was a beautiful thing.

A few days later Wilhelmina sent me over to see another photographer, Mike Reinhardt. Like Patrice, he was part of the nefarious French Mafia—this despite being the American-born son of German parents. He was shooting a lot of stuff for *Glamour,* working with top girls like Patti Hansen, Beverly Johnson, and Lauren Hutton.

"All the girls love him," Wilhelmina warned me. "So don't be stupid."

I got to his studio and an assistant let me in and introduced me to Mike Reinhardt. He nodded, barely acknowledging me, then crossed the room and picked up the phone and called someone and reamed him out. He was very handsome. And solidly built. He saw me studying him, said he'd be with me shortly, then went off and busied himself in another room.

I sat there for forty-five minutes, getting increasingly pissed off. There was a copy of *People* on the couch, and I started flipping through it. The magazine was new on the market. American's love affair with fame was under way. And God, did I want to be part of it! I looked at some of the faces and thought, *I'm as beautiful as they are. And I can be shallow, too.*

Then I noticed a portfolio—some of Mike's recent work—and looked through it. He was good. The photographs were natural, the lighting soft. And the models all looked as if they were about to ask you to fuck them. Maybe they were.

Mike reappeared once or twice, made some more calls, ducked into the kitchen for a bottle of Perrier, rolled a joint, smoked it, rearranged the lights, looked for a lost wide-angle lens—everything but acknowledge my existence. I felt like part of the furniture. Finally, as he walked past me for the tenth time, I tripped him.

"Remember me?" I said. He looked at me as if he were trying to place me.

"Yes. Of course. Why don't we get started?"

He spent the next two hours testing several new lenses. He never spoke to me. Didn't even say good-bye. But of course: I was a nobody. I was never going to be one of the *People* people. He made me feel meaningless, unimportant, ordinary. Some day, I swore, I'd make that arrogant bastard pay for his rude behavior. And I did. But I'm getting ahead of myself here.

WOKE UP
THIS MORNIN'

I celebrated the New Year in Las Vegas with Ron Levy. B. B. King and the band had a gig at the Hilton. Nineteen seventy-four had come and gone. I had moved out of the Gralnicks' Upper East Side co-op and into an apartment on 14th Street and Fifth Avenue that Ron and I had found together. The building looked nice—it had that redbrick thing going—but the place was a little funky. And there were some pretty sleazy characters around, including a psychotic drug dealer just down the hall.

Of course, I didn't care. I was crazy in love with Ron by this time, and he with me. And, no, it wasn't just about the unbelievable sex. Ron wanted to be around me all the time. He practically cried whenever he had to hit the road with the band. He called me every day, at unimaginable hours, to tell me he missed me, and that he was crazy about me, and that I was the best thing that ever happened to him. To be wanted like that—you have no idea what it did for me.

You'll never amount to anything. That's the message my father had pounded into my head since I was a child. But here was a man who loved me. Me, Janice, a little nineteen-year-old nobody, struggling—like ten thousand other girls—to make it in the Naked City, and he loved me just the way I was.

A few weeks after we came back from Las Vegas, Ron

took me out to Brookline, Massachusetts, to meet his parents. I was so nervous we had to park a block from the house until I could pull myself together. Anxiety Dickinson indeed!

It was a beautiful house on a tree-lined block in the ritziest suburb I'd ever seen. His parents met us at the door, and hugged me as if they'd known me all their lives. Ron had obviously told them all about me.

His father, Joshua Levy, had invented some kind of plating process that NASA took to the moon. He was gentle and very refined. "Hey, Dad," Ron said. "Look at this beautiful little bird that flew all the way up from South Florida." Ron's brother, George, was also there. He was quiet and warm and—like his parents—went out of his way to make me feel welcome.

Best of all, however, was Ron's mother, Jeanne. She had the most beautiful, chestnut-brown hair and the same sparkling green eyes as Ron. She also had a wonderful

RON LEVY (FARTHEST LEFT) AND B. B. KING (FARTHEST RIGHT). JEANNE LEVY IS FOURTH FROM THE LEFT.

laugh—more of a cackle, really—and I couldn't get enough of it.

She had strong opinions, too. Over dinner, she told me she hated Ron's lifestyle. "He's wasting his talent on B. B. King," she said. And there was no denying his talent: People in the business said he was the best white blues piano player around—even if he couldn't read a stitch of music. "He should be at Juilliard, studying to become a real musician," she said.

Ron protested from time to time, but he was smiling. It was obvious he'd been through this many times before, and he seemed to find it kind of amusing. From time to time, he'd look over at me and wink, *That's my mother.*

She didn't approve of his drinking and smoking, either. She meant the *cigarettes,* of course; she didn't have a clue about the pot. And the *notion* of cocaine wouldn't have entered her head. *My nice little boy?*

Me? I wasn't big on pot, but every now and then I enjoyed a line or two of coke. Mostly, though, I was into Courvoisier in those days: Courvoisier with O.J. back.

A week after we returned to New York, Ron had to go on the road again.

"Why don't you come with me?" he said. We were in the apartment on 14th Street. We could hear someone coming up the stairs, en route to the drug dealer's. Ron bent over the table and snorted another line. "It's only Ocean City," he said. "Right down in Maryland. There's plenty of room on the bus."

I refilled my cognac snifter with Courvoisier, nurturing a pleasant buzz. "Okay," I said. "If you don't think B.B. will mind."

We left the next afternoon. The bus was so thick with smoke you couldn't *not* get stoned. It was a hoot. B.B. kept smiling at me and Ron and shaking his head. "Man, you two," he said, grinning his big warm grin. "I smell trouble." He meant it in the nicest possible way. Or so I thought.

Ron and I couldn't get enough of each other. We made love around the clock. The night we reached Ocean City, I did a little striptease for him in our hotel room. I was flying. He was flying. "Oh, baby," he kept saying. "Oh, baby, baby. Oh baby, I love you so bad."

The next night Muddy Waters showed up for the show and stayed long after the last member of the audience had gone home. He and Ron and I and a few of the band members and their girlfriends were sitting around, chatting and riffing and getting stoned. And Muddy told a very funny story about how to sing the blues.

"Well," he said. "If a song begins with 'Woke up this morning,' that's the blues. Especially if you repeat the line. And if it's about a woman, and she's a nice woman, that's *not* the blues. But if the woman's mean as a rattlesnake, and ugly as a junkyard dog, *that's* the blues.

"If you're young you got no business singing the blues," he said, "because you ain't fixin' to die. Only ole people can sing the blues. You got to be older than dirt. But if you're young, it's best to be blind. Or maybe you shot a man in Texas or Memphis. Or maybe you're missing a leg. But you can only sing the blues if a alligator got your leg. If you lost your leg in a skiing accident, that ain't the blues."

Muddy bent over the mirror and a huge line of coke leapt into his left nostril. He looked a little dazed for a moment, then turned his eyes on me. "Janice," he said. "Can you sing the blues?"

"No," I said. "I'm not mean as a rattlesnake."

Muddy laughed. "You can sing the blues, woman. Body like that, you *gotta* know how to sing the blues. You be exonerated, girl."

They jammed for a while. People drifted in and out of the place. We killed a couple of bottles of Courvoisier. Hours later, Muddy turned to me again and *insisted* I could sing.

So I said, "Well, I'll try anything once." I was young and stupid in those days. And very drunk at that moment. Muddy plucked his guitar and I recognized the tune and got to my feet and sang: "Take me to the river and wash me down / Take me to the river and put my feet back on the ground."

Everybody cheered when I was done. I guess they must have been pretty stoned. The only ones who didn't cheer were the bums who were passed out all around us. On the floor. On the couch. By the edge of the stage.

"Well, you didn't wake none of them up," he said.

"Is that a good thing or a bad thing?" I wondered.

"*I* think you can sing, Janice. And I'm Muddy, so I must know."

One Sunday morning, about a month after the Ocean City trip, Ron and I were sitting in the claustrophobic kitchen of the 14th Street apartment, nursing coffees, trying to plan the day ahead. I had a little Courvoisier-and-coke hangover. He didn't feel all that good himself. He kept saying drugs were evil, a duplicitous bitch; he was going to quit once and for all.

He looked at me, his other bitch, the less evil bitch. And he flashed a mysterious smile.

"What?" I asked.

The smile just wouldn't quit.

"I'm thinking," he said.

"A thought of yours would die of loneliness," I said.

He laughed and had another sip of coffee and looked up at me and the smile disappeared. "Janice. Baby. I. Was.

Wondering . . . " The words came slow and heavy. He was making me nervous. Then he blurted it out: "How would you feel about marrying me?"

We were married in his parents' living room, in front of the fireplace. It was a small affair. Just family. Along with a rabbi, of course, and a minister. The rabbi was a friend of the family, and the minister was the rabbi's idea: For some reason, he thought he wasn't legally able to marry a *shiksa*.

Okay, that was the weird part. Here's the *really* weird part: My parents came to the wedding. Yes, it's true. My mother and the rat bastard showed up.

And the oddest thing of all: Shortly after Ron proposed, we came back to Brookline to tell his family. His mother was elated. The next day she and I went out and did girl stuff in town. Shopped. Had our nails done, side by side. Ate lunch at her club. Like that . . . I was floored. I felt so close to her. I found myself wishing that *she'd* been my mother, instead of the mother I had. And on the way back to the Brookline house I began to cry. She pulled over and asked me what was wrong. I couldn't hold back. I told her everything. I honestly couldn't help myself. I told her things I had never told anyone in my life.

The night before the wedding, both families went out to dinner. My father was trying hard not to be impressed by all that wealth and power. His little girl, the piece of trash who'd never amount to anything, had clearly hooked a man who thought otherwise.

At the restaurant, as we were waiting for our table, Ron's mother took my father aside. I could see them at the far end of the bar. She was doing all the talking. She was smiling, but I could read don't-fuck-with-me in the creases on her face. My father—well, he looked terrified. All the color had drained out of his cheeks. When they were done,

Ron's mother rejoined us. "I love your daughter," she told my mother. "My son is a very lucky man."

My father recovered and joined us at the bar, and a few moments later the maître d' led us to our table. We had a lovely evening: The rat bastard didn't say a word all night. He just nodded his head like a bad little boy who'd received the scolding of his life. And every time I glanced in his direction, he quickly turned away—as if he were afraid of me or something.

After dinner, my parents went back to the motel. The rest of us returned to Brookline. When we got back to the house, I took Jeanne aside. I was dying of curiosity.

"What did you say to my father?" I asked her.

"I told him I knew everything," she said. "And I told him if he said even one wrong word, that if he even *looked*

SELF-PORTRAIT FIRST THING IN THE MORNING BEFORE COFFEE.

at you funny, I would make it my mission to destroy his fucking life." I had never heard Jeanne curse before. "Excuse my French," she said.

I hugged her. I felt so hopeful. I had married a wonderful man from a wonderful family. I was barely twenty years old and my Real Life was taking off in all sorts of new and exciting directions.

Ron and I got back to New York and resumed life as a married couple. We joked that our sex life would probably crash to a stop now that we were man and wife, but it didn't. It slowed down some, but that was because of the drugs.

To be honest, though, I was getting concerned. A little toot now and then was okay, but I worried about us.

I was still calling Willie every day, pushing the agency for work—any kind of work. But things were slow. And that worried me, too. I have never been, and will never be, the kind of woman who's taken care of, the Edna Gralnicks of the world notwithstanding. I wanted to pay my own damn way. And, hell, it's not like we were loaded. Ron made a decent living on the road, but we had expensive tastes: Courvoisier. Three-star restaurants. Cocaine. Funny how you forget about the rent . . .

I sat down with Wilhelmina a week later and told her I desperately needed money; our landlord was no longer our friend. Willie said she had something for me. She knew it wasn't going to make me happy, but the money would be fast and tax-free.

That night I was waiting tables at a smoky little bar on 37th and Madison, which attracted a clientele of rich middle-aged men with a penchant for hookers. The owner was a guy named Mark Fleischman, whom I'd get to know better later, when he became co-owner of Studio 54—though he tried very hard to get to know me better right then and there.

Some of the hookers were fine-looking girls. A couple of them seemed oddly familiar. Hadn't we crossed paths on go-sees here and there? Suddenly, I was terrified. I would *never* fall that low. Willie knew that. Right? I mean, even if I weren't married, even if I'd been junkie-desperate, she knew I'd never sell my body. *Right?*

I brushed that crazy thought aside. I was being paranoid. She was just helping me out. After all, I had Ron. I was loved. I was *loved*.

So I buckled down and worked hard and hated every fucking minute of it. But a few nights into it, guess what? The rent was paid.

So here it is, weeks later. We're okay with the landlord, and Ron's getting ready for a little gig in Tarrytown, New York. He should be happy, but he's not. This is the first time I've seen him go off to work unhappy, and it bothers me deeply. We get into an argument about drug use. He shouts, and waves his arms, and tells me I'm crazy. I apologize. He apologizes. We hug, and off he goes to hook up with the guys, and I tell him I'll take a bus after work and be there for the last set.

I go to my hooker bar and lay on the short-skirt charm, like I learned to do at the Orange Bowl. I cut out early with two hundred bucks in tips, and make it to Port Authority just as the Tarrytown bus is getting ready to pull out. I haven't had time to change. I *know* I look like a hooker. Some guy propositions me on the bus and you can hear the slap all the way back to Manhattan.

I sleep, comfortably, for the rest of the trip.

* * *

Now I'm in Tarrytown. Get to the concert hall. Go through the rear entrance, don't hear anything, and assume I'm late. I run into B.B. He gives me a quick hug and tells me they're just taking a break; last set hasn't even started.

I go look for Ron. Walk into the dressing room.

I find Ron. Ron who loves me so much he cries whenever he has to leave town. Ron who tells me over and over, "Girl, you are the best thing that ever happened to me." Ron who has never felt like this about anybody, ever, and never will and never wants to.

I find Ron with another woman, pumping away with all the force and splendor of a man possessed.

"NOOOO!" I scream.

Ron's head whips round so fast he falls off the couch. The woman just lays there spread-eagled, staring at me. She doesn't even have the courtesy to cross her fucking legs. I turn to go.

"Honey baby—"

But I'm already out the door. Ron follows, stumbling over his pants and struggling to pull them up. He catches up with me by the stairs and I whip round and slug him and he stumbles against the wall.

"You *sonofabitch*!"

"Honey—"

But I'm not there anymore. I'm blind with rage. He comes at me again and I kick him and he falls backward down the stairs. He lands with a heavy thud.

I run outside and hurry through the parking lot and run run run, blinded by tears.

That's a husband's love for you.

Cars go by. Men hoot and holler. It's a miracle I'm not raped and left to die in a Dumpster. I certainly look the part.

Miles later, numb, lost, I find myself at a gas station

near a freeway off-ramp. There's a heavyset truck driver getting ready to hop aboard and pull out. He's looking at me more with lust than sympathy. I open my mouth to talk, but no words come. I'm having an anxiety attack. I lean against the side of the truck, trying to draw breath. He doesn't know what to do. He pats me on the back—*pat pat pat*—and the tears come. Those fucking buckets of tears again.

"You okay, miss?" the trucker asks me. He seems like a decent guy. I shake my head from side to side. *No, I am not okay. Do I look like I'm goddamn okay?*

He gives me a ride to Manhattan. I don't say much. I listen. He tells me he's married. He has a boy, seven. He and the wife had trouble getting pregnant, which is why he looks like he could be the boy's grandfather. I take my cue and tell him he doesn't look like a grandfather. He loves his boy, he says. He says that until he had his boy, he didn't really understand what it meant to truly love someone. But now he understands.

Weird. This guy just does not look like the New Sensitive Man type. I mean, if you were going to cast him in a movie, he'd be the truck driver with a weakness for doughnuts and bondage porn, maybe even in that order.

We get to Manhattan. I thank him. We shake hands. He tells me—I kid you not—that he knows good things are in store for me. Maybe even in the next day or two. He has this *feeling,* see. His mother was a Hungarian gypsy, a psychic, and he seems to have inherited a little of the old knack; that's what his friends tell him, anyway. I give him a kiss on the cheek and tell him I hope he's right and get out of the truck.

I walk up the street. It's three in the morning. I still look like a hooker, a miserable fucking hooker.

I remember that I have two hundred dollars in tips in my

purse and hail a cab and make my way to my friend Alexandra King's apartment, on 72nd Street near Madison. The cabdriver asks me how business is. I tell him to fuck off.

Alexandra is home. Yes! I go inside and collapse on the couch and and tell her everything. She's my buddy. My bosom bitch. A fellow model. Gorgeous. Her fucking parrot wakes up and starts squawking the one phrase it knows: "Fuck me Fuck me Fuck me." No, fuck *me*.

"Love sucks," Alexandra says.

"Yes," I say. "But what else is there?"

"Fuck me Fuck me Fuck me," the parrot says.

We look at each other and laugh. Yeah, there's that.

I got back to 14th Street late the next morning to find Ron passed out on the floor. He had a bed and a couch to choose from, but he took the floor. His mouth was open. He was snoring. Someone had bandaged his thumb.

"Wake up, you fuck," I shouted.

He didn't move. I kicked him. He opened his eyes and looked up at me like he was in a coma.

"Hey." That's what he said. *Hey.* No apology. Nothing.

"I hate you," I told him.

I locked myself in the bedroom and popped a couple of sleeping pills and went bye-bye. As I drifted off, I began to wonder who the fuck I'd married, and—more to the point—*why*. He'd wanted me, right? Really, truly wanted me. And to be wanted like that—well, it can go to a young girl's head. Or maybe—God help me—maybe it was the orgasm. An orgasm can make a believer out of any girl, especially a *first* orgasm.

"Fuck me fuck me fuck me," I moaned, burying my face in the pillow. I felt about as intelligent as Alexandra's foulmouthed parrot.

When I woke up, it was early evening. Ron was gone.

There was a note taped to the fridge. Shows how little he knew me: I never went *near* the fridge. He was off to Atlantic City for a week; the band had a gig. *Call you in a day or two*. Not a fucking word about what happened. Not even a *hint* of an apology.

I spent the next few days eating junk and watching TV. Sometimes, just to get my heart started, I'd add a shot of Courvoisier to my morning coffee.

I began to understand the appeal of television. *Brady Bunch* reruns. *Kojak,* with that old lollipop-sucking perv Telly Savalas. *All in the Family. Baretta.* (Robert Blake! Jesus, even back then, any fool could see the guy wasn't all there.) *Barney Miller. Happy Days. Mary Tyler Moore. Rhoda.*

Pretty soon I was talking back to the TV. "Hi, Rhoda. Love that dress." Who needed a life? Who needed a family? By the third day I thought I'd never seen anyone as handsome as the fucking Fonz.

Then the phone rang. I couldn't believe it. Three days had gone by and this was the first time my phone had rung. I was really popular. My own fucking husband wouldn't even call me. I was in such shock that by the time I picked up the receiver the person at the other end was gone. I put the receiver back in its cradle. I willed it to ring again. It did.

"Hello?"

"Janice?" It was one of the assistants at Wilhelmina.

"Yeah?" I said.

"Don't forget. Those two guys from Christa are coming in this afternoon."

Shit! It was next week already!

"Don't worry," I said, trying not to panic. "I'll be there."

I hung up. Oh my God! The Silverstein brothers, from Willie's sister agency in Paris. They were looking for hot new faces. They needed girls in Paris.

I ran into the bathroom and saw *my* face and freaked. I mean, it was like a cartoon. *Yaaaaaaargh*! I looked like a hooker after a high-profit holiday weekend. I mean, tired as hell and totally *fucked*. Then I thought, *No. This is not possible. That isn't my face staring back at me.* I shut my eyes real tight and said a little prayer, and when I opened them again I was still there.

I was hosed. I had an hour to pull myself together. One lousy hour.

No problem. I'd been bullshitting myself into action my whole life:

"I am Janice Dickinson, motherfucker! I am unstoppable. I'll show them. I'll fucking show all of you!"

"Shut the fuck up!" It was the asshole in the apartment across the alley. Scared the shit out of me. "People are trying to sleep around here!"

Two hours later I arrived at Wilhelmina for the cattle call. The place was crowded with desperate girls. You could smell the flop sweat.

When it was my turn, I put the last three days out of my mind—wasn't hard; couldn't remember much anyway—and entered the room slowly, long legs first. I guess I'm a bit of a Drama Queen at times. The Silverstein brothers introduced themselves. Jacques and Dominick. A pair of good-looking French guys, very pleasant, with warm, Cheshire-cat grins. I could have done without the gold chains and the pointy shoes, and the pants—so tight you could tell their religion. But who was I to judge? Wait a minute! Let's back up here. I'm Janice Dickinson. And don't you forget it!

There was a woman with them. Face like an angel. Lorraine Bracco. She was Jacques's girlfriend. She'd been modeling for Wilhelmina since she was thirteen, but she was destined for bigger things.

Dominick opened my portfolio, turned the pages slowly.

"Stop!" Lorraine hollered. "I *love* that one!" This in that wildly nasal Long Island Sopranos voice. She was pointing at one of Patrice Casanova's photographs of me. Very Lauren Huttonish: I'm leaping through the air with my alligator grin. "I like this girl!" Lorraine said. "Let's take her to Paris. She's hot."

Jacques laughed. Dominick laughed.

"Okay," Jacques said. "Done."

I literally fell to my knees, bowing and scraping. "Thank you thank you thank you thank you!" I told the men. Then I turned to Lorraine and actually curtsied. "And thank you, kind stranger, whoever you are!"

THE GIRLS
IN THE ATTIC

➤➤➤➤➤➤➤➤➤➤➤➤➤➤➤➤➤➤➤➤➤➤➤➤➤➤➤➤➤➤➤➤➤➤➤➤

Here's the advice I got from Lorraine the day before my flight to Paris: Drink a lot of water; you get dehydrated on the plane. Don't eat the airplane food; it's salty, and it'll puff you up. Pack light. They've got plenty of stuff to wear in Paris. "If you're good, you might get to bring some of the clothes back," she said. "Of course, if you're bad, you'll bring *all* of it back."

She also taught me a few important French phrases. *Ou est l' hotel? C'est trop cher. Encore du vin.* And, in times of trouble, a simple English phrase everyone understands when properly delivered: "Go *fuck* yourself, you pig ass ugly frog motherfucker!"

Ron got home the morning of the day I was leaving for Paris. He was a mess. It was obvious he'd been on some sort of binge, and just as obvious that I hadn't wanted to see it. After all, this was the man who had told me, repeatedly, that I was the best thing that ever happened to him. What did it say about me that he was a junkie?

"About that night—" he began.

"I don't have time for this," I said. I went into the bedroom. He followed. He saw that I'd started packing. He looked like a whipped dog. No, he looked *worse* than a whipped dog. He'd lost weight and his teeth were rotting and his skin had a sickly, yellowish pallor.

"You're leaving me?" he asked. "Jesus, Janice, don't tell me you're leaving me."

"I'm going to Paris, you dumb sonofabitch. If you really want me, I'm sure you'll find me."

"Paris?"

Just then, the phone rang. You'd think a normal husband, pleading for his life, would have ignored it. His wife was on her way out the door. But Ron wasn't a normal husband—not anymore, anyway. He looked at the phone, next to the bed. It rang again. He hurried into the living room, for the other phone. He wanted privacy.

"Hello?" He was whispering, but I could hear two things in his voice. The first was desperation; the second was relief. It didn't take a genius to see he was talking to his dealer. He hung up and came back into the bedroom and told me that he had to go out for a minute. Business; very important. He'd be right back. Please wait.

I told him I'd wait. The minute he was gone, I finished packing, hurried outside, and hailed a cab to JFK. I cried my eyes out all the way to the airport. I cried at the Air France counter when I was checking in. I cried when I boarded the plane.

"Are you okay, miss?" one of the flight attendants asked me shortly after takeoff.

Sure I'm okay. My marriage is over. I've never felt more alone in my life.

"Yes," I said. "I'm fine."

I was on my way to Paris, goddamn it. Going abroad for the first time in my life. This was the break I'd been waiting for. I should have been *beyond* fine. So I got up and made my way down the aisle to the bathroom and locked the door behind me and really fucking bawled for a good five minutes. Then I pulled myself together and took a few deep breaths and washed my face and went back to my seat and told myself I was fine, goddamn it. Life is *good,* motherfucker. And the black cloud began to lift.

I began to think only of the future. I fell in love with the *idea* of the future. I fell in love with my French fellow passengers, with the sound of their oh-so-refined language. With the French airline wine. With the gorgeous flight attendants and their perfect makeup and the way they had their hair up in those elegant chignons. I fell in love with every word in my little French phrase book. I was sitting in my seat smiling at nothing, giggling, laughing out loud, out of context, out of control. . . . And by the time the plane descended into Paris, I was ready for My New Life.

Dominick Silverstein met me at Orly airport, carrying fresh daisies and a sign with my name on it. He gave me a big hug and kiss and we went outside and hopped into his Peugeot and drove to Paris.

It was early morning—I'd been on the red-eye—and Dominick took a few detours to point out the sights. The Arc de Triomphe. The Champs Elysées. The Pont Neuf. The Louvre. The Picasso Museum. Notre Dame. The goddamn Eiffel Tower! Me, Janice, a rube from backwater Florida—and I'm standing in front of the Eiffel Tower. Yeah, I know, call me Mary: If I'd been wearing a beret, I'd have tossed it with gay abandon. But I couldn't help myself. Every cell in my body was being fed. The architecture, the monuments, the weird little cars, the weird little *dogs,* the Vespa motorcycles, those big baguettes people carried under their arms . . .

"I love it already," I told Dominick.

"And it loves you," he shot back.

He parked near the agency and we stopped briefly at a

little café across the street for espressos and croissants. It looked like a movie set. Unreal. Perfect. Perfect little waiters with perfect little curled mustaches. I started laughing, giddy with happiness and hope.

Then he took me into the magnificent six-story building that housed the Christa agency. There was a kitchen on the ground floor. A short, red-faced Frenchman approached, smiling broadly. *"C'est Janice Dickinson,"* Dominick said, introducing me. "This is Raphael. He takes care of us. Anything you need, ask Raphael."

"A votre service," Raphael said, and snapped his heels together smartly. I'd only seen that done in the movies, by German SS officers. Evil omen?

The agency itself occupied the next three floors. Dominick took me through, introducing me to everyone. They fawned beautifully. I felt like a homecoming queen. People shook my hand warmly. Some of them kissed me on both cheeks. Everyone welcomed me in French and bad English.

Finally Dominick walked me to the top floor—the goddamn attic. Five flights up, me dragging my bags. There were three little rooms up there, tiny, and a bathroom the size of a broom closet. He led me to one of the rooms. There were five mattresses on the floor. It was like they figured it out mathematically: If you put this one here and this one just so, well—you can squeeze another bitch into the far corner. The last futon on the left was mine. I was the "other bitch." I tried to hide my disappointment. I don't know what I was expecting exactly . . . the Plaza Athenee?

Dominick could see the horror in my eyes. "I know it's not much," he said. "I'm sorry."

"No no no!" I protested. "It's perfect."

"You will have your own place soon," he assured me.

"You are beautiful. *You* are perfect. Now freshen up and come downstairs and we'll talk about your future—yes?"

My future—yes!

I spent the rest of the day meeting the staff, discussing my (sadly lackluster) portfolio, and talking about the days ahead. Unfortunately—or fortunately, depending on your point of view—the agencies were in the middle of a bitter war with some of the top magazines, including European *Vogue, Marie-Claire,* and *Elle.* The issue, as usual, was money: They felt their models were getting the shit end of the stick. I oohed and aahed and expressed deep concern over the horrible working conditions, but I would have posed anytime, for anyone, in any state of dress or undress, for two bucks an hour. Of course, I didn't tell them that.

Everything will be *magnifique,* I was assured over and over again. *Absolument magnifique.* I wanted desperately to believe them. I'd been grinning my big old alligator grin since I landed, and my jaw ached. But I didn't give a shit. I was in Paris. I'd do my shuck-and-jive for anyone who asked.

As I was making the rounds, moving from one department to another, a very handsome Frenchman walked through the front door. He had dimples, which I immediately liked, and a coarse five o'clock shadow. His name was Guy. I had heard about him in New York. He was a very talented illustrator, only twenty-four, and a magician with the airbrush. He had a great smile. He told me to call him. He said he'd be glad to show me around Paris. "I know how hard it is when you know no one," he said. "But now you know me."

That first night, Dominick took me and a few of the other girls to the Maison du Caviar, a wonderful restaurant on the Place de la Madeleine. He ordered the best beluga caviar and kept the champagne coming. An hour into it, I was very contentedly buzzed. The other girls seemed downright pleasant.

I went to bed that night drunk, happy, and full of hope. So what if I was sharing a room with four struggling models! They were darling girls! What a darling attic! Life itself was darling!

In the morning, I waited for my turn in the bathroom—last, of course—and then worked my way downstairs to the booker's office. An elderly French woman told me I was expected at *Marie-Claire*. I had no idea where it was. She gave me the address and turned her attention to other things, dismissing me. I was a little taken aback, to be honest. It's not as if I'd been expecting a limo, but a little friendly direction would have been nice. It didn't happen. People were busy. I was invisible.

I went to the nice café across the street and tried to get help from a waiter. He told me, in broken English, where to buy a Metro map, where the nearest station was, where to get off. I wrote down all the strange names. Braced myself. Hurried off.

It was simultaneously terrifying and exciting. I was walking walking walking, as I'd walked in New York. I hoped the results wouldn't be the same.

I bought a map at the entrance to the Metro station. Got on the right train. Found the right stop. Walked some more. Arrived at the *Marie-Claire* building, where I was greeted with profound indifference. *Attendez. On vous vera tout suite.* Wait. We'll be with you shortly. Shit! Just like New York, only in a foreign language.

An editorial assistant appeared a while later, smiling a tired smile, and took me out back. She looked at my portfolio. She seemed profoundly unimpressed and did nothing to hide it. She said something in French. I told her I didn't understand French. She said something else in French, and I don't know what it was, either. But I look back on that first day now and I'm *glad* I didn't understand. I'm sure she was saying, *Sorry, we have nothing for you. We're looking for a thin-lipped all-American blond.*

I got lost on my way back to the agency, but I didn't care. I liked the way people sounded. I liked the way they looked. Everyone seemed so fashionable and cultured, like something out of a nineteenth-century novel—not that I'd ever read a nineteenth-century novel, but you get the idea.

The sidewalk cafés were overflowing with chic people at tiny tables, slurping oysters and shelling shrimp and drinking endless amounts of wine. They laughed big French laughs. Gesticulated grandly. Spoke with great passion about God knows what.

I had no money, of course. I'd spent the bulk of my nest egg on that cab to JFK. I found a small corner grocery store and went inside and bought some blueberry yogurt and told myself it was the best yogurt I'd ever had. It probably was, but it didn't exactly do the trick.

I got back to the agency at dusk, desperate for a friend. Dominick was out. Everyone else was busy.

I went to my attic. Making my way up the stairs felt like some kind of punishment, though I couldn't for the life of me understand what crime I'd committed.

My roommates—the ones who'd seemed so charming the night before, in that champagne haze—turned out to be unpleasant in the extreme. They had been in Paris longer. Knew their way around. Had better portfolios. More money. Rich Eurotrash boyfriends who took them shopping at Louis Vuitton, Chanel, and St. Laurent. And each night they'd go off to Castel's, Club Set, Le Bain Douche.

I wasn't invited along. Not that night nor the next nor the night after that. It was okay, though. I couldn't be bothered. Really. I mean, I was a married woman, right? I wasn't going to let my morals be corrupted by the living arrangements in this bordello of beautiful women.

So I sat down one night and wrote a long letter to my husband. "Dear Ron," it began. "I love you and I don't want to lose you." Given that he still hadn't apologized for his little indiscretion, I thought that was going well beyond the call of duty. But I *did* love him. I went on to tell him what an amazing human being he was, how happy he'd made me, how he had come along and changed my luck and life. "I owe you," I wrote. "But you owe me, too." I asked him to please clean himself up. His lifestyle was going to destroy us. And I really, truly didn't want to lose him.

In the days ahead I trudged through a string of go-sees, all of them as underwhelming as the first one at *Marie-Claire* (and eerily reminiscent of the go-sees in New York). I went to department stores I'd never heard of. Magazines I'd never heard of. Met with characters who looked dangerous and desperate. But the department stores didn't want me, and the magazines didn't want me, and the dangerous characters weren't desperate enough for me.

I'd return at the end of the day for more abuse. My roommates talked as if I wasn't there. They talked about Paul's huge cock. Or Pierre's little one. Or about Ahmed, the Saudi prince who liked to take care of himself, loudly, as he watched.

They showed off their new dresses. Their new jewels. Their new shoes.

I hated the sound of their voices. Their laughter. I couldn't wait for them to go to their fucking snooty nightclubs with their trashy, overcologned boyfriends so I could

sit alone in my lumpy little corner bed in that claustrophobic little cell.

By that second Friday, I didn't know what to do with
myself. There was a TV downstairs, and I found myself
watching a rerun of *I Love Lucy,* in French. I couldn't take
it anymore. I turned off the TV. It was eleven o'clock and I
was wide awake and lonely. I went into the reception area
and picked up the phone and got through to an operator
who spoke English and made a collect call to the only
home I had . . . Ron answered. I could hear voices in the
background—*high-pitched* voices.

"Hey, baby!" Ron said. "How's Paris treating you?"

"Great," I said. "Did you get my letter?"

"Oh, yeah, babe," he said. "Great letter. Loved it."

Great letter? Loved it? Not exactly the response I was
hoping for.

"What's going on?" I asked. "Sounds like you're having
a party."

"No," he said. "A few of the boys came over for a little
poker."

I did the math. It was a little after five p.m. in New York.
Ron and the boys were off to an awfully early start. On the
other hand, you never knew with them. Maybe they were
still partying from the night before. Then I heard a
woman's laughter, the sound of breaking glass, more
laughter. I hung up.

I picked up the phone and dialed another number. Guy
answered. The airbrush genius. "It's Janice," I said. "I
know it's late and I'm not sure you remember—"

"What are you talking about, *late*? I was just getting
ready to go out. Sit tight. I'll pick you up in ten minutes."

He was there in eleven. Not that I was counting. He
asked if I was hungry, and took me to the Brasserie Lipp,

which to this day is one of my favorite places in the world. He ordered the *assie·'e de fruits de mer* for two. Suddenly I was one of *those* people. Eating oysters, mussels, shrimp, munching on crab legs. The wine flowed; he ordered a very nice Sancerre. I was in heaven.

Of course, as they say, there's no free lunch. And I guess that goes double for dinner. I went back to Guy's place. I was torn. But not badly torn.

"You don't understand," I said, vacillating. "I'm a married woman."

"It's you who doesn't understand," he said. "That doesn't bother me in the least. And *I* have a girlfriend. And it probably doesn't bother her. And if it does, that's not my problem."

That right there is the difference between European men and American men. Don't ask me if I like it. I'm not sure I like it. No, in fact, come to think of it, I hate it. There's real arrogance there. Then again, the arrogance is coupled with disarming honesty. *I fuck who I want to fuck when I want to fuck, and fuck anyone who's bothered by it.*

Call me crazy. We fucked. And it was pretty fucking good.

I woke up the next morning to see Guy sneaking out with his motorcycle helmet under his arm. A moment later I hear his moped starting up in the alley below and puttering away. I closed my eyes and fell back asleep and half an hour later he walked into the bedroom with breakfast on a tray. Fresh strawberries, buttery croissants, slices of glistening ham, and an assortment of the finest cheeses. And the best French coffee in the world, which we drank out of huge, handleless mugs. I mean, God—me, Cinderella! I used to have to get down on my hands and knees and scrub floors. Now look at me! This was the life. I loved France. I loved French room service. And I especially loved French men: They may cheat on their women, yes—but they sure know how to treat 'em.

We spent the entire weekend together. With service like that, it wasn't hard.

Guy told me I was going to make it. But it was all about the photographers, he said. That was the key. You have to get endorsed by the name shooters. They're the ones who pick and choose the models for both the fashion shoots and the prestige designers. They know who's hot today and who's going to be hot tomorrow. "Get the photographers behind you, and you'll soar," Guy assured me.

He mentioned Jacques Malignon and Patrick Demarchelier. He liked Alex Chatelein, too. He said Pierre Houles was doing some incredible work for *Elle.* And Guy Bourdin was just a genius—incredible. "Mike Reinhardt is very good, too. Maybe even great. You have to meet Mike. He's part of that same French Mafia. He's half the time in New York, half in Paris."

I told him I'd already met Mike, and that I disliked him intensely. Mike was the sonofabitch who'd treated me like a piece of furniture for forty-five minutes, refusing even to acknowledge my existence. Bastard hadn't even offered me a hit off his joint.

"That sounds like Mike," he said. "He can be as difficult and self-absorbed as the women he shoots."

The Monday after my wild weekend with Guy, my luck began to change. I got a call about doing a shoot for DIM, a well-known stocking company. The money was lousy, they said—but it was like *now,* this second. So I found my way over to the studio and a perverted little photographer half-greeted me at the door. He led me inside, pawing me, touching me, and started blathering away in French. I didn't understand a word, so I just nodded and smiled a lot and put up with his restless hands until the makeup girl came along to do what she had to do.

Within an hour my hair had been poofed out to here, my eyebrows had been plucked to within a centimeter of their lives, and I was standing in front of the bright lights in fuck-me pumps, a one-piece dress open to the waist, and DIM pantyhose with no underwear. The pervy little photographer barked at one of his assistants and suddenly there was a huge roar and I got hit with a blast from the biggest wind machine I'd ever seen in my life. I thought I was going to get blown right through the wall, but somehow—with my hair blowing back, and the dress lifted clear off my body like a sail—I managed to smile smile smile . . . And then, *boom!*—it was over. *Zenk you for coming, American bitch.*

I got back to the office, feeling a little insecure and hoping for a bit of positive feedback, but they had no time for feedback. French *Playboy* was doing a fashion spread with Jacques Zolti, who at that moment was the most sought-after male model in France. The Silversteins had pushed hard, and the people at *Playboy* had shown my photos to Michel Berton, the photographer. He *loved* me. The genius!

They weren't paying much either—nobody was paying much, that's what the strike was about—but I didn't give a rat's ass. Work was work, money was money.

I met Jacques and Michel at the Paris airport—Jacques with a bushy trademark mustache, Michel with the harried look of a photographer with too much on his mind—and we took a small plane to La Rochelle, in the south of France. On the way, I sat next to Jacques, who was very charming—didn't come on to me at all. He was even nice to the giggly young girl who came over during the flight and asked for his autograph.

We arrived late and were put up in a small *pensione*. We had a light dinner and some wonderful red wine and were told to get a good night's sleep. "We start first thing in the morning."

In the middle of the night, I was awakened by a noise at the window. I looked up, startled. Jacques, grinning his bushy grin, was climbing through. I leapt out of bed and whacked him with the pillow and he toppled out. Luckily, we were on the ground floor. I looked out at him. He was unhurt, at least physically.

"But women find me irresistible!" he complained.

"Not this woman," I said.

He smiled. I smiled. We understood each other.

The shoot went flawlessly. It had this sort of barnyard motif. I changed in and out of clothes and posed with cows and chickens and even did a Little Bo Peep number with a lamb. It didn't look like much—it didn't even feel like work—but it nailed the cover.

When I got back to Paris, the work kept coming.

I was flown to the Club Med in Martinique for a spread

IN EUROPE
I BECAME
OBSESSED WITH
SELF-PORTRAITS
AND LEICA
CAMERAS.
➤➤➤➤➤➤➤➤➤

in *Marie-Claire,* and I thought I'd died and gone to heaven. I shot in the Loire Valley. In castles mountains vineyards rivers rooftops. I was everywhere.

Then the results of that DIM stocking shoot hit the streets. I remember it with incredible clarity. I was leaving Guy's apartment one morning and I'd barely reached the sidewalk when I thought, *I'm hallucinating.* A bus was just going by. I was on the side of the bus. *Me.* My dress and hair flying, my long stockinged legs out there for all the world to see. I watched the bus round the corner and disappear from view. Jesus! I ran back to the apartment, and Guy was in the shower, and I was so excited I couldn't get the words out.

"It's me! There was a big picture of me on a bus!"

Guy laughed and hugged me. "What did you expect, *ma petite*? I told you you were going to make it."

He didn't understand. Three months ago, I was getting every door in New York slammed in my face. Now I was everywhere. Billboards. Shopping malls. Every magazine in Europe. *Elle. Marie-Claire. Marie-France.* I felt powerful. Invincible. I felt like I did that first time I'd done coke, back in New York, with Ron. Only it wasn't wearing off. I wasn't coming down. And every time I saw a new shot of me, I'd get that little cocaine rush all over again.

And it didn't stop with DIM. There I was in *Playboy.* There I was in *Marie-Claire.* There I was in *Elle.* There I was in *Vogue France.* I was on top of the world. I would rush out to the nearest newsstand and buy half a dozen copies of each magazine and take them back to Guy's place and pore over them. *See,* I'd tell myself. *I knew you could do it.* Still, the elation was short-lived. Before long, that little voice inside started casting the usual aspersions. *You were just lucky. You don't deserve this. It's a fluke.* Then I'd take a closer look at the photographs and see nothing but flaws. *Too much makeup. Look at the baby fat in your face. You better cut back on the push-ups, girl—those arms are getting way too buff.* I couldn't even enjoy my success. I was turning into my own father.

"What's wrong?" Guy asked me one night. I was in that dark, self-destructive place.

"Nothing," I said. What was I going to say? I was up one minute, down the next. Soaring and crashing and crashing and soaring; the roller coaster from hell.

"You're doing great," he said. "The photographers love you. Just keep working them."

Okay. Deep breath. *Work the photographers.* I went off to work Alex Chatelein, one of my favorites in those early days. Alex had started out as a painter, but he couldn't sell much and decided to try his luck with photography. One of his first jobs had been as Richard Avedon's assistant—what an incredible education. He was another member of the French Mafia, and a good friend of Mike Reinhardt's. He kept telling me I should work with Mike when I got back to New York. I wondered why everyone kept pushing Mike on me.

"You look wonderful," he said. And I was flying.

I saw the pictures a few days later: I crashed.

When I was back in Paris, home between assignments, I usually stayed with Guy. He was insatiable. I knew there were other girls, but I didn't care enough to ask. It wasn't like I was falling in love with him. After all, I was a married woman—not that my husband seemed to remember. He never called. I'd lost him.

One night, Guy took me to the Tour D'Argent, one of the most fabulous restaurants in Paris. It was such a well-heeled crowd, a long long way from ham sandwiches and brewskis. And it made me think: I guess fame is the great equalizer. These folks didn't care that I was poor, white trash. Or at least they didn't care enough to notice me. Or maybe they *didn't* notice me. Or maybe I was having a good night; maybe I passed as one of "them."

"What are you thinking about?" Guy asked me.

"That I deserve this," I said.

Toward the tail end of dinner, he announced that his girlfriend was on her way back to Paris. I don't know what he expected. Tears? I wasn't upset. As I said, Guy was all about recreational sex. And that's all I'd ever wanted from him.

"I'm not going to get all bent out of shape," I told him. "I knew this was coming."

I think he was a little disappointed—men love it when women fall apart over them—but he hid it well. "You know something, Janice? You're amazing."

"I know."

"You're not going to make a scene?"

"Tell you the truth, I'm more concerned about living arrangements."

I was sick of the "charming" girls from the Christa attic. I was always running into them at the clubs around town. They'd come over and fawn and tell me how fabulous I looked and go on and on about whatever layout they'd seen on the stands. And I would grin my alligator grin and hate them. Power does corrupt, I guess. And I had power. I was taking Paris by storm. And some of the girls, well—all they had was their masturbating Arabs. One of those poor things was so strung out on heroin she'd started hooking to keep the cash flowing. She looked worse than I'd looked on that fateful morning of the Christa cattle call. A *lot* worse.

"I'd still like to see you from time to time," he said. "I hope you don't mind."

"Does your girlfriend mind?"

After dinner, we went to Castel's, a way-hot club, and bumped into John Casablancas. Casablancas ran Elite, a very happening Paris-based modeling agency. He told Guy that Mike Reinhardt had just done a fabulous shoot for him. Guy introduced us. Casablancas couldn't have been less impressed. He looked me up and down with zero interest. That was his style. It was his way of telling me I'd never make it.

"What an asshole," I told Guy after he left.

"It's his loss," he said.

I could have fucked Guy then and there. In fact, that's what I did.

At the end of the week, just before Guy's girlfriend arrived, I went to Noumea, New Caledonia, for a bikini shoot. (I really didn't have to worry about living arrangements much; I was never "home.") Benny Truitman was the photographer. He was a fat, mischievous guy who had made a name for himself taking pictures of Fiats, and I knew I was a lot better-looking than any car he'd ever photographed. He had one shot where he got me in the ocean, half under water, half out—he had a camera made especially for the occasion—and there was a fucking great white shark hovering in the background. I didn't know about the shark until one of the assistants told me to get the hell out of the water. Which I did. With alacrity. I love that word: *alacrity*. Go look it up in the dictionary.

After a quick trip to Thailand for *Marie-Claire*, with Patty Oyai, another model, I took the train to Saint-Tropez to meet the great Helmut Newton. I checked into the beautiful hotel and there was no one around and I went outside and sat by the pool and had a drink. There was a cool breeze blowing and I felt very peaceful. Life was good. I closed my eyes for a minute and enjoyed the feel of the sun on my skin. When I opened them, I saw this old guy watching me from across the pool. We were the only two people around. He kept staring at me. I ignored him and lit another cigarette and looked away.

He came toward me. He looked like a horny old fucker, out to ruin my perfect afternoon. I wished he'd go away.

"Take off your clothes," he said.

"What!?"

An elegant middle-aged woman had come out of the hotel and was watching us from near the door.

"You heard me," the man said. "Take off your clothes."

"Fuck you, you dirty old perv!" I said.

I got up and stormed off. As I was approaching the hotel, I noticed that the woman was smiling. I didn't understand what was so goddamn amusing. When I was within earshot, she said, "Helmut can be so difficult."

Now I was really confused. "Excuse me?" I said.

"That's my husband, Helmut Newton."

"Oh my God," I said. I'd totally blown it. I turned around. Helmut was coming toward us, on his way back to the hotel. He was seething.

"Mr. Newton," I stammered.

"You'll never work again," he said, and moved past us into the hotel.

I buried my face in my hands. I thought I was going to die.

The woman laughed. "Forget about him," she said. "Why don't you let me photograph you instead?"

"You?"

"Sure," she said. "I'm a photographer, too. Maybe not so famous, but not so temperamental as my husband, either. I'm Alice Springs."

I was in shock. "Come on," she said. "You are so beautiful."

We went inside—she took me by the hand and *dragged* me into the lobby—and she stopped to make a quick call on the courtesy phone. When she got through, she started barking at someone in French. *Vite vite. Maintenant. Tout suite.* I just stood there, dazed, numb, writing my own modeling obituary in my head.

The next thing I know I'm down at the beach with Alice and her two assistants, in a gauzy cotton shirt, my hair glistening with globs of Brylcreem. And then I'm coming out of the water looking like Jacqueline Bisset in *The Deep*, but *sans* tits, admittedly. And Alice is snapping away, laughing, loving it, telling me I'm *magnifique, incroyable, delicieuse.*

I made the cover of *Elle*. It was my very first cover. I was up at the crack of dawn the morning the magazine hit the stands. I couldn't believe it—there I was, staring back at me. What a feeling! On the *cover.* I looked like a water leopard in that tight, wet T-shirt. And my alligator grin wouldn't quit. It was genuinely overwhelming. I started laughing like a crazy woman. People stared. I didn't give a shit. I bought four copies and hurried back toward the apartment, but in my excitement I stumbled near the corner and one of the magazines slipped to the sidewalk. There was a man in a dirty white apron standing a few feet away, in front of the fish market, shucking oysters. He set down his knife and leaned over and reached for the magazine. As he handed it back, he noticed me on the cover. He looked from the magazine to my face and back again.

"C'est toi, non?" he said, smiling.

I shook my head from side to side, grinning like a madwoman. *"Non,"* I said. *"C'est pas moi."* No. It's not me.

"Mais oui!" he said, laughing. *"C'est toi!"*

I took the magazine from his big cracked hands and thanked him and hurried away, still laughing.

Patrick Demarchelier called later that day. He had seen

the cover and heard parts of the Helmut Newton story. "Is it true you told the old man to go fuck himself?" he asked. Those were the first words out of his mouth.

"Yes," I said. And I gave him the short version.

"I love it," he said, laughing. "I want to hear the whole thing. In detail. You can tell me on the way to Morocco."

And that was my next big shoot. Fucking Morocco! We drove up to the Berber Mountains and posed with the Blue Mountain Men. Patrick was brilliant. We were out in the dunes and he would wait until the sand and wind and light and breeze were just perfect—and *boom!*—he'd get his shots. He was the Ansel Adams of fashion.

"You know who you should work with?" Patrick said that night, over dinner. And I said, "If you say Mike Reinhardt, I'll kill you." And of course he said Mike Reinhardt.

When I got back to Paris, people began to notice me. I'm not just talking about people on the street, either. Reporters started calling. *Who are you? Where did you come from? We've never seen anyone like you!*

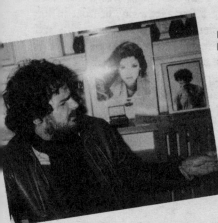

PATRICK DEMARCHELIER.
I LOVE PATRICK!

It was a trip. I loved the attention. I felt energized. I would leap out of bed in the morning, excited about the day ahead. And so *grateful*. The French photographers were turning me into the star the Americans had said I'd never become. Back then, there was this crazy notion of American beauty, like it was the goddamn gold standard or something. And I'd been told I didn't have it—which was true, I guess. I wasn't blond, and I was too exotic, and my almond-shaped eyes made me look Asian. But what the fuck is wrong with that, people?

Most models—hey, they just show up and look beautiful and they're off. Me, I had to fight like hell to *convince* people I was beautiful in my own Polish half-breed way. The French were the first to go for it. And I love them for it.

Of course I wasn't making much money. Editorial shoots didn't pay well in the States, and they paid even less in Europe. And they *still* pay shit. But I had to start somewhere, and the European magazines were easier to crack than the American ones. So I fought like hell to be seen, to get my face in their faces. Because the magazines are really no more than catalogs. Within those pages, Fashion's Decision Makers will find the next Revlon girl, or the girl behind the wheel of a Mercedes-Benz, or the new face of Versace. And *that's* where the real money is, not in magazines. Because here's a horrible, ugly secret, people: Even Cindy Crawford gets the standard hundred and fifty dollars when she's on the cover of *Vogue*. And she doesn't give a shit about the money; it's about the prestige of being on the cover, about keeping that face alive.

And that's what I needed; that's the dream. You take your lousy hundred bucks from *Elle* to sell tacky silk sheets, because—*Hello!*—Bloomingdale's just called: They want you for a catalog shoot at $15,000 a day, and they're figuring on three days.

So, yes—you take all the shitty, no-money gigs in the world to become The Next Big Thing—even if The Next Big Thing is fucking *Corn Flakes*.

"There's always one person who comes along and turns things around for everyone," Dominick Silverstein told me one day. "Everything people have been saying about what a model needs to look like, well—you're proving them wrong. You're redefining the whole notion of beauty." Dominick liked to wax lyrical. "You're going to open doors for all sorts of interesting women."

Did that go to my head? You fucking bet it did.

One day I walked into Christa and everyone was all aflutter. Peter Knapp wanted to meet me! This was a big deal. *Huge*. Peter Knapp wasn't just a fantastic photographer; he was the art director for *Elle*.

I took the Metro to his studio, a copy of *People* with me, and I flipped through the pages like an addict, admiring all those beautiful faces. Fame was taking on a life of its own.

I got to Knapp's studio and rang the bell and a sweet little gay man let me in. He asked me to wait inside, showed me the way, and disappeared. I looked around. It was a huge open space, filled with incredible art of all kinds. A pair of giant thumbs was parked in one corner of the room, looking like they were made out of cheese—which reminded me I was hungry. I stole into the kitchen and assumed the position in front of the fridge.

A few moments later, I heard a man behind me. "Anything good in there?" he asked.

"Yes," I said, turning around to look at him. He looked lost, as if he'd stumbled into the kitchen by mistake. "Lots."

I found some excellent Brie and attacked it with gusto. The man smiled at me and left the kitchen. I noticed a bottle of Chateau Margaux on the counter, found an opener, and popped the cork. The man came back. "So you're thirsty, too?" he said. He was grinning ear to ear. I wondered what function he filled in that busy studio; he was such a happy guy.

"It's delicious," I told him. "Grab a glass."

The little gay man walked in on us. *"Excusez moi, on vous demande a l'appareil, Monsieur Knapp."*

Monsieur Knapp! Shit! It was Peter Knapp! This was *his* cheese I was eating, *his* vintage wine I was drinking, *his* kitchen I was invading. Knapp reached for the phone—there was a call for him—and chatted for a few seconds. I was dying. I had a hunk of Brie in my mouth and thought I'd be wise to just choke on it and die. Knapp hung up and turned to look at me.

"So, Janice," he said sweetly. "Anything else I can get you?"

I swallowed the cheese, not without difficulty, then noticed a box of Swiss chocolates on the counter between us. They looked very expensive. "I wouldn't mind a little chocolate," I said. "I love chocolate."

That grin of his wouldn't quit. "I like you," he said. "I'm going to put you on the cover again." And he did. I had four back-to-back covers in *Elle.* I went island-hopping in the Caribbean for them with Sascha, a French photographer, and her Tunisian slave-boyfriend. She'd bark and he jumped. Next stop, Tunisia. A week later, I'm working with Guy Bourdin—one of the masters.

A photo session with him was almost as good as sex. He was on top of you. Touching, posing, rearranging. He generated heat—creative heat. He made me feel like the most incredible woman on the planet.

Suddenly I am hot hot hot. Everyone was asking about that American girl who didn't look like all the other American girls. The Polish mutt was on fire!

One night in Paris, at a party with Bourdin, I told him everything Eileen Ford had said about me. That I was too ethnic; that my lips were too big; that I'd never work.

"She's an idiot," he said. "What does she know about real beauty?"

Bourdin spelled out what the other French photographers had been trying to teach me. "Be yourself, Janice. That's what I love about you. That's what turns everyone on. Your craziness and big mouth and bad-girl attitude. Your desire to be *shockant*. You are one of a kind, girl." I could've kissed him. In fact, I *did* kiss him. A woman needs to hear shit like that from time to time. And me? I needed to hear it more than most. Especially now, when I had something to lose . . .

The fact of the matter is, I'd always been insecure—I'd been raised that way—and success was suddenly making me *more* insecure. I would think, *It's all a bad joke. Everyone's in on it but me. They're just building me up to knock me down.* So, yes—I was still that hyperanxious, hypervigilant, cripplingly self-conscious little girl; I honestly couldn't get my mind around the fact that I was really beginning to make it.

"What is it?" Dominick asked me at lunch one day. We were at a sidewalk café, near the offices. I was studying the women at the neighboring tables. They were so classy. They dressed beautifully and their hair was done just right and I loved the way they raised their forks to their mouths, unlike me—who bent down to meet it somewhere near my plate. These women even *chewed* with class.

"Nothing," I said, and I smiled the way Dawn Doyle had taught me to smile. My *confident* smile. She'd shared a whole repertoire of smiles with us: happy sad pouty smirky flirty fierce . . . *I'd learn to fake it,* I decided. I'd learn to sit the way they sat; eat the way they ate; walk the way they walked. And of course I'd cultivate that touch of haughtiness that seemed to come so naturally to them. I was uncomfortable in my own skin, yes; but why the fuck did anyone have to know it?

"I've never been happier," I said, and I raised the fork to my mouth and chewed with class.

I'm sure you're wondering about Ron. I was wondering about him, too. I'd written him that long letter, but you know where that got me. Ron didn't seem to care. I waited for him to call and when he didn't I swallowed my pride and tracked him down at home and on the road and begged him get help, to clean up his act. I suggested he come to Paris. He said he didn't need help, that he was clean and just too busy to come to Paris. He never called on his own. Never wrote. And it felt lousy. I had a big jones for love and affirmation, and he'd gone out of business as my supplier. So I thought of him less and less, and called him less and less.

On the other hand, I did think—and worry—about my sister Debbie. I'd just turned twenty. She was fifteen. She'd just written me a long letter telling me how much she missed me, how unhappy she was. She'd enclosed a

MY SISTER DEBBIE LOOKING STUNNING AT TAVERN ON THE GREEN IN NEW YORK CITY.

picture of herself on the beach with a group of crazy adolescent friends. Most of them had pimples; Debbie glowed.

I called her and told her how beautiful she was. Debbie cried. It was the end of summer and she was really, genuinely unhappy and didn't want to go back to school; she wanted to go to New York to sing and act.

And suddenly I had this crazy idea.

I phoned the Silverstein brothers and told them to take me to lunch. We met at the Brasserie Lipp, my favorite hangout. "How would you like another Janice?" I asked them. I was pretty full of myself at this point.

"Another Janice?"

"I have a little sister. Debbie. She's beautiful. Very wholesome, all-American looks. You'll love her."

I set the picture on the table in front of them. "Guess which one is Debbie," I said.

I was amazed when she arrived. She was drop-dead gorgeous. It had been almost two years since I'd seen her, and the girl had *bloomed*. She was closer to the "ideal," too. She was good product. A traditional Cheryl Tiegs type, only more beautiful: pure home-baked apple pie.

We went back to Christa's and she got the futon next to mine. She wasn't even vaguely disappointed. Debbie is a survivor. Her attitude has always been "No matter how bad it is, I can fix it." We talked all night. Families are complicated, but they can also be wonderful. I would have done anything for Debbie—was it guilt over having abandoned her to the rat bastard?—and I did.

I took her downstairs the next morning and everyone fawned over her, just the way I'd asked them to. (So sue me! There's not much about this business that's genuine.) But the fawning paid off. By week's end, she'd booked a couture show for Louis Feraud. This was a good thing. On the very day she booked the job, Guy Bourdin called and told me we were going to Milan for Italian *Vogue*.

Before I left for the airport, I gave Debbie some valuable advice about the shoot. One, be on time. Two, don't chew gum—it's not classy. Three, don't act like some goddamn superior queen with the assistants: They're there to help make you look good, and looking good is what it's all about. Four, you're great, remember that, and if you don't feel great, fake it.

Finally: Always always always make sure he wears a raincoat.

I wish someone had given me advice that good when *I* started out.

MILANO

For those of you who don't know the business, Milan is the capital of the Italian fashion industry. Armani, Prada, Versace, Valentino, Gucci—all the great design houses are clustered together here, and, twice a year—during show seasons in February-March and September-October—everyone who's anyone descends on the city.

So Bourdin took me to Milan in September. Me and all the medium names. Our plane was filled with desperate wanna-be models. I felt a little sorry for them, but not *too* sorry. I'd paid my dues—why shouldn't they?

When we got off the plane, the first thing I saw was a bunch of handsome-if-oily Italian playboy types, waiting around with big colorful bouquets in their arms. It reminded me of the day I arrived in Paris, when Dominick Silverstein met me at the airport with daisies, except that all these guys looked kind of sleazy.

"Who are these creeps?" I asked Bourdin.

"Rich boys who like to fuck models," Bourdin said. "It's a seasonal thing. They show up with flowers and their fathers' Ferraris and fuck their brains out for a couple of weeks. The locals call them *figli de papa*—Daddy's boys."

It wasn't like that for me. There was a limo waiting for us at the airport. The driver got into some heavy fawning. I liked it. This was the A-list ticket, and I'm thinking, *I'm the Flavor of the Month, yes. But I'm going to make my month last forever.*

We checked into our hotel and went off immediately to do a shoot for Charles Jourdan shoes. The next day, we did a spread for a Bloomingdale's lingerie catalog (which has since become a collector's item, thank you very much). Then Bourdin took me to the city of Parma.

It was my first time in Italy, and I was seeing it in grand style. I discovered prosciutto. And Parma ham, which is even better. And Parmesan cheese. Everything was delicious—the food, the people, the views. I promised myself I would return to Italy someday and sit around and eat and get fat and be happy. I couldn't stop stuffing my face. There's a Bourdin shot of me in a spectacular gown, with a hunk of prosciutto literally crammed into my mouth. It was red-hot sexy.

"That's you, Janice, all the way," Bourdin said. "That's

POSING WITH MYSELF. MY FIRST ITALIAN *BAZAAR* COVER, SHOT BY JAMES MOORE.

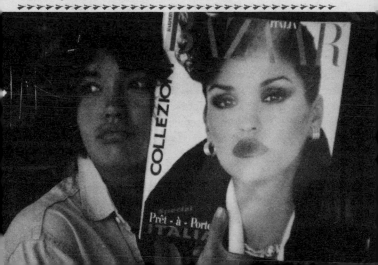

how you are in real life. Hungry. Big appetite for everything. What is this word you use all the time?"

"Gnarly," I offered.

"Yes," he said, laughing. "Gnarly Janice."

Of course, the trip wasn't all gluttony and happiness.
From the *figli de papa* on, the whole affair had a decidedly
dark side. What you have to understand is that a lot of
aspiring young models go to Milan to try to make their
mark. They have to fight for the all-important tear sheets
that will launch a real career back home. And, in Milan,
they actually have a shot at it: There are so many magazines and so many photographers and *faux* photographers
and *fashionistas* that you can literally get discovered on the
street. Of course the chances, at best, are still pretty slim.

Most of the girls stayed in a hotel the locals called the
Fuck Palace; those who couldn't afford it shacked up in the
less expensive Pensione Clitoris.

At night, in restaurants and clubs all over the city, you
could see girls of fifteen, sixteen, seventeen—girls who
hadn't made it and probably would never make it—resort-
ing to good old-fashioned sex to survive. Some of them
were so desperate they'd fuck a guy for a decent meal.

The Arabs came over, too, in droves—and not for the
fashions. A thousand dollars to them was chump change,
and if you're a pretty girl, in need, and your inner voice is
telling you, *Hon, you ain't making it as a model,* well, that
thousand dollars will help you get home, right? And of
course then you figure a second thousand won't hurt—*I'll
take a few gifts back to Des Moines, for the folks*—and then
a third and fourth . . .

The fact of the matter is, there are American girls in
Milan who have been there for years and years. They get
rough around the edges, fast, but they're still pretty. You
can find some of them in the Yellow Pages.

The night before we returned to Paris, a young girl over-dosed in the rest room of the nightclub where we were celebrating. The paramedics carried her out, trying hard to be discreet, but there's nothing discreet about early death. I was thinking about that poor girl on the plane back to Paris. What lies would they tell her family, home in the States? Whatever they needed to hear, I guess. "Your daughter was a wonderful girl. Very gifted. She was on the verge of making it. Another month or two and she would have been a major star."

Bourdin was seated next to me. I turned to look at him. "This business is pretty tough, isn't it?" I said.

"It's just business," he said. "No worse than any other. When the stakes are high, people get nasty. It's inevitable."

"You really believe that?"

"Yes. I have a friend in real estate. You should see the backstabbing that goes on there. And another friend who moved to Hollywood a few years ago. The things he tells—it's wild."

"Like what?" I asked.

"He told me something funny the other day," Bourdin said, clearly trying to cheer me up. "He said, 'In Holly-wood, it's not dog-eat-dog. It's dog-doesn't-return-other-dog's-phone-call.' "

I laughed. I've never forgotten that line. It's funny but it's also pretty sad. I didn't understand it then, but it really goes to the core. If you're not even important enough to get your phone call returned, you must be next to nonexistent. It made me think of my father. *You'll never amount to anything.*

Fuck you, Ray. Wait till I get home.

I arrived back in Paris to find that Debbie had had a very good week. Without me. Imagine that! The couture show

had gone so well that she'd already lined up her next gig—
for *Elle*. And she was being courted, in high style, by a
bunch of local photographers.

I had mixed feelings about Debbie. This was my little
sister, after all. Why had I gone and invited her to Paris? To
corrupt her? No, she'd done a perfectly good job herself,
growing up in sunny Hollywood, Florida. So why did I feel
so much conflict, for God's sake? I was helping her big-
time. If anything, I was making things *too* easy for her. I
was proud of her, and jealous and angry and protective, all
at the same time.

I took her to the Maison du Caviar for beluga and champagne and told her I was going home. I had a portfolio the
size of a fucking phone book, and I was ready. I wanted her
to fly back with me.

"I only just got here," she whined.

"You're fifteen years old."

"So what?"

"Debbie, you're a *child*."

"I don't want to go back. I love it here. I love the
agency, I love the people, I love the men. I love my life—
for the first time in my life."

What can you say to that?

Guy took me to the airport for the flight home. I liked him.
I'd been in Europe for seven months and he was the only
man I'd slept with. (Okay, I let one other guy go down on
me, and maybe there was some fellatio one night when I
was blindsided by some excellent cocaine, but what's a girl
to do?) I hadn't wanted anything from Guy except sex. At
the time, that was a good thing. Later, as my life became
increasingly complicated, I would demand much more
from men . . . Unconditional love. Validation. Approval. I
went prospecting for everything my father had never given

me. No, that's wrong. I was looking for a man who could undo the damage my father had done. He'd ripped a huge hole inside me, and I needed someone to fill it.

But I'm getting ahead of myself again.

I had things to look forward to in New York. And one thing I wasn't looking forward to. I didn't tell anyone to meet me at JFK because I wanted to take care of the unpleasantness first. I took a cab to 14th Street—God it was nice not to have to think about money!—and went home to Ron.

When he first opened the door, my husband didn't immediately recognize me. I thought for a moment he was going to ask me who I was, but then the synapses clicked in and he said "Jesus!" and he hugged me. There was something frightened and tentative about the hug. He was a mess. And the place was a mess. I stepped through, literally watching where I put my feet, and turned to look at him. He had lost weight; his clothes hung loosely on his frame. His beautiful hair had lost its luster. His teeth were brown, stained with nicotine. And his eyes—I don't know how to describe it—there was no light in them. His eyes looked *dead*.

"You look good," I lied. "You could gain a little weight, but you look good."

He knew I was lying.

I stole a look toward the bedroom. The door was open, but the bed was empty. I guess I half-expected to find him with a woman.

"Jesus, Janice. I can't believe it's you."

"It's me."

"I missed you, girl. God how I missed you!"

I knew he was lying.

We ordered Chinese from the roach-infested place around the corner—a long way from the Brasserie Lipp—and Ron worked hard at making conversation. He asked about some of my adventures and talked about some of his own. The band was off again the following afternoon, he mentioned with feigned regret.

After dinner we sat on the couch, and Ron oohed and aahed over my portfolio. It *was* getting pretty good, and Ron was clearly impressed, but his mind was drifting. He started getting antsy as the evening wore on. I told him I was exhausted, and took a shower and got into bed next to him. Propped up against two pillows, sitting on the covers, he looked miserable. It was a Sunday night. He'd been watching *60 Minutes* without really seeing it.

"What's this segment about?" I asked.

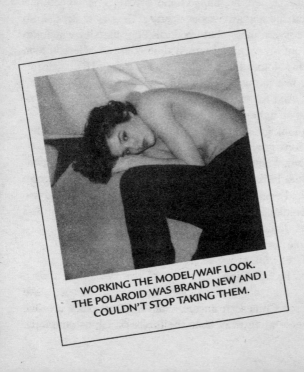

WORKING THE MODEL/WAIF LOOK. THE POLAROID WAS BRAND NEW AND I COULDN'T STOP TAKING THEM.

"I'm not sure," he said. He smiled a nervous smile and put his arm around me and told me again how much he'd missed me, how glad he was to have me back, and how upset he was that he had to leave the next day. There was no feeling in the words, and the gestures were just gestures. It was excruciating.

A few minutes into this he got up and went into the bathroom. I muted the volume on the TV. It was awfully quiet in there. Then I heard some strange sounds that I wasn't sure I could identify coming from within. Next was the clink of a spoon falling onto the tiled floor. I turned out the light and tried to blink away a tear. When he came out of the bathroom, groping through the darkness and whispering my name, I pretended I was asleep.

In the morning, I was up early. Everything looked so shabby. I missed my buttery croissants and those French cheeses and the porcelain mugs the size of soup bowls. Ron stumbled out of the bedroom as I was making the coffee.

"Try to get home early, babe," he said. "I leave tonight." B.B. and the boys were heading south, to the Chitlin Circuit, for what promised to be a very long trip.

I dressed up like a French whore and went off to see my agents. I was received like the queen I had become. Everyone was fawning—and you know how I feel about fawning. It's right there on the Top Ten list of things that make me happy. Wilhelmina herself came out and hugged me and whisked me into her office. She had three cigarettes going at once.

"Well, you did it," she said.

"I guess I did, didn't I?"

"The phone's been ringing off the hook for weeks. 'When is Janice coming back?' 'Can we get Janice?' 'We want to hold this for Janice.' Janice Janice Janice." She named names. Most of them belonged to the same people who'd spent the previous year slamming doors in my face. "How does it feel?" Willie asked.

"Fucking great," I said. "When do I start?"

"Well, I have someone who has been calling for weeks. He knows everyone in France, and they've gotten him all worked up about you."

"If you say Mike Reinhardt, I'll kill you," I said. I was smiling broadly.

"Well, then—consider me dead."

Here is the fucking thing about Mike Reinhardt. He didn't even fucking remember. He walks over and shakes my hand and does the usual I've-heard-so-much-about-you shit and starts talking about how he's going to change my life.

"My life doesn't need changing, honey," I told him. "I'm here because you know how much I can do for your career."

Mike smiled. But he seemed a little wary. "Everyone told me how nice you were," he said.

"You don't remember, do you?"

"Remember what?"

"I was here once. Last year. You treated me like shit."

"Did I?"

"Yes," I said, mustering my dirtiest look.

"In that case, I apologize." He lit a joint and offered me a hit—a huge improvement over my last visit—but I declined. "Maybe I can do better this time," he said. "You mind sitting over there? I want to test the lights."

"I don't test," I said. I was being a major bitch. And loving it. "That was last year. You should have had one of Willie's testers come over earlier. Obviously you're not prepared for me."

"Was I that bad?" he asked. He was smiling. Motherfucker knew I liked him. Could I help it? He had the nicest eyes.

"You were awful," I said. We were sitting in a haze of smoke.

"I've improved with age," he said.

"How old are you?" I asked.

"Thirty-eight," he said. Not quite old enough to be my father, but close. "You?"

"Twenty-one."

"Nice age," he said. "But way too young for me."

"You ready?" I said. "I'll give you half an hour. I've got *real* photographers waiting."

He laughed and got to work. The man was a master. Remember I said that shooting with Guy Bourdin was like having sex? Well, this was like having sex and coming. And by the way, I hate to break it to you—but all that shit you see in the movies: *Yeah, baby. Camera loves you, baby. Fuck me, baby. You make me so hard.* It's bullshit. The truth is closer to, *Very nice, Janice. Yes, Janice—perfect. A little more, Janice. A little less.* And I don't know about you, but I think straight talk can be pretty hot. I had to fight the urge to fuck him then and there. I wanted him so bad my Little Flower barked.

I hailed a cab and hurried home. I was in a great mood, Ron notwithstanding. I'd been in New York twenty-four hours and was on top of the world.

I found my husband in the bathroom, stoned or drunk, I wasn't sure. He looked up at me, glassy-eyed, and mumbled something that sounded like an apology. He looked like a dog that had messed the carpet and knew trouble was coming. Tears welled in my eyes.

"I was just on my way out," he said. It was true. His suitcase was packed and waiting by the bedroom door. He struggled to his feet. Looked at me. Didn't know what to say.

"I'll call you," he said.

And I said, "Good."

Then he kissed me—once, lightly, on the cheek—and picked up his suitcase and walked out. I heard the front door close. I listened to his fading footfalls. Growing fainter. Making their way down the stairs now. Then I went into the bedroom and cried myself to sleep.

In the morning I went to see Willie and spilled my guts. She gave me the number of a divorce lawyer and told me not to look back. I didn't know what to do. Somehow, that didn't feel right.

The secretary buzzed her. It was Mike Reinhardt. I reached for Willie's phone and took the call.

"What?" I said. I wasn't in the mood for chitchat.

"What are you doing?" he asked.

"What's it to you?" I said.

"I'm at Kennedy Airport," Mike said. "I have to go to Paris. Why don't you come with me?"

"You have a lot of nerve."

"I'm on assignment for French *Vogue*."

That gave me pause. He pressed on. "Come on, Janice. You know something happened between us yesterday. Don't pretend it didn't."

"Good luck," I said, and hung up.

I did a shoot for Bloomingdale's later that day and made a few calls between setups. One of those calls was to Ron's mother. I guess you could call it a telephone intervention, though that was in the days before the word became part of our everyday vocabulary. I told her I was worried about Ron. It broke my heart, but he needed help and he wasn't listening to me, and I knew he loved his mother. It also broke her heart, but I knew how tough she was. I'd seen her put my rat-bastard father in his place the night we got married; I figured she was up to this.

"You've always been good to me," I said. "I'm sorry it didn't work out for Ron and me. I really am. I tried. I hope you can do something for him."

I finished my shoot and got back to the office. Mike had called twice more; Ron had called a dozen times. Mike was in love. My husband was out of control—and he called again as I was leaving the agency. I took the call and couldn't understand a word—he was cursing and screaming at the top of his voice. He sounded possessed. Fucking whore cunt, and a hundred other things. He reminded me, at that moment, of my rageaholic father.

"I'll *kill* you, you bitch! How could you tell my mother!? What the fuck *did* you tell her? I will fucking kill you."

I hung up and dug out the lawyer's number and called to tell him I needed a divorce. He was on his way out, but since I was a friend of Willie's he took a moment and listened. I told him I needed nothing from Ron. I could take care of myself.

"All I really want is my name back," I said.

SHOT BY MIKE
REINHARDT FOR
FRENCH *VOGUE*,
1979.

He seemed surprised. Surprised and impressed.

Mike called again the next morning, this time from Paris.

"How did you get my home number?" I asked.

"Patrick Demarchelier gave it to me," he said. "He thinks we should be working together."

"Is that what he thinks?"

"Yes."

"This is my home," I said. "In the future, I'd advise you to call my booker."

He ignored that. "You know," he said in that beguiling voice of his, "it's crazy . . . I can't find a single girl in Paris that's right for this *Vogue* shoot. And the pity is, it's a cover."

I took a beat. "I travel first class," I said.

There was a flight later that day. He told me he'd be waiting for me at Orly.

I hung up and called Willie.

"You're crazy," she said.

"I don't want to be here right now," I said. "My husband is out of his head. I hate that dump on 14th Street. I miss Paris."

"You just got back," she said. "You're a star. You are solidly booked for the next three months."

And I said, "Something happened at Mike Reinhardt's studio."

"Watch out for him," Willie said. But I could feel the smile in her voice. "He's trouble."

I didn't care. A little French trouble sounded pretty good.

Arriving at Orly was like a replay of the first time, with Reinhardt in the Dominick Silverstein role, red roses for daisies, and a limo with Cristal waiting for me outside.

"That's a lot of props you've got there," I told Mike. "Flowers, champagne, a limo. Are you really that insecure?" Mike laughed. He knew I was just messing with him.

"If you think I'm trying to seduce you, you're wrong," he shot right back. "I'm simply apologizing for past sins."

The limo dropped us in front of a gorgeous building on the Left Bank, near Notre Dame. I half-expected to see Quasimodo loping past, on his way to the bell tower.

Mike took me upstairs. The apartment was bright and cozy, but it had only one bedroom. Hmmm. I wondered where poor Mike was going to sleep.

I showered and we went to the Brasserie Lipp for lunch. I sat there drinking white wine from one of their green-stemmed goblets. If he was trying to get on my good side, he was doing a pretty good job. I loved this place. I smiled at him. It was more of a tease than a smile. He smiled back, hopeful. "What are you smiling about?" I asked. "I hope you don't think you're going to get lucky. I'm here to work."

He laughed and paid the bill and we spent the afternoon walking around Paris. It's the best walking city in the world.

We didn't get back to the apartment till nightfall. I was hungry again from all the walking. Mike opened a nice Burgundy and I sat with him in the kitchen and watched him get to work. He made a simple pasta with *haricots verts* and tiny tomatoes. It was delicious. I liked the way he handled himself in the kitchen. I like men who cook. Men who cook are generally good lovers.

"So," I said, "I get the bedroom, right?"

"If you insist."

"I insist."

I got the bedroom. I wondered how long it would be before I heard his footfalls. And I must tell you, Dear Reader, it wasn't long at all . . .

I couldn't get enough of Mike, but—and I'm genuinely sorry about this, Mr. Reinhardt—it wasn't about sex. It was his mind I fell in love with. He was all about culture and good breeding. He spoke flawless English, of course, along with Italian, French, and German. He gave me tours of the city's finest museums—in four languages. He explained expressionism and impressionism and degenerate art. He took me to see the *Mona Lisa*. He spent hours showing me how much he had

MIKE REINHARDT
LOOKING GORGEOUS.
SOUTHAMPTON, 1981.

learned about light and composition and depth of field from Leonardo Da Vinci.

Here I was, a Florida pom-pom girl, getting a real education from a man who actually knew what he was talking about. Who cared if sex was an afterthought? It was over fast, anyway.

I was in awe of him. I didn't speak; I listened. He was flawless. Mike Reinhardt was the man I'd been waiting for my whole life. (Love has some side effects, including tremors and delusions.) And there was an added bonus: When those first proofs came back, I looked better than I'd ever looked in my life.

On the third night we took a break and went out to dinner with Debbie and a "new friend" of hers. Debbie looked great, but I didn't like the guy. He was close to forty, older than Mike. She was a kid. I wondered what kind of evil father-daughter thing was at play here. It's amazing how much a parent can damage a child. I wanted to say something to Debbie, but who was I to talk? I could see myself in her. We'd been shaped by the same forces.

Worse still, the next day I found out that the son-ofabitch was running around claiming that he'd had his way with Debbie, not because of who she was, but because she was my sister—the sister of Janice Dickinson, the hot model. I was a little flattered, sad to say, but also furious. So here's what I did: I called the guy and told him I found him irresistible, and I wondered why he was settling for my little sister when he could have the Real Thing. I said I was doing a shoot the next day at the airport, miles from town, and suggested he book a room for us at the Hotel Sofitel. *The penthouse would be great. Oysters and champagne. Lots and lots of both.* I'd sneak away at lunch and join him. "I must have you," I said. I swear to God, I heard him whimper.

Poor sap. I had planned it so beautifully. Mike was gone all afternoon, riding his beloved ten-speed bicycle, and I was out shopping. But I stopped at pay phones every hour on the hour to call this character. *I'm coming. Please wait; I've been delayed but the shoot is almost over and I'll be there momentarily, honest.* I made my last call around midnight, shortly after Mike had fallen asleep.

"Hello?" he said.

"Hey, shithead, it's me," I said. "I'm not going to make it, so why don't you just fuck yourself?"

I went back to New York two days later and called Willie in advance to let her know I was ready to book and boogie. When I set the phone down, it rang immediately. I was sure it was Mike, but it was Ron. He was coming home. "I'm sorry I went crazy on you last time, babe," he said. "But I'm good now. I'm clean." Uh huh. He could barely speak.

I hung up and headed for the salon. My hair was fine, but I was feeling lost, and I wanted to see a new friend of mine: Edward Tricome, this wiry, high-energy kid from Brooklyn who worked at *the* hottest salon in town, on East 57th Street.

"What's wrong, Janice?" he asked. He was standing behind me, the two of us reflected in the mirror. He had his hands on my shoulders. I told him the Ron story. He thought about it for maybe two seconds, then said, "Why don't you move in with me?"

I packed a few things and went over to his apartment later that night. "You can't live here," I said. "This is a dump. We've got to find a new home."

Mike reached me at the agency the next morning. "Where the hell were you last night?" he asked.

"I moved out."

"Where'd you go?"

"To Edward's place."

"Edward? The hair guy?"

"Yes," I said.

"But he's not gay!" Mike exclaimed.

"I know," I said. "Neither am I."

"Janice—"

"Would you relax!"

"This isn't working for me," Mike said. "I don't like this at all."

I should have been smart enough to see right then and there what fate had in store for me, but I was foolishly, blindly in love. "Mike," I said. "You're the only man for me."

Guys like to hear shit like that from time to time.

He called every day. He was completely in love, he said. I swore I'd hang up if he told me I was the best thing that ever happened to him. It's a line I hope never to hear again.

Of course, love is never uncomplicated. Mike was "sort of" dating another model at the time, Barbara Minty.

"Have you told her yet?" I asked.

"As soon as I get back," he promised.

I worked like a banshee that next week. But every night after work, no matter how tired I was, I'd hook up with Edward and this mousy little broker and we'd trek from one apartment to the next. On the third night we found ourselves in a duplex on East 59th Street. There was something really tacky about the place. We loved it.

The following Saturday, Edward and I moved into our new digs. In the middle of the afternoon, the doorbell rang. Edward answered the door. A middle-aged man was standing in the corridor.

"Is Kathy here?" he asked.

"There's no Kathy here," Edward said.

The man looked confused and left.

Twenty minutes later another guy stopped by. He was looking for Sybil. Ten minutes after that it was a Haitian businessman looking for Candy.

"This used to be a fucking whorehouse!" Edward said, doubled over with laughter. We couldn't believe it. We went back to our unpacking but a few minutes later the doorbell rang again. A big guy was standing there. He looked like a mobster.

"Is Alice around?"

I couldn't resist: "Alice doesn't live here anymore."

"Who the fuck are you?" the guy said. He pushed his way inside and began to look around.

"Hey! You can't do that, pal," Edward said. Edward, who was half the guy's size. The guy ignored him. We followed him into the kitchen. There were boxes everywhere. What did he think, that we were bullshitting him?

"The girls are gone," I said. I wanted him out of there.

"Oh yeah?" The mobster turned and took me in with his lopsided grin. "You look pretty good to me."

Edward grabbed a butcher knife and put it to the guy's throat.

"Hey, pal, I don't think you're listening too good. There's no hookers here no more. They went bye-bye. And you better go fucking bye-bye, too."

The guy left. I slammed and bolted the door behind

him. I was terrified. "Jesus! Edward! I can't believe you did that! You're my hero."

"Don't look now," Edward said. "But I think I peed my pants."

When Mike came back from Paris two weeks later, he invited me over to his studio at Carnegie Hall and cooked me an amazing dinner. By the time we got to dessert he told me he'd broken up with Barbara and asked me to move in with him. I said I'd think about it.

I did think about it. But not too deeply. My last stab at conjugal bliss hadn't exactly been a resounding success. I wanted to get to know Mike better, not get in too deeply too quickly. Plus I liked my newfound freedom. And I liked living with Edward. Well, *living with Edward* is a bit of an overstatement: I was at Mike's about four nights a week.

This went on for several months. And it was working. Mike kept begging me to move in with him, and I kept saying no. Still, it's nice to be asked, nice to be wanted.

Then Debbie came back to New York and crashed with me and two nights later I came home and found her in bed with Edward. It was kind of weird. My little sister and my roommate, lying there, grinning up at me like naughty children.

I called Mike. "I've thought about it," I said. "You're right. We're a great couple. We should be living together." He came over and helped me get my things and that was that.

I worked and worked. I began making oodles of money. I was hot and knew it and it went to my head. Photographers started learning to send limos for me. The other girls took the subway, but not Janice.

I'd go home after a hard day's work and there'd be flowers waiting for me. *Thank you, Janice. You were wonderful, Janice. You are beautiful, Janice.* I would get a call from the office at night to make sure I was safe in bed, and a wake-up call in the morning to see me on my way.

I loved the way the photo studios smelled. They were usually cold and damp, with a hint of chemicals in the air. Coffee, too. Fresh-brewed, and tons of it. And doughnuts. You could always tell the bulimic models: They're the ones who ate the doughnuts.

I was starting to take an increasingly aggressive interest in my career. Starting with the pictures. The agency was always sending new shots of us to its clients. Most models didn't get involved: Sifting through all those photographs was hard work, so they let the agency handle it.

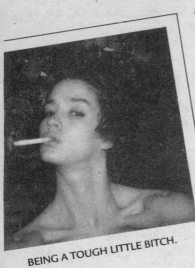

BEING A TOUGH LITTLE BITCH.

But I was very picky about what got sent out. I had opinions. I wanted more control, and I got it. I had a good eye for the way pictures worked. I knew more about photography than they suspected—more than *I* suspected—and what I didn't know I was determined to learn.

Willie took me to lunch or dinner two or three times a week. She'd fawn over me. She'd invite clients along, and sometimes they brought their wives. They all fawned. One woman asked if I'd be good enough to autograph a menu for her teenage daughter. "She's in awe of you," she said. I took the pen and scrawled my name across the menu and thought, *You bet she's in awe of me. She should be. I'm fucking great.*

Funny what success will do to a girl, particularly a girl with a split personality. The insecure, hyperanxious, self-loathing Janice was nowhere in sight.

The money started pouring in. Editorial was nothing: seventy-five dollars a day. I doubled it. They offered me twelve hundred for a lingerie shoot: I asked for two thousand and got it. I became the guinea pig. "If we can get twenty-five hundred for Janice, we'll try to get it for Iman."

I could hear the bookers in the office. "No, sorry. Janice isn't available." "Janice? You can't afford Janice." "I'll talk to her, but, you know—Janice is picky."

I weighed myself twice a day, every day. I was five nine and a half and 134 pounds when I'd first come to New York. I was still five nine and a half, as far as I could tell, but now I kept my weight at an even 125. And I had to work at it, people. You could find me jogging around the Central Park reservoir five mornings a week. Riding my bike Sunday mornings, when the park was closed to traffic. Practicing yoga with Zen Master Mike.

I was in total control for the first time in my life. I was *driving* this rig. And I felt *good* about it. I could look at myself in the mirror—my surface self—and see beauty there. Beauty and power. I would think, *Fuck you, Ray, you rat bastard. Never amount to anything? Look at me now.*

They wanted me for a shoot with Luciano Pavarotti. I said, "Fine, but if you're going to put his name in the piece, I want my name in there, too." I wasn't about to hide in the background. I became my own publicist. And it worked.

There it was. *Luciano Pavarotti and Janice Dickinson Paint the Town Red. Janice Dickinson and the New York Mets Do Manhattan.*

The thing is, I made it *fun.* I would do anything. I was game. I remember flying to Tobago for Sir Norman Parkinson, *the* preeminent British fashion photographer for damn near fifty years. "Janice," he said in that tweedy uppercrust voice. "Would you very much mind scaling the side of a mountain in a thong?"

"No problem, Normy," I said, and I scaled away.

"You know what I like about you, Janice?" he said later, as we wrapped up for the day.

"Slay me."

"You do the work. You're not a diva like most of the girls. And you make me laugh."

There was no stopping me. One day I showed up to audition for a JVC Handycam campaign. It was a major gig, and I wanted it. I walked into a conference room and found myself alone with six Japanese executives. They were all dressed exactly alike, each with his hands clasped in front of him. They all just sat and stared, not even moving: If you told me they were breathing, I would have asked for proof. No warm hellos, no niceties, a big zero.

"Gentlemen," I said. "The search is over."

Still nothing.

"I am the new face of JVC."

Still nothing. The fucking guys looked like statues. But I wasn't going to let them get to me. No. I wasn't going to let them see Janice the Terrified, Janice the Loser Who Will Never Amount to Anything. Hell no. Today, I was Janice the Magnificent, Janice Who Could Do No Wrong. *Prepare to be dazzled, motherfuckers!*

"You see these almond-shaped eyes?" I asked. I walked across the room, slowly, dramatically. Their heads moved in unison, like spectators at a slow-motion tennis match. "These are the eyes of my Japanese great-great-grandmother."

Jesus! Where was I getting this bullshit?

"That's right, gentlemen. My great-great-grandmother was Japanese. And in a moment of weakness, admittedly, she had the poor taste to sleep with an Irishman. That Irishman was my great-great-grandfather. And I'm not saying he was a nice guy. He wasn't. But my great-great-grandmother was a fine woman, a fine *Japanese* woman, and if you think about that, gentlemen, I don't know why you would even consider another model."

I left without another word. What a fucking performance!

I got back to the agency and was told that Willie wanted to see me right away. I walked in and batted my way through the cigarette smoke.

"What's up?" I said.

"The JVC guys called. They want you."

My heart was beating a mile a minute, but I acted very cool. "I want twenty thousand a day," I said.

"Don't be ridiculous!"

"Willie," I said. "The business is changing. Can't you see it? These guys have money. I want to make the jump to the next level. You have to be more aggressive."

"You'll aggress yourself right out of a job," she said.

"Are you going to ask for the twenty thousand or not?"

"I'm going to ask for five thousand, and you'll be happy to get it."

I laughed and turned and walked toward the door.

"Janice!"

I kept going. I walked right out of the agency and across the street to Eileen Ford's to see Monique Pillard, now the head booker. Monique had believed in me from the start, from the first time she set eyes on me, that afternoon when Eileen dismissed me as *too ethnic*. And she *still* believed in me. I told her about the JVC guys: I knew I had them, I said. And then I took another chance: I told her I wanted to speak to Jerry, Eileen's husband, not Eileen. This was highly unusual, to say the least, a real slap in the face to Eileen—as Monique understood only too well.

"Eileen is sensitive, you know," she said. "Are you sure about this?"

"I'm sensitive, too," I said.

She nodded and headed for the inner sanctum. A few minutes later she returned to lead me down the corridor.

We went into Eileen's office, Monique and me and my big fucking lips.

Eileen and Jerry stood up. She was so nicely put together. She had a big smile for me. But she knew I remembered; I could see it in her face.

"Hello, Janice," Jerry said. "Nice to meet you."

"So nice to see you again, Janice," Eileen cooed.

"Here's the deal," I said, plunging right in. I told them about the JVC campaign, just as I'd told Wilhelmina and Monique. And I told them I wanted twenty thousand a day.

"Janice, really—" Eileen began.

But Jerry cut her off. "You'll get it," he said.

"Good," I said. "I get my twenty grand, you get me."

MONIQUE PILLARD—
AN INCREDIBLE FRIEND.

Jerry said he'd negotiate the deal himself. We left Eileen's office together. Jerry made the call, and I got my twenty grand. I called Willie and told her to send my books over to Ford. "I got what I asked for," I said, and hung up. Okay, so I wanted to rub it in. Sue me. It felt great.

THE GOOD
DAUGHTER

Once a week, Sunday afternoons, regular as clockwork, I called home to speak to my mother. I don't know why I bothered—she'd never been much of a mother—but I guess part of me felt bad for her. Her life seemed so empty and horrible. She'd never seen Paris or Milan, and never would, and she'd never get out of that backwater because she was never going to find the courage to free herself from the rat bastard.

I was always anxious before I called, but a little wine or champagne did the trick. It was like magic. *Boom!* I'm okay now. And I'd pick up the phone and dial.

"Oh, honey, another magazine cover! I clipped it out and framed it. You are just such a star!"

"How are you, Mom?"

"I am great, thank the Good Lord." The sound of her voice was enough to make me cringe. "I am just so happy to be alive, and to have a wonderful little girl like you, and oh, yes, I forgot to thank you for that beautiful silk blouse you sent me last week! I wore it to church this morning. I got so many nice comments on it!"

She was into God now, easing herself off the drugs and into a nice anesthetic church buzz. Debbie told me about the little pictures of the Virgin Mary, hanging all over the house, and how Mother never went anywhere without her blessed rosary.

"Glad you liked the shirt, Mom."

"Have you talked to your sister?"

I told her Debbie was doing fine. She and Edward had broken up and she'd moved to the Upper East Side and was booking jobs left and right.

"And how's our darling Alexis?"

Alexis was living in Pennsylvania, staining glass and making jewelry and hanging out with an older man who treated her less than nicely. I resented the way Mother always called her "our Alexis," as if somehow we shared the blame for what the rat bastard had done to her.

"She's fine, Mom."

By this time, I was starting to get pissed. I *always* got pissed. I tried to be civil, but I couldn't seem to get beyond my anger. She had never protected Alexis. She had never been a mother. She was too busy shutting herself down.

"The weather has been terrible here . . . a new administrator at the hospital . . . could use a nice pair of comfortable shoes . . . the mechanic says it's the crankshaft, whatever that is . . . " I would let her drone on, not really listening, getting angrier, guzzling my wine to take the edge off. I was usually pretty buzzed by the time I had eased her off the phone. And I usually kept going until Mike returned from his Sunday power ride around Central Park.

"Are you drunk?" he'd say, all pissy. "Don't you know drinking is bad for you? You're not getting enough exercise. The body is a temple, and you're treating yours like shit."

So, yeah—things weren't perfect. In due course, I discovered that Mike was not merely opinionated, but fucking tyrannical. I was allowed to have opinions of my own, yes, but I was urged to keep them to myself. Whenever I

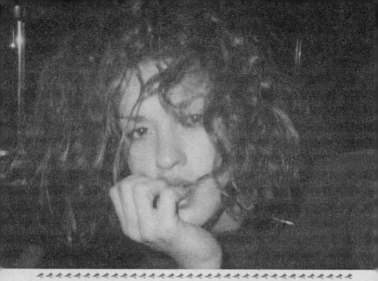

TRYING TO FIGURE OUT HOW TO SET A LEICA TIMER
AT CARNEGIE HALL STUDIO.

ignored this unwritten law, we would argue. Loud, *fuck-you* arguments. Mike had to be in charge. Mike had to be in control. Mike worked on convincing me that I was nothing without him, and, since I'd been trained to believe that I *was* nothing, I was an easy sell.

Still, I found it hard to bite my tongue. So we argued constantly. Bitterly. We argued about how I should look in a shot. About what I was wearing. About the way I held my fork. And we argued, incessantly, about other men. Mike was so fucking jealous it drove me nuts. Couldn't he see I was devoted to him? He was even *retroactively* jealous. He was curious about men I'd slept with long before I met him. He wondered if I'd slept with any photographers—and whether they were any good. As *photographers,* not as lovers.

Men! Go figure.

Still, confused as I was about life with Mike, my career was going strong. I was so hot I was burning. All the big jobs were beginning to roll in. Revlon. Max Factor. Clairol. And all the name designers were after me. Halston. Bill Blass. Perry Ellis. Oscar de la Renta.

Mike shot me half a dozen times. He *insisted*. He was still the Genius of Light, as far as I was concerned, and I was curious about how he managed it. I started getting seriously interested in photography. I'd watch him set up and pepper him with questions about lenses, distortion, shadows. Eventually, he stopped answering my questions. I guess he was worried I might learn a little too much.

No matter: There were other masters. I was out there all day, day after day. Posing, vamping, learning. And these others appreciated my interest in the work. I hate to be immodest, but what the hell—this is my book. So I'll spell it out: I wasn't just about looking good. I had personality. I was a fucking hoot to work with. (I even got laughs out of old, stiff-upper-lip Normy.) I was interesting and *interested*. I asked questions, made suggestions, tried to make it fun for everyone. And that came through in the pictures. And it changed things for everyone. Hell, before I came along, models were just supposed to stand around looking like, well, *models*. I made it okay to have personality. And of course I went overboard. I was Personality Plus. And the others followed. (Well, they *tried*.)

At around this time I was booking so many jobs that Monique was starting to worry. I'd be doing a Saks catalog in the morning, a shoot for French *Vogue* in the afternoon, and a test for a commercial in the evening. One frenetic day I actually walked out of a shoot and into the wrong limo, and only discovered my mistake as we were crossing the Brooklyn Bridge.

Monique begged me to slow down. "Who do you think you are?" she asked in her thick French accent. "Super*mon*?"

"No," I said. "Super*model*."

And lo and behold! I'd coined a phrase!

Mike was so jealous. "Supermodel!? What is that shit? What about Superphotographer?"

I told him he was lucky to have me. "Look at all the breaks I've given you. Me, Supermodel."

"*You* gave *me* breaks! Ha! I fucking made you," he said.

"Fuck you," I said. "You're nothing without me."

"Right!"

We had huge fights about who was doing what for whom, who was doing the using.

Mike had this line: "We're all prostitutes. Every last one of us is a whore." He'd started out as a law student and joked that he'd opted out because he couldn't deal with all the snakes. By the time he discovered that there were even more snakes in the fashion biz, it was too late to back out. "It's mutual abuse. Everyone uses everyone, in work and in life. That's what all relationships are about."

"Is that what *our* relationship is about?" I asked.

"Of course. Why should we be any different?"

"So what happens when we've used each other up?" I asked.

"We'll find someone else to use," he said.

It made me sad.

So I lost myself in work. And there wasn't anyone I *didn't* work for. I was in all the magazines. I did layouts for Hush Puppies, Cutex nails, Max Factor, Keiko bathing suits. I did billboards for Virginia Slims. Yes, I sold cigarettes to the young. This was the mid-1970s. What the fuck did we know? We didn't even care. I was in love and in money, and people recognized me on the street. Ah, fame. Who knew how many adolescent boys across the country were locked in their parents' bathrooms at that very moment, their little cocks in their hands, trying to will the picture of me to leap off the page and into their laps.

Like I said, I'm here to make it fun.

One day, a Venezuelan photographer told me: "You are the first dark superstar. You opened the doors for all these other girls." He was right. I represented hope for all the girls who'd been told they were too ethnic. They looked at me and knew they could be as beautiful as—hell, *more* beautiful than—any white-bread blond. And about time, too! America was a melting pot. Why shouldn't the fashion world be stoked over the same fires?

And he was right about opening doors. Suddenly there were other "mutts" sniffing around the fashion business, especially at the runway shows. Dalma, a Brazilian model at Zoli, who had the most amazing, long-legged, rhumbalike walk I'd ever seen. Apollonia, the Polish princess, who kicked her legs like a prima ballerina. And Pat Cleveland, so light-skinned she could have passed for white. Pat was one of the greatest runway models ever. When she moved, she painted the air around her with the clothes—a veritable riot of living color. She was Halston's favorite.

"Baby, when I saw you in *Vogue,* I knew there was hope," Dalma once told me. And Apollonia echoed the sentiment: "I love you, you big Polack. But watch your butt; I'm right behind you."

They still had trouble getting into the magazines, though. That felt too permanent, too risky. Who were these girls? What would readers think? And—most important—would they sell product or magazines? And while it was true that *Vogue* had taken a chance with Beverly Johnson, it wasn't as if the doors had opened; it wasn't as if the offers were coming in fast and furious.

Of course the print girls were now clamoring for the runway shows. It hadn't started out that way—runway shows were something you did in Milan or Paris, and they were hard work and not much fun—but suddenly they became chic. A runway show was like a stage play. You were on, and you were live. It was terrifying—but that's what made it so exciting.

But enough about them, darling. Let's get back to *moi* . . .

Monique kept getting calls from the French. They wanted me back. After all, they said they'd discovered me, and they felt entitled. (That fucking word again—*entitled*. Just like the rat bastard, may he rot in hell.) She put them off until the offers were too good to refuse. I flew to Paris and booked gigs with Yves Saint Laurent, Issey Miyake, Yamamoto, and Kenzo. Then I hopped over to Milan for back-to-back meetings with Gianni Versace and Giorgio Armani—a trip in and of itself.

Ricardo Guay, my Italian booking agent, was waiting for me at the Milan airport. "Don't be nervous," he said,

APOLLONIA AND JERRY ON THE WAY
TO LONG ISLAND FOR A SHOOT.

helping me into the limo. Then he turned to the driver and barked, "Versace!"

I *was* nervous, of course. I was crazy about Versace's designs, and the initial meeting with a designer is always a little intense. You want to impress them; you want them to like you; you want them to want to drape your body in their genius clothes.

We crawled through downtown traffic as Ricardo made small talk about life and love and misadventures—mostly his—then, finally, there we were, pulling up in front of Versace's atelier. I took a deep breath and stepped into the building. They were waiting for me. A good sign. A very hip young assistant ushered me into the spacious studio and the master himself turned toward me. He had the warmest smile; it matched the warmth of his eyes.

"Jan*eeeece,*" he said, taking my hand in both of his. "Thank you so much for coming."

For the next half-hour he had me in and out of leather jackets, fall sweaters, jodhpurs, more leather, and more sweaters. He handed me a leather riding crop and made me feel like the queen of the Horsey Set. He asked me to walk a little, so I did. But after a minute my giddiness ran away with me and I broke into a trot, whinnying like a thoroughbred. Versace laughed. He came over and hugged me. "I like you," he said. "We will be seeing much of each other, yes?"

"Yes," I said. "I certainly hope so."

He walked me out and gave me a little kiss good-bye and I hopped into the car and sped off to Armani's. "How'd it go?" Ricardo asked.

"He loves me," I said.

The atmosphere at Armani's was a little different. Some woman who looked like she'd just stepped off the space shuttle directed me to a small, sterile waiting room. I sat and waited. And waited. I waited so long I fell asleep. When Little Miss Astronaut returned to fetch me, I noticed I'd been dozing for over an hour.

"This way," she said. She led me down a stark corridor and through a large door into the inner sanctum. Giorgio was sitting on an elevated throne—an actual throne, I kid you not!—on the far side of the room. He watched me approach with a mystifying lack of interest. He was handsome; his hair was starting to go white, and he combed it straight back, proud like a lion. Something in his hand caught the light, and I found myself mesmerized by the largest pinky ring I'd ever seen.

"Hello, Gianni," I said, parking myself directly in front of his throne. I had to tilt my head back to look at him—he was way above us commoners—but I was feeling pretty chipper. I'd done a number on Versace and was primed to impress Armani, too. I almost whinnied with excitement.

But something was wrong. Armani's boredom had turned to anger. His eyes flashed. *What had I done?* Little Miss Astronaut crept up behind me and whispered in my ear. "Giorgio. *Giorgio.*"

Good Christ! I'd called him Gianni.

Giorgio raised his left hand—the one with the massive pinky ring—and directed my attention to door. *What!?* The motherfucker was dismissing me? Jesus!

"Are you putting me on?" I said. But he wouldn't even meet my eyes. Instead, he just stared at his Little Astronaut, and when he snapped at her in Italian she jumped and literally took me by the arm, dragging me toward the exit. I couldn't believe it. I took my arm back and turned back to Armani. That ring, that throne, that *attitude.* "Jesus, dude—who the fuck do you think you are? The goddamn pope?" Then I spun round and marched out the door.

"How'd it go?" Ricardo asked when I got back into the limo next to him.

"Take me back to Versace's," I said, and I burst into tears.

Versace's assistant was surprised to see me again. But he went off to get the boss. I was still crying, but I managed to tell Gianni what happened. He gave me a hug and dabbed away at my eyes with a cashmere scarf, laughing in spite of himself. "You called him the pope! That's wonderful! She called Giorgio the pope! *Il Pappa!*" Everyone else laughed, too. Versace draped the cashmere scarf around my neck and kissed me on both cheeks, like the pope might have done. "I bless you, my child," he said, laughing. And everyone laughed with him, me included. "Janeece, you and I are going to be great friends!"

Ricardo drove me to the airport for my flight back to Rome. I was relieved and happy. "I wish Versace wasn't gay," I told Ricardo. And I did; he was the perfect man.

A few days later, Mike—the not-so-perfect man—came to visit me in Rome. He missed me, he said. And, unlike Ron, he was willing and able to do something about it.

But the minute he landed, we were fighting. We fought about everything. About who got what side of the bed. About where we were going for dinner. About the clothes I wore. Even about money, though we were both rolling in it.

Most of all, we fought because Mike was pathologically jealous. It seemed there was nothing I could say or do to convince him that I was faithful, that I was his, that I was a one-man woman. In addition, he couldn't handle all the attention I was getting. And that first night he was in town I was getting plenty of attention, more even than I'd bargained for . . .

I was doing Valentino's haute couture show. It was held outdoors, at the base of the famous stairs outside the Colosseum. A huge tent had been erected off to one side, a few yards from the runway. I'd already made the trip up and down that goddamn runway two dozen times, and I was dog-tired. It was getting late; we were near the end of the show. Valentino came over to make sure I looked perfect. He was tall and rail thin and deeply tanned; every last hair on his head was glued into place, stiff as a helmet.

"You look marvelous, darling," he said.

I reached for another Baccarat flute of champagne and finished it off in a gulp. "VaVa," I said. "This dress is too tight. I can't breathe."

"Breathing is for amateurs," he said.

I had another glass of champagne and braced myself, and when my turn came I stepped out onto the runway and wowed the crowd. It felt great to be loved. I was blowing kisses, puckering up for the photographers. I saw Mike scowling at me from the third row, but resisted the urge to give him the finger. Then I reached the end of the runway and it wasn't there. *Gone*—just like that. And for a brief moment I found myself sailing through the air—held aloft, no doubt, by the bubbles in the champagne—only to crash into the lap of the great Sophia Loren.

The paparazzi went nuts. They trampled each other to get at us.

"Oh, Miss Loren," I said, all safe and warm on her lap, nestled in her celebrated bosom. "I am so so sorry."

She was sitting with Marcello Mastroianni and now turned to look at him as if to say, *Do something*. And he did. He stood and helped me to my feet—flashbulbs exploding all around us—then bent low and kissed my hand. The crowd went wild. Marcello took a bow and smiled. He raised my hand—a victory salute—and helped me back onto the runway. I curtsied, much to everyone's delight, then turned to go on my merry way. But Marcello wasn't done with me yet: He smacked me on the ass, hard, and the crowd roared with laughter. So did I, to be honest. I roared all the way back to the tent.

"Ay Jan*eece!*" VaVa moaned. "You're something else!"

He wasn't the only one who thought so. By midafternoon, my hotel room was overflowing with congratulatory cards and flowers.

"Can you get rid of some of these fucking flowers?" Mike groused. It was later that night; we were dressing for dinner. "I feel like I'm at a fucking funeral."

"Not *my* funeral," I said.

We had a peaceful enough stroll to the restaurant, but we'd barely ordered when Mike began giving me shit about Pierre Houles, one of the photographers I'd been working with. Pierre was another French wiseguy; he also happened to be one of Mike's best friends. He was very cool, a sort of European cowboy, and I was so sick of Mike's jealous badgering that I started playing into it.

SHOT BY MIKE REINHARDT
AT BREAKFAST. WE
LOVED TO READ THE
NEWSPAPER TOGETHER.

"Well, you know, Mike, you're good, but you're no Houles."

"What the fuck does *that* mean?" he snapped, raising his voice. People at the neighboring tables turned to watch. The Italians love good drama.

"What's wrong?" I said. "You think I'm sleeping with him?"

"Are you?"

"Fuck this!" I said. "I don't have to put up with your ridiculous insecurity." I threw my napkin down and stormed out.

I ran across the Piazza della Repubblica to the fountain by the Grand Hotel, feeling pissed off and belittled as I always did after a blowout with Mike. It was ninety degrees that July night in Rome; I grabbed my blouse in a frenzy of overheated anger, and it ripped. That got me so pissed that I started ripping off the rest of my clothes, and before I knew it I'd jumped into the fountain, butt-naked. Traffic stopped. I was mooning people and screaming at Mike and he was screaming at me and horns were blaring and the Italian men were cheering. A couple of guys tried to jump into the fountain with me. Fights broke out. The police came. A bellman ran over from the hotel with a big fluffy bathrobe for me and the police hustled us out of there and started traffic moving again.

I went back in our hotel room, and found Mike there. He pulled off my robe and fucked me.

"Is this love?" I asked him when it was over. (And it was over *fast*.)

"I don't know," he said. "You tell me."

He was asking the wrong girl. I didn't know what love was. There were times when I thought I was using Mike to be mean to me. Does that make any sense? *Meanness*. It's what I knew. It was familiar. And they say we're attracted to the familiar.

Still, I tried not to analyze it too deeply. Spend your life trying not to think about something, and eventually you discover you're afraid to start. So we'd fight and fuck and fight, and we called it love. And there were times when it felt like the best thing in the world.

In fact, when we got back to New York, there were moments of genuine domestic bliss. We'd sit home Saturday nights. Cook together. Lie in the tub in the candlelight, glowing with good feeling. We'd watch *Saturday Night Live* and fall asleep in each other's arms, like a pair of newlyweds who were finally taking a much-needed break from sex. But it didn't escape Mike when our ardor began to wane.

"There's an old joke," he said.

"Tell me."

"There are three stages of sex in married life," he began. "The first is Household Sex. That's where you fuck in every room in the house, in every imaginable position. The second is Bedroom Sex, which is where you fuck in the bedroom, but with less and less frequency and less and less enthusiasm . . . "

"And the third?"

"The third stage is Hallway Sex. That's where you pass each other in the hallway and say, 'Fuck you!' "

It was a pretty funny joke unless you thought about it. If you thought about it, it was pretty sad. It was sad because it was the goddamn truth. All that jealousy from Mike, and he was the one doing the cheating. I knew it. He traveled constantly, and every time he came back there would be whispered phone calls and odd charges on his credit card and this look about him like he'd been a bad little boy. He denied it, of course. Told me I was crazy. Told *everyone* I was crazy. And I accepted his denials because I wanted to believe he was faithful.

It's true what they say. We believe what we want to believe.

MODEL WARS

In the spring of 1977, with the snow gone and New York City awash in April sunshine, the business started growing cloudy. The turmoil was about money. But then it's always about money, isn't it? Money and sex . . .

The thing is, some people were getting very, very rich. Halston was already in the stratosphere, but photographers like Avedon were now demanding—and getting—million-dollar contracts. That was a lot of cash in those days. Photographers began to grumble—*Who the fuck is Avedon? I'm better than Avedon!*—and hot on their heels were the models, some of whom were making upwards of $100,000 a year. Not me, of course. I was still too different. I wasn't as black as Beverly or as white as Cheryl—a couple of Cover Girls who were really raking in the dough. And I was a little too ethnic, a little too sexual, a little too threatening—unlike, say, Lauren Hutton, who had a juicy contract with Revlon.

So, yeah—I found it hard to listen to their endless whining. Most of these girls had never dreamed of that kind of wealth—half of them were trailer trash—but suddenly a hundred grand wasn't enough.

I would have killed for a hundred grand. I had to *work* for my money. Sure, I traveled all over the world, and I was treated like visiting royalty. Flowers, limos, champagne, caviar. But America wasn't exactly embracing me. In fact, there was this nasty little man at Conde Nast—the publishing empire responsible for *Vogue, Glamour, Vanity Fair,* and countless other magazines—who downright hated me. He told a client that my eyes weren't the "right shape," that they wouldn't sell product. Plus I was just too sexual, not sweet and approachable and girl-next-doorish like Cheryl. Maybe he was right; maybe I had the kind of look that would have offended or threatened American sensibilities. And maybe the stuff I was doing in Europe *was* too provocative . . . Me, stark naked, arms and hands strategically placed over my tits and crotch. On a beach in the Bahamas, with my nipples at attention. Wading through a piranha-infested swamp in the African bush, looking like I'd just been laid—by an entire village . . . But right or wrong didn't matter: He was a powerful little man, and he hurt me—personally and professionally.

It was also hard to listen to the whiny photographers. Everyone wanted what Halston and Avedon were getting: juicy contracts, security, and long-term commitments.

"We should be getting residuals for our pictures," Mike said one night. We were having a few friends over for dinner, all of them in the business. "Why the hell are the magazines entitled to use my images over and over again without paying for them? Why am I giving up the rights to my work?"

We'd all started at the bottom. We'd paid our dues. Now it was time to start getting what was coming to us. And of course things did begin to change. Nowadays, photographers own the rights to their photographs; they get paid every time the image is reprinted. And some of the big names—Herb Ritts, Patrick Demarchelier, Steve Meisel, Bruce Weber—command fees of $100,000 a *day.*

Of course, real geniuses think beyond day rates. Halston, for example, was one of the first people in fashion to get into licensing. He would put his name on perfumes, cars, luggage, bath towels, sunglasses—you name it. Then he would sit back and watch the checks roll in. People hated him for it. What's that old line? "Every time one of my friends succeeds, I die a little."

That same month, while people were still being appropriately catty about Avedon and Halston, Studio 54 opened its doors. Ian Schrager and Steve Rubell had long dreamed of creating a nightclub for Beautiful People, and here it was. We loved it. We were those people. The club was for *us*. You walked through the front doors and immediately felt like you'd arrived, like you *belonged*. There were other clubs, yes—but they were nothing like Studio. I can't even remember their names. Studio, hell—I'll never forget it.

They threw their first major party the following month. It was Bianca Jagger's birthday. Halston was the host. Bianca made a grand entrance atop a white horse, led through the club by a huge black guy who was wearing nothing but gold glitter. *Are we getting your attention, people?* Everyone was dying to get into Studio. Everyone wanted to be beautiful, to rub shoulders with the beautiful. But few are chosen. Tough shit.

I loved it. I had worked hard to get where I'd gotten and part of the fun was being recognized for it, going out and partying and having Steve Rubell tell you how great you looked, and *Would you like to step into my office, sweetheart?*

Mike, on the other hand—he hated it. Mike was into the temple of his body. If I stopped in for a quick drink without him, which I did from time to time, he'd find a way to punish me for it.

"You're falling apart," he said one night.

I had just walked in. I guess he smelled the cognac on

my breath. He had just finished meditating and giving himself a fucking colonic or something—he was turning into a monk—and he couldn't help himself.

"So who were you with? Stephanie? Andie? Iman. Was Truman there?"

Mike found the place repellent. It was loud and stank of sex and amyl nitrate, and everywhere you turned people were fucking like animals, but with less shame and less self-consciousness than street dogs. I was put off by that part of it, too, to be honest, but I loved the energy and the deafening music and the writhing bodies on the dance floor and the feeling that we were oh-so-special.

"I stopped in for one lousy drink, Mike. Is that a crime?"

"*One* drink? I don't think so, Janice. You're drunk. Keep it up. Your ass is starting to sag."

"Really?" I said. "I must be in horrible shape. *Sports Illustrated* called today. They want me for the swimsuit issue."

"The *swimsuit* issue!?" He was stunned.

"Yes," I said.

Mike rubbed his chinny-chin-chin, lost in thought, then made up his mind. "Okay," he said, "I'll let you do it. But I want you to call Julie Campbell"—the photo editor—"and tell her *I'm* shooting you. No one else."

The next day I called Julie Campbell and told her Mike wanted to shoot me. "Thanks, honey," she said. "We'll pass." She wasn't going to let Mike take over her shoot. He was a control freak in a world of control freaks. It wasn't all that dissimilar from the film industry. The director—or, in fashion, the photographer—thinks he's God. And everyone from the clients to the producers to the lowly models had to kneel before God. Julie was not a kneeler. She was going to run her own show.

So of course I lost the gig. And I was way pissed. I called

Iman, and we met for drinks at Trader Vic's, in the Plaza Hotel. I loved Iman. We went all the way back to the Wilhelmina days, and I thought she was one of the most ravishing creatures on the face of the planet. She'd been discovered by Peter Beard, who was a genuinely great photographer. But the stories about her were genuinely bullshit. I mean, Beard told everyone he'd found her in the African bush, and suddenly reporters were describing her as this Somali tribeswoman, part of a fierce nomadic family. The truth is, they met in Nairobi, on a dirty, noisy city street filled with tourists. And Iman's father was a respected gynecologist, not a fucking warrior.

Iman had a great sense of humor. She had this attitude that you should never correct anything anyone says about you, good or bad. I thought it was a great attitude. And she was a great storyteller. She was madly in love with her husband, Spencer Haywood, the legendary basketball player. Life! It gets so fucking complicated. Here she was going on about her great husband, and I'm whining about Mike. He was running my life, and *ruining* it, but somehow I couldn't break free. He had a sick hold on me, like my father. He was handsome and smart and talented and successful and multilingual. I was dumb. I was lucky he wanted me, right? Even when he screamed at me and called me stupid and went off and cheated on me. No, not right; *wrong*. But I guess I was hooked, because every time I felt myself thinking about trying to end it, it was like he sensed it. He'd have roses waiting for me when I walked through the door. Or I'd come home from work, exhausted, and he'd be in the kitchen shucking oysters. Naked.

The thing is, even when the work was going well, I needed a man to tell me I was great and good and wonderful and beautiful and amazing. I believed in myself, yes; but there was a limit to what I believed. Deep down, I couldn't drown out the rat bastard's voice: *You'll never amount to anything. You'll never amount to anything. You'll never amount to anything.* Sometimes I felt like a split personality, caroming between extremes of self-confidence and crippling insecurity. I wondered if everyone was like that. I *hoped* everyone was like that.

But who had time for introspection? The next thing I knew, John Casablancas came to town. For many years, he'd been running Elite as a European associate for Eileen Ford and Wilhelmina, in a friendly, noncompetitive way, much as they worked with Christa. But suddenly he wasn't feeling friendly anymore. (Money again! The business was making people filthy rich.) He decided to open his own office in New York. He promised the girls fatter paychecks, reduced commissions, and plenty of *fun.* He knew how to seduce women. Limos, dinner, roses, caviar, diamonds. He told each of them—me included—that she was *the best, my very favorite, destined for greatness* . . . Many girls jumped. Christie. Iman. Bitten. Kelly Emberg. Nancy Donahue. My sister Debbie. There's not much loyalty in this business. In fact, betrayal is the norm.

Eileen Ford sued. Wilhelmina followed. The Model Wars were on.

In a strange way, though, it was kind of exciting. Everyone was making such a fuss over us. We were being courted. We felt valuable. The business was really about buying and selling the most beautiful girls in the world, and I was one of them. Casablancas knew how to treat girls. Especially young girls. He was a businessman and lover both. And he was emerging as the clear winner in the Model Wars.

By this time, with money to burn, I talked Mike into renting a house in Southampton. Our friend Patrick Demarchelier, the French photographer, along with Mia Skoog, his fiancée, a gorgeous Scandinavian model, decided to join us. We got this great place on the beach, a mansion. And we were supposed to go there to kick back and *relax*. But even when we weren't working we were working. Out there on the sand, shooting, posing, vamping.

I borrowed one of Mike's old cameras and started fooling around. It was incredibly liberating. When I was modeling, I was being manipulated. When I was taking pictures, I was in control. Ask me which I preferred?

So of course I got serious about the work. I read books about light and composition. I looked at the work of modern geniuses—George Hurrell, Horst P. Horst, Avedon, Irving Penn—as well as that of past masters like Cartier-Bresson, Lartigue, Bill Brandt, and—one of my all-time favorites—Andre Kertesz.

Right from the start, Patrick was impressed with my photography. Mike was less generous. "Stick to modeling," he said. It pissed me off. But I still bought him a fucking platinum Rolex for his birthday.

We usually drove out to Southampton early Friday afternoon, but one Friday things got crazy with work and I didn't get home till six. Mike didn't want to bother with the traffic, so we went to dinner and found ourselves near Studio 54.

"Come on," I said. "One night isn't going to corrupt you."

He called Patrick from the restaurant pay phone—believe it or not, there were no cell phones in those days—and told him to meet us at the club. "Janice will make sure you're on the list," he said. He hated having to say that; he hated having to admit that I was getting us through the front doors, not him.

We walked the few blocks to the club. There was a huge

line snaking its way down the block. Most of the people were part of the Bridge-&-Tunnel crowd, kids from the outer boroughs who didn't have a prayer of getting in, especially on a Friday night. But me—well, they knew me here.

"Hey, Janice! Come on up." The doorman ushered us over and slipped me a handful of tickets. "Have a few drinks on us."

"One drink," Mike muttered under his breath. "Sure."

Okay. So they knew me pretty well. Big deal.

As we slipped past, I heard a girl say in her nasal Brooklyn twang, "Hey! That's Janice Dickinson! That was Janice Dickinson!" Like I was God or something. Ask me if it felt good.

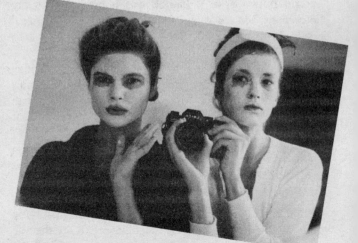

ME AND CHRISTIE IN GREEN TEA MASKS.

It was packed inside. And you couldn't turn around without seeing another famous face. I found myself being ogled by a very stoned John Belushi. He hugged me and gave me a big fat kiss on the cheek, like we were dear old friends. It was surreal. Here's a guy that Mike and I had been watching on TV, with religious fervor, and he acts like we're closerthanthis. It didn't stop. There was Andy Warhol, with his mop of white hair; Liza Minnelli, with that permanent grin you wanted to slap off her face; Keith Richards . . . I wondered if Mick was around.

People kept coming over and introducing themselves, like they were trying to make points or something. That's one of the things about fame I was still trying to get used to: the way complete strangers behave as if they're part of your life. It's odd, yeah, and off-putting. But it's also weirdly seductive. You get hooked fast. You feel loved (and

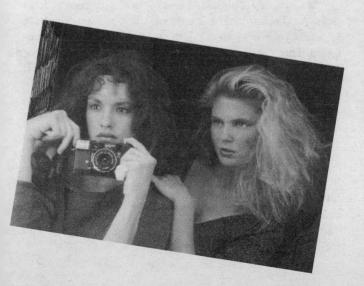

God knows I've never turned down a chance at easy love). I looked over at Mike and smiled at him. He wasn't having a good time, but I didn't give a shit. I wasn't leaving. And we had to wait for Patrick, anyway.

Steve Rubell came over, gave me a big kiss hello, and introduced me to Andy Warhol. "But we've met already," he said. Yes, we had, mostly in passing, but Andy seemed to know me better than I knew myself. He talked about spreads I'd already forgotten! It was uncanny.

"You seem to know an awful lot about me," I said.

"Fame, Janice. Get used to it."

We got into a long conversation about fame. He wasn't selling that old fifteen-minute line, but what he *did* go on about was timing. Stuff that really made me think. He said fame was all about timing. Timing and luck, especially luck. I told him I didn't agree: I said that some girls might have gotten lucky just sitting around looking pretty, but I'd had to fight like hell to get as far as I'd gotten.

"Yes," he said, "but that's one of the things people don't understand about luck. Luck doesn't just happen. You have to make your own luck." I thought that was pretty profound. That's why he was Andy Warhol.

The big phrase at the time was "of the moment." It made me sick. I swore I'd kill the next person who used it. But in the seventies you heard it nine hundred times a day. That magazine is of the moment. This new collection is of the moment. She's so *of the moment*. I could have puked.

The problem with being "of the moment," Andy told me, was that moments pass, and people don't know how to live *in* the fucking moment. Instead of enjoying themselves, they worry about who or what is creeping up behind them, or where they're going to be the next day. "You should live as if every minute is your last," he told me. "One day, you'll be right."

He was wonderful. He had the sweetest, meekest, mildest voice, and he would take hold of both my hands when we talked. He had the softest hands.

In the middle of my philosophy lesson, we ran into Christie Brinkley. She was also at Ford, and she was very shy, and we were becoming quite friendly. She liked me because I was ballsy and outspoken, and I liked her because she was smart and cultured and spoke fluent French and smoked those wonderful Gitanes and had gone to all the best private schools in Los Angeles. I guess she had the life I felt I should have had. Or wanted to have. I don't know. I guess you can't exactly live your past vicariously, but that's what I seemed to be doing.

She was beautiful, Christie, except for that big flat butt she was always trying to hide. She summed up the ideal: the blond, blue-eyed California girl. She was doing all sorts of wholesome girl-next-door work for Sears and people like that, but she was desperate to get into edgier things—like some of the stuff I was doing. For a while, we were like the two poles of modeling—one light, one dark.

After Warhol got dragged away, we went over to chat with Mike, who was standing in a corner alone, looking like a miserable fucking wallflower. Christie made a big fuss over him, but I didn't mind. When she mentioned one of his recent spreads and called him a genius, his mood suddenly improved.

Patrick showed up a little later, with John Casablancas and a coterie of girls. Casablancas came over to say hello, but I turned my back. He hadn't shown much interest in me when I was struggling in Paris; he could go jump in the Seine for all I cared.

I saw my friend and short-lived roommate, Edward, across the room, and I hurried over. Edward was really making a name for himself as the go-to hair guy in the fashion biz. He was with Sandy Linter, the fabulous makeup artist. She ran the salon on 57th Street where I'd met Edward, and she was dating the salon's French owner. Of course, this was before Gia Carangi came along and bulldozed her way into her life. I'm not blaming Gia. Gia was madly in love with Sandy. Their relationship turned into a fucking Greek tragedy. I still get upset when I think about the two of them.

Gia showed up as we were leaving. She had this way of touching you, her hand on the small of your back. Of looking at you—as if she were really interested, hanging on every word. It was strangely seductive. I'd met her before and liked her—liked the edge on her. Plus there was something seriously damaged there that I related to. She was eighteen, just starting out. She was very boyish, and kind of rough. (She never went anywhere without her switch-blade.) Her stepfather owned a hoagie joint in northeast Philadelphia. It was obvious that that was where she'd learned her good manners.

Mike came by, urging me to leave, but just then Steve Rubell showed up and insisted on taking us to his office. Mike rolled his eyes, but I wasn't ready to leave—and Patrick and Casablancas were still partying. The little girls followed Casablancas like puppies.

Rubell closed the door and laid out a fucking ounce of cocaine. There was something kind of repellent about him, to be completely honest. Repellent and charismatic at the same time. You felt like running away, but he'd smile his wicked smile and you knew good times were just around the corner.

He chopped up a few lines and offered me a silver straw. I plunged in. Mike didn't. He gave me a dirty look, but I was in a fuck-you-don't-tell-me-what-to-do mood. Then I asked Patrick to dance with me. As we fought our way through the crush of writhing bodies, everyone seemed so happy that I couldn't help feeling good, too. Who cared if it was all chemical? I was going to take Andy's advice and live in the fucking moment. All this analyzing the Deeper Meaning of Life, what had it ever done for anyone?

"I hope Heaven's half as much fun as this!" I hollered in Patrick's ear.

We didn't leave for Southampton until two in the morning. Patrick was driving, I was in the front seat next to him, and Mike was fast asleep in back. He was pissed, and he had a way of falling asleep when he was pissed. It must have been some kind of Zen Master bullshit.

The bad news is, John Casablancas and a couple of his trashy little girls were in the car behind us. Patrick and Casablancas had been friends for many years, but I still didn't like the idea of having him out to the house. He had treated me with such disregard in Paris, but I was still expected to be the charming hostess. I don't think so. Still, at the end of the day, the house was certainly big enough. I guess we could stay out of each other's way.

The next morning I walked into the kitchen and found him with one of his girls. I have no idea how old she was. She was sitting on his lap, topless, and the way she smiled and said good morning made me want to slap some sense into her. I managed a forced smile and poured myself a coffee.

"Janice," Casablancas said, "you should come work with me." I laughed and left the kitchen and ran into Mike. He was all decked out in biking gear; he was pushing forty but was still thinking he might take a shot at the Tour de France.

"Come on," he said. "We're doing thirty miles today."

I went. Bicycling gave me these beautiful legs. Ah, vanity, vanity! All is vanity. Like every other model, I'd been obsessed with my body since the day I'd noticed it. And like every other model, I tried to stay in shape. Of course, now that I was successful, I didn't have as much time for jogging and bike riding and yoga. But there was coke and binging and purging, and I had taught myself to stop eating a third of the way into my meals. Like confused women everywhere, I was turning food into the enemy.

Christie showed up later that day to hang out, and we had dinner out back—or a *third* of a dinner, in my case—facing Wooley's Pond. The house was between the pond and the ocean, near a marina. It was perfect. I loved it there. Pierre Houles showed up, too, in time for dinner. He and Christie liked each other right away, but of course she knew who he was. He could do things for her career. Nothing wrong with that, right? *We all used one another.*

Sunday morning I was up early and called home.

My father answered the phone. I asked him to please put Mother on and he didn't seem to understand. I thought he was fucking with me, but then I realized he was genuinely confused. He started screaming at me, going on about how he was sick and tired of people calling at all hours of the day and night asking for money. Then he hung up. When I called back a few minutes later, my mother answered. I asked if everything was all right.

"Oh, fine," she said. "But I think I'm going to need a new car."

Not a word about my father. But I didn't care to ask, frankly. I sent her a check for the down payment on a new car. I was making oodles of money. I didn't know how to handle it, but that didn't seem to be a problem. I just wrote checks—to my mother, the grocer, the liquor store—until the bank called to tell me I was overdrawn and would I be good enough to come in and do something about it.

The thing about money is this: You have to have enough money so that you don't ever have to think about money again. And that's not an easy place to get to. What I had, I spent. I bought a Jeep. A Roballo boat. I'd go into town and buy lobsters for twenty guests. The best champagne. Beluga caviar because it reminded me of Paris, of the time I'd spent being an innocent little nobody . . .

And of course I worked for my money. Only it didn't feel like work. This is what you have to understand: It was fun. *Then.* I would sit there surrounded by fawning assistants and hair and makeup people and dressers and think, *I can't believe I'm getting paid for all this fawning!* And I couldn't. Really. So I didn't stop. And it kept being fun.

I remember meeting the legendary Scavullo for the first time. He shot me for *Cosmo,* with whom he had a contract. He worked out of a carriage house in the East Sixties, where he lived with his lover, Sean Byrnes, who was also

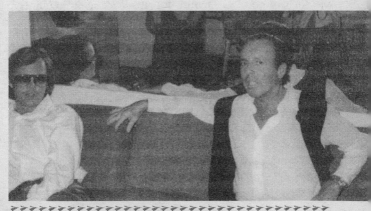

SEAN BYRNES AND FRANCESCO SCAVULLO
AT SCAVULLO'S STUDIO.

his chief stylist. They were a real hoot, those two. "If you don't behave yourself, Sean, I'm going to cut you out of my will," Scavullo would say. Sean was the party animal in the relationship, and the threats kept him in line. He would bite his tongue, and go quietly about his business, but within a few minutes he'd be studying Scavullo with a sharp, appraising look.

"What?" Scavullo would snap.

"Oh, nothing," Sean replied, the picture of innocence. "You look like you're retaining water."

The truth is, they were inseparable, and they knew it, but they went at each other like an old married couple. They even started to look alike. It was always quite the show.

Scavullo was nuts about me. He kept asking me back. I was in *Cosmo* every month for about six months, until I finally had to beg for a break. I thought I was getting overexposed, and I wanted to spread my wings.

I went off and did a session for *Vogue* with Arthur Elgort, who had made a name for himself as a ballet photographer. He said he loved the way I moved, which—from him—was a major compliment.

Richard Avedon saw the result and sent for me. I was nervous. I admit it. Here was this kid from New York whose career began in the U.S. Merchant Marine when he was asked to take ID snapshots of the sailors, and he went on to become The Master. Intimidating? You bet. I mean, JVC was a fucking advertising campaign. Avedon—well, we're talking *art*. And art—well, that's another world.

So there I was, heading off to Avedon's place in the

West Seventies. The whole way there, I told myself I was wonderful, amazing, good enough for Avedon. Then I rang the bell and a chubby little assistant opened the door and walked me through. I had to remind myself to breathe as I waited. I felt like I was meeting one of *The Beatles,* or getting an audience at the Vatican—which kind of scared me, frankly: It brought back memories of Pope Giorgio.

Moments later, Avedon appeared: a little bespectacled waif of a man, smiling, oddly normal. And he shook my hand and took me into the studio and—with no fanfare, no fuss—quietly introduced me to the two geniuses who had been working with him for years and years: Way Bandy, who did makeup, and Ara Gallant, on hair. Way took great pains with his outfits; he was partial to flowing Japanese robes that made him look like a geisha. And he had this wacky Prince Valiant do that was so weird you couldn't help staring. Made me wonder why Ara didn't fix it. Ara wore a pin-studded black leather biker cap and matching leather pants. That was *it;* I seldom saw him in anything else.

"Janice," Way said, flailing his arms like the queen he was. "I love you. I've always loved you."

And Ara said, "I love you more."

And Way began to sing, "I love you more today than yesterday . . . "

And Ara joined him.

Now, I'm here to tell you, *that's* entertainment.

Avedon was over on the far side of the room, conferring with

**RICHARD AVEDON:
THE MASTER OF MASTERS.**

Gideon Lewin, his lighting guy. It was surreal. Things hadn't happened exactly the way I'd envisioned them—Avedon and Lauren Hutton didn't discover me in a lousy Florida pizza parlor—but they were happening just the same.

When the musical interlude was over, Ara took me by the hand and said, "I need you to come to all my parties from now on, *comprende?* And I won't take no for an answer." Ara's parties were legendary: A-list all the way.

"I'll be your date," Way said. "It'll ruin my reputation, but what can you do?"

Gay men—gotta love 'em. They were as damaged as I was. They had grown up the way I'd grown up: with fear and shame and no sense of self-worth and the feeling that there was no place on earth for them. They were my spiritual next of kin.

WEARING A PATRICIA FIELD BLACK WIDOW WEDDING DRESS IN GIDEON LEWIN'S STUDIO.

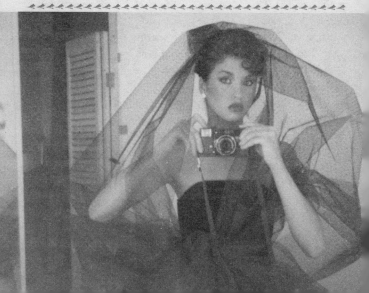

Suddenly, Avedon cleared his throat. He was ready. He took his place behind his large-format camera. Way and Bandy blew me kisses, told me I looked like a goddess, and moved into the wings.

Now Avedon turned his attention to Gideon Lewin. He worked with handheld reflectors, controlling every ounce of light in the room. This was a far cry from the French Mafia's kamikaze approach to fashion photography. This wasn't about pumping off a hundred motor-driven pictures and hoping for one lucky shot. This was about masterminding every inch of every setup, every photon in the air . . .

For the next few hours, Avedon worked his magic. I was in and out of a dozen outfits, one more beautiful than the next. Avedon directed the show with little fuss. His voice calm, a rock. I grew increasingly comfortable, increasingly confident. He urged me to *feel* the clothes against my skin, to forget I was in the studio, to imagine myself en route to the Academy Awards/on a hike in the Alps/at the beach—depending, of course, on what I was wearing. And he was so goddamn gentle. If I went over the top, he'd ask me, in a whisper, to tone it down a little. And if I was too subdued, he'd urge me to give it a little punch. Avedon knew how to make a girl feel loved—you can see it in the pictures—and that's no small part of his genius.

The result was a twelve-page spread in *Vogue*. The magazine was so happy with it that they booked me for a cover. With Irving Penn. Jesus! Did it never stop? Scavullo, Avedon, Penn. If Scavullo was the Genius and Avedon the Master, Penn was God.

I was *really* nervous about meeting Irving Penn. The thing is, not all that long ago, I'd been a little nobody, getting turned away, rudely, by these very people; now I was a sort of half-somebody from Wilhelmina. And it *was* fucking scary. There's no manual that tells you how to behave. And I didn't come from the kind of family that teaches you much in the "class" department. But you wing it. And I decided I'd wing it. I cabbed over to the studio, on lower Fifth Avenue, took a deep, bracing breath, and rang the bell.

I was ushered inside by an assistant—I thought I recognized him as one of the smarmy little assholes who had turned me away when I was a nobody—and Penn came over to say hello.

He had a huge studio. He must have had twenty underlings running around, getting ready for the shoot. Everyone was very quiet. It was almost sterile in there, like a hospital. Everything reflected his personality.

"Hello, Janice," said the short little man approaching me. "I'm Irving Penn."

We shook hands. He had small, soft hands. He reminded me of the Imp of Spring; a little munchkin. He was wearing a conservative coat and tie and he was polite and very soft-spoken. Old World to the core.

"Do you have any music?" I asked. There was a look on his face. *What?* "I have a hard time working without music."

It was clear Penn preferred silence, but he humored me. Before long, we were all listening to the *Rolling Stones*. I went over and jacked up the volume and watched as he prepared his equipment. He was very methodical. Calm. Centered. His assistants did all the nervous scurrying for him. It was wonderful to watch. Penn ran the show with quiet grace.

Finally, when everything was ready, he nodded at two beefy guys who were standing in a corner. They looked like moving men. They ducked out back and returned moments later with a huge hunk of ice on wheels, rolling it into position on a dolly. It was as big as a steamer trunk.

Penn came over and stood me in front of the giant ice cube. I was practically sitting on it. He shot and shot some more, and moved me this way. *Gorgeous, wonderful, let's have a smile, please.*

I loved watching him work. Like Avedon, he was all about control, all about making the perfect image. These men predated idiot-proof cameras; this was before autofocus, autolights, autoinspiration. This was before the Almighty Digital Image. These men were artists in the truest sense of the word.

By the time we took our first break, my butt was freezing. I went over and parked it next to the radiator.

"What are you doing, Miss Dickinson?" Penn asked.

"I'm warming up your dinner, Mr. Penn."

A couple of assistants looked over at me in horror. But Penn just smiled.

"You're quite something, Miss Dickinson," he said.

"So are you, Mr. Penn."

Three weeks later, he called me back for another shoot. He took me out to Jones Beach with Patti Hansen and Shawn Casey, and we modeled bathing suits all afternoon. Penn seldom left the studio, so it was quite the big deal. His twenty assistants looked nervous and out of their element on the sand. But not Penn; he was quiet, commanding, relaxed. He was the opposite of Reinhardt and that ilk; there was no shouting, no ego, just a steady, calming presence.

At one point, all three of us were lying on the sand in red, one-piece bathing suits, so close we were almost touching. "I used to do this in South Florida," I told Patti, remembering how I would lie on the beaches, on

Quaaludes, dreaming of becoming a famous model. "I can't believe I'm getting paid for it."

Between shots, I asked Penn questions about natural light and reflected light. He was incredibly generous about it.

I got home that night and told Mike how much I'd learned from Penn in the course of a single day. I was wired; I couldn't wait to whip out my cameras and put Penn's lessons to work. Mike didn't say anything. He just looked at me and laughed a nasty, disparaging laugh. For a moment, I saw my father's face in his. I was livid. I stormed out and went downstairs to see Bill Cunningham, a *New York Times* fashion photographer and one of my all-time favorite neighbors.

"Fucking French Mafia," he said. "They're a bunch of pretentious amateurs—and that goes double for Mike Reinhardt!" I felt better instantly.

Bill only shot with Leicas. And he never went anywhere without his velvet beret. I used to go to visit him with my contact sheets and we'd pore over them with a loupe and

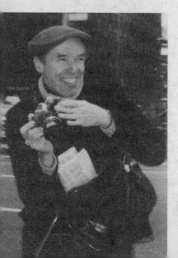

he'd give me pointers. *This shot has no depth. This one is poorly centered. This one makes me feel claustrophobic.* He'd tell me how to fill the frame. He advised me to get right into people's faces. He told me to keep working on my style.

"What style?" I asked. "I didn't know I had a style."

"It's getting there," he said,

BILL CUNNINGHAM

showing me. "There's something casual and edgy about your shots. And a little rough, like photojournalism. I like it. Stay on track."

On my twenty-second birthday, Bill gave me a photograph of Greta Garbo. It was one of those paparazzi-style shots: the reclusive Garbo glaring at the lens, her eyes awash in venom. I loved it, still have it today. And, no, it's not for sale.

But Bill gave me something much more valuable than a photograph and his undying friendship: He gave me confidence in myself as a photographer.

LOVE'S A BITCH

◄◄◄◄◄◄◄◄◄◄◄◄◄◄◄◄◄◄◄◄◄◄◄◄◄◄◄◄◄◄◄

At around this time I started working with one of the hand-somest men in the business: Calvin Klein. He was wonder-ful. He talked to me about my ongoing battles with Mike, about life love drugs self-esteem and the crazy business that ran our lives.

Whenever I had a moment alone, a moment to think, I felt depressed. I wasn't in love with Mike anymore; I wasn't sure I'd ever been in love with him. I didn't feel good about it, either. Or about myself. Sure, I felt beautiful. People made a living telling me how beautiful I was. But that didn't do much for me on the inside. And nobody was asking.

"So I guess they don't give a shit, right?" I asked Calvin.

"Of course they don't give a shit," he said. "This busi-ness is about surfaces. People don't care to dig too deeply. They'd rather not know."

So who was I? A successful supermodel? Mike Rein-hardt's doormat? The frightened little girl who wouldn't suck her father off?

"Janice," Calvin joked. "Models aren't supposed to *think*."

He was right. Models are supposed to be dumb, right? That's what they tell us, anyway. And, yes, there are plenty of pretty girls who are thick as posts. But most of us can actually walk and talk and snort coke at the same time. And some of us even ask ourselves Big Questions, like, *What the fuck does it all mean?*

Christ, this *thinking*—it was exhausting. I needed help.

I called my old friend Alexandra King—the one with the foul-mouthed parrot—and got the name of a respected Upper East Side shrink. I went to see him. He was in his mid-forties, good-looking in a blandish sort of way. With his round glasses and graying temples, he reminded me of an owl.

I gave him my life story in about ten minutes. He nodded from time to time, but his expression never changed. I thought maybe he was thinking about fucking me, but I was wrong. He was actually paying attention.

"A great deal of what happened to us in the past searches for expression in the present," he said when I was done. "Every relationship contains within it the ghosts of everything that *wasn't*." Huh? Okay, I'm a model. Slow down.

I wish I'd brought a tape recorder, because everything he said was brilliant. And of course I never put any of it into practice. But this is basically what I remember—and I know I'm not doing him justice.

All of us are fucked up, he said. Some worse than others. And much of what happened to us as kids, well—we want to fix it. No matter how many years have passed, we're determined to fix it. So what we do, see, is we keep getting into relationships that mirror the relationships we had with our parents. And the reason we do is that we want to undo the damage by reexperiencing it and finally getting it right.

So, yeah, what he was saying was that Mike Reinhardt was the latest version of my own personal Lost Ark: my abusive father. And, in some ways, I think I saw what he meant. Like my father, Mike made me feel I would never amount to anything. He would put me down at every turn. He would criticize the way I spoke, walked, talk, ate. And if I tried to do anything on my own—take pictures, for example—Mike was quick to put me down for it.

"The psychiatric term for this is 'repetition compulsion,'" the wise old owl was saying. "People spend the bulk of their lives recapitulating old conflicts, trying to undo the damage that was inflicted on them as children. But most of them never break free of it."

Well, thanks a lot! *Never break free of it.* That's really fucking heartwarming.

I walked the thirty blocks to Carnegie Hall, trying to understand what he was telling me. What did I want from Mike? Was I really looking for men who would mistreat me? No—that was insane. (Was *I* insane?) And this business about history repeating itself—surely there was some way to avoid that, no? I mean, if I actually understood what I was doing, why couldn't I just stop doing it? But what *was* I doing exactly? I just wanted to be wanted. That's all.

And then it hit me. Christ! He's right. My

CHRISTIE BRINKLEY IN PALM SPRINGS. I WAS TRYING TO GET HER TO QUIT SMOKING.

father didn't want me. He wanted lips and a warm mouth, not the person who was attached. Me, Janice. And then I thought about my conversation with Calvin, about this crazy business, how it's all about surface. Nobody cared about the real Janice, about what I had going on inside. And then I wondered, *What if I look inside and find nothing?* And that scared the hell out of me.

So I decided thinking was too fucking hard. I would stop thinking. Period. I mean, I was just a dumb model, right?

When I got home—my head still reeling from Deep Thought—Mike told me he'd just booked a job with French *Vogue*. He was supposed to go to Palm Springs and shoot some desert stuff. The French are big on sand and cacti.

"I told them I was using you," he said. He said it like he was doing me a favor. Very off-the-cuff. But the truth is, he needed me. He was lucky to have me. And he knew it.

"Fine," I said. Janice the Doormat.

"We'll fly to L.A. and drive down."

"Is it just me?" I asked.

"Yes."

"Why don't we take Christie?" I suggested.

"Why?"

I told him I wanted to take some pictures of her, which was true. I was honing my skills as a photographer. But in retrospect I think I might have had something else in mind. If I didn't have the strength to call it quits with Mike, maybe there was another way to break free.

We stayed in a motel in the middle of nowhere, a few miles from Palm Springs. Christie flew out with us. She had a friend in Palm Springs—Delphine, a French girl with whom she'd gone to the Lycée Français. Delphine came out to see us the second day we were there. She was sexy in a trashy, stripperish way—which was appropriate, since that's what she was, a stripper.

She watched us work in the broiling sun, and I got the feeling modeling must have seemed pretty unglamorous to her. When we got back we had dinner, drank too much wine, and Christie went to bed early. But I was kind of intrigued by Delphine. I asked Mike if he was interested in getting together with both of us. I asked him in front of Delphine. Delphine smiled. What was Mike going to say? *No?*

It was, well, *different*. The taste. The smell. Sort of unexpected, though I don't know exactly why: I've got one of my own.

Delphine and I were going at it long after Mike was finished. I enjoyed it. So did she. You know why? I'm a woman, I know where everything is, I know what feels good. You'd be surprised at how many guys can't find their way to the clitoris, even when you're pushing their faces in it.

Delphine was gone in the morning. Mike and I never even talked about our little adventure. We shot some more pictures that morning and went into town for lunch. Late in the afternoon, when it had cooled off somewhat, I took some pictures of Christie. I never told her about Delphine.

When we got back to New York, I showed my desert shots of Christie to Pierre Houles. "You're better than Mike," he said. (And he was one of Mike's best friends!)

"And you made Christie look so beautiful. I see things here that I didn't see in her when we first met."

Pierre called Christie and invited her to his studio for a shoot. She was delighted. And of course they ended up in bed.

In December, Mike and I went to Saint Moritz and we asked them along. Mike had a nine-year-old son, Sandro, from a previous marriage. He lived in Paris with his mom. The Christmas visit to Saint Moritz was an annual tradition with his father. I didn't want to go, but I didn't want to disappoint Sandro.

We arrived at night and crashed early. I remember waking up the next morning and drawing the shades and looking out at the most majestic snow-capped mountains in the world, feeling horribly sad and empty.

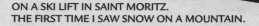

ON A SKI LIFT IN SAINT MORITZ.
THE FIRST TIME I SAW SNOW ON A MOUNTAIN.

The next morning we all went skiing together. Mike and Pierre and Sandro and Christie and me. But I got lost— deliberately. I found myself standing on a snowy ledge, looking down at the village, sparkling below, and realizing that part of my life—the part with Mike Reinhardt—was coming to an end.

The next day, Christie and I took lessons with an irresistibly gorgeous ski instructor. When a woman's in love, she doesn't even notice other men. Well, okay, she might notice them, but she never *wants* them. She's in love, for Christ's sake. And I wanted this guy. I was *starving* for him.

The last night of our vacation, Mike cooked an amazing dinner. It was a very homey scene. Sandro went to bed early, and the rest of us sat around drinking and eating; Mike and I smoked a little dope. But I slipped Mike and Pierre a little something extra with their wine: crushed Valium.

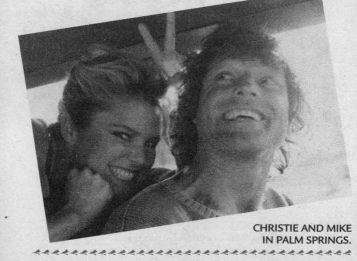

CHRISTIE AND MIKE
IN PALM SPRINGS.

After they'd passed out, I told Christie I was going to pay a call on our ski instructor. I made her come with me. We trekked through the crunchy snow, beneath the low-hanging moon, and found our way to his chalet. We got a little silly, and I necked with him, and we both got pretty hot and bothered. But I'd brought Christie along to keep me honest. And I stayed honest.

At about three in the morning, we went back. I opened the door and stepped through and *boom!*—confrontation time. Mike closed the door, and I just stood there against the wall as he called me every ugly name in the book. I didn't say anything. There was nothing to say.

In the morning we drove down from the mountains to the airport. Nobody spoke. Mike flew to Paris to take his son home. Pierre and Christie and I returned to New York.

I called a realtor the moment I got home from the airport and was out looking at apartments the next day. I found a place on 93rd Street, a three-story walk-up. I was alone and scared and almost didn't go through with it, but in the end I signed the lease. It was mine. I had a home of my own for the first time in my life.

A few weeks later, Christie dumped Pierre and moved in with Mike.

PARTY GIRL

After I got the news about Christie I sat in my new apartment for days, staring at the walls, wondering how I'd made such a mess of my life. On the fourth day, Calvin Klein called.

"What's wrong?" he asked. "You sound strange."

"I'm fine," I said. My tongue seemed to have grown too big for my mouth.

"I'm about to launch the biggest runway show of my career," Calvin said. "Tell me you're available."

I almost wept with relief. Work was just what I needed. In work there is escape. "Well," I said, trying to keep my emotions in check, "I'll see what I can do."

It was a slamming show. Calvin rounded up all the hottest models, male and female, and made it a party. There's an energy in runway work you don't find anywhere else. It's electric, full of passion and adrenaline. Everyone becomes your New Best Friend. *We're all in this together,* you think. *And aren't we just fucking great!*

I loved working with Patti Hansen. She was seeing Keith Richards, who hung out in back telling outrageous stories about Mick and Jerry Hall. He looked like an insect; no, he looked like an ad for chewing tobacco—with those hollowed-out cheeks and his evil teeth. Beverly Johnson was there, too. She was very cool, almost detached. I suspected there was a lot going on inside her—but this was a surface business, so I knew better than to ask.

The men were dreamy—and, no, not all of them were gay. Charlie Haughk was a fine specimen, though he didn't have much of an edge. I heard he lived with his mother, out in Brooklyn. But he had style. He wore Hawaiian shirts before anyone else had even heard of them, and he had a collection of straw fedoras. Tony Spinelli was there, too. I had worked with him and Irving Penn; he was luscious. I just wanted to fuck him. And—*oops!*—guess what? I did.

Here's what happened. We're backstage before the show. Everyone is running around like crazy. Half-naked, excited. You can hear the audience starting to arrive and take their seats. Anybody who means anything in the business is going to be out there, watching, judging, and that only adds to the nervous buzz. So you're excited and half-naked and hot and nervous and surrounded by the most beautiful people in the world, and suddenly you find yourself horsing around with a perfect-looking man who wants you—and what do you do? You find a closet and you lift up your skirt and you fuck him. And you fuck faster because the show's about to start—the G-rated show—and then you come and he explodes inside you and you barely have time to catch your breath and, *boom!*—you're disengaged and heading for the runway.

And Calvin is screaming, "Where the fuck have you been? I've been looking *everywhere*!" And the dressers are hovering around you, their hands flapping like nervous birds, trying to undo the mess you've made. And then you feel the come dripping down your leg, and you smile at Calvin and say, "I was fucking Tony Spinelli, and it was great, thank you very much," and then you're on the runway, trying to keep your knees from buckling.

And I was good at that runway stuff. Sure, when I'd

started, I was as nervous as the next neophyte. All the shit you have to remember. It's not just about walking, people. You have to hit your marks for the photographers. At the midpoint, you pause and give them the full shot, head to toe. At the end of the runway, it's the bodice shot, so you give them your trademark smile. On the return trip they want a shot of the back of the dress, so you turn your head a little and give them a nice profile. And, if you can swing it, you make sure they can squeeze the designer's logo into the shot.

I was a pro by this time. As you start getting comfortable with the routine, you learn how to work the crowd— which is what it's all about. My friends would all score front-row seats and egg me on, and I'd dish with them as I sashayed my way along. There's real energy out there. And the photographers—Jesus! They're shouting your name— "Janice! Janice, over here!"—like they can't get enough of you. It's pure performance. They love you and you're flying and you began to feel like a rock star out there and you think, *I could get addicted to this.*

Speaking of addiction, I was becoming quite the regular at Studio 54. On one level, I guess it was just plain fun. But I had a broader definition of "fun" in those days. Steve Rubell, the eternally stoned co-owner, was very generous with his drugs—mostly cocaine—but you could get anything you wanted from those cute, shirtless bartenders. I also became addicted to the noise. It was so loud you couldn't hear yourself think, which was fine, since I didn't *want* to think. And the sex—everything you've heard is true, and then some.

Guys making out with guys. People fucking in the bathrooms. Drug-addled girls bent over the bar snorting while some sleazoid took them from behind. Sex sex sex. And somehow, since the common denominator was sex, all these crazy groups—the druggies, the fags, the black-leather set—managed to coexist quite nicely, thank you very much.

It's strange. Decadent as it seems now, I look back on it and think there was a certain honesty to the scene. It's like people were saying, *Yeah, we're animals. We fuck. You can put us in nice clothes and take us out to watch Shakespeare in the Park but we're still animals deep down, and we like fucking best of all. It's all about fucking. Life is about fucking. Shakespeare is about fucking. Beethoven is about fucking. Name one thing that isn't about fucking.*

And they were all there (though, admittedly, not all of them were fucking). All the people from *People,* glossy pages come to life. Smiling and cooing at each other. *Look at us. Aren't we special? Aren't we interesting?*

One night I was there with this mildly interesting conga player who didn't understand why I refused to go to bed with him. "Well, you know, we've had dinner all of two times," I said. "I'm an old-fashioned girl. I believe in courtship." He didn't like that, and I got tired of listening to him whine, so I excused myself to use the bathroom. A girl was going down on another girl in the stall next to mine—*yawn*—and I did my business and left and bumped into Warhol. "Janice," he said in that sweet voice. "Come over here and fill me up. I've been feeling so empty all day." He always had his camera around his neck. He took it off and held it up and snapped another in a series of self-portraits, *Andy and Janice at Studio, # 317.* Some geeky guy was watching us. He was looking at me like he wanted to fuck me, again, since clearly he'd already fucked me—in his head—and come. Andy took me by the elbow and hustled me off. "How did *he* get in?" he wondered. "Who's manning the barricades?" There was another guy wearing leather chaps and nothing else. He looked like something out of *Midnight Cowboy,* something that hadn't made the final cut. Andy whinnied in my ear and led me to a quiet corner and sat me down.

"So?" he said. "Talk." Andy had many gifts, among them the ability to really listen. He'd ask you a question and look at you with this sort of gentle intensity, genuinely wanting to hear your answer. He was curious about a spread he'd seen in an Italian men's magazine. "You looked like you were about to blow the camera," he said. "Those lips must reduce grown men to tears."

"Thank you—I think."

Then Iman came over and asked me to take her to Rubell's office, so I kissed Andy good-bye and off we went. I saw the conga player, scanning the crowd, looking for me, and I yanked Iman into a corridor until the coast was clear.

"What was that all about?" she asked.

"He doesn't think I'm putting out fast enough," I said.

Rubell greeted us like royalty. There was no incense or myrrh, but there was plenty of nose candy.

Calvin Klein showed up. I thought he'd be mad at me, given our recent blowup at his runway show, but he was very friendly. No, that's not right; this went well beyond friendly. He kept telling me how hot I looked. *Fabulous. Yummy.* And I *did* look hot. I was wearing a beautiful Sonya Rykiel cashmere dress, with pearls, and my hair was fucking perfect. Just thinking about it now makes me hot. Excuse me for a moment . . .

So where was I? Oh, right—in Rubell's office, with Calvin and Iman. And Calvin invites us back to his place. And we score a cab on 54th and get dropped at his Upper East Side apartment. And up we go. And Calvin makes us drinks and he keeps ogling me and saying, "You look hot, Janice. No, *seriously.* Really hot. I mean, *hot.*"

And Iman says, "I think she gets it, Calvin."

And Calvin leaves the room and comes back a few moments later, having slipped out of his pants, to get comfortable. So now he's sitting there in a boxy silk shirt and no pants and Fruit-of-the-Loom underwear and fucking knee socks. It was bizarre. Maybe he thought *he* looked hot. So I told him, "You look really hot, Calvin. I mean, *hot*. I *love* the socks." But he didn't catch the irony. Then I said, "Why don't you do a line of underwear? Just put your name on it. I bet it'll sell." And his eyes lit up, but he didn't say anything. He should have said, "Janice, you're a genius. I'll cut you in for ten percent." But he didn't.

And then Iman changed the subject, saying, "That Studio. Those boys are really raking it in, huh?"

It sure looked that way. And I guess the Internal Revenue Service was curious, too. They'd probably heard about the garbage bags full of cash that left the club every night. I wondered if they knew that Rubell liked dumping the cash on his bed and getting naked with young boys and *coming into money,* as it were.

CALVIN KLEIN, IMAN, AND BARRY SCHWARTZ
DURING THE STUDIO 54 DAYS.

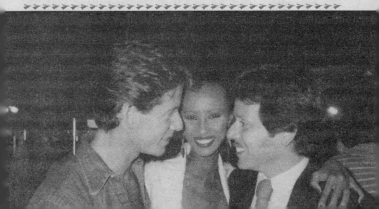

In December 1978, the Organized Crime Strike Force raided the club. It was big news. The U.S. Attorney's Office claimed that Rubell and Schrager had two sets of books, one of which they cooked to avoid taxes. Apparently, along with the two sets of books, they found other books with lists of names—the *People* people, and next to each name a little notation about the drugs they liked and the kind of sex they enjoyed. Hey, it was a full-service club. Gotta keep the clients happy.

There was a big party for Rubell and Schrager before they were sentenced. Halston was in charge. Everyone was there. Bianca, Warhol, Liza Minnelli. Richard Gere. Janice Dickinson . . .

Diana Ross sang for the guests. I envied her, up there on the stage, bathed in light, looking like an angel . . .

But the truth is, it was all very sad. The party was over. It felt like a funeral. Studio 54 had been a place to run to when you were lonely. Just getting through the front door made you feel special, anointed. And once you were inside, you were with family. You felt accepted, validated, *loved.* So what if it wasn't real? It felt real. And we all need our illusions.

For a while, to fill the gap left by Studio's disappearance, people concentrated on dinner parties. Diane von Furstenburg gave great dinner parties. Then it was skating parties. Everyone would meet at the roller rink and get stoned on mushrooms and go happily crazy. I kept running into Charlie Haughk at these things; you couldn't miss the Hawaiian shirts. One night after work he took me to John's Pizza, on Bleecker Street. Best pizza in New York. We ran into his father, Charles Sr. He was wearing a shoulder holster. I was a little taken aback, admittedly: Charlie never mentioned that his old man was a detective with the NYPD. And, shit!

I had a gram of coke in my purse. I kept thinking he was waiting for me to finish my pizza before throwing me against the wall and busting me. He didn't, of course. He was a very sweet guy. Told me he was a big fan. Told me *Charlie* was a big fan. It was odd. I almost felt he wanted to see us together, me and Junior, out in Bayside, maybe, dodging rugrats behind a white picket fence.

Meanwhile, the work kept coming. But not at home. I went to Mexico City for Mexican *Vogue;* the cover. Mexican *Vogue,* not American *Vogue.* Big difference. But I wasn't going to complain. Then I went to Greece, to shoot a cover for *Vogue;* Greek *Vogue.* Next, I was on a plane to South Africa, sitting in the first-class section next to a large woman, admiring the pictures Irving Penn had taken of me at Jones Beach, along with Patti Hansen and Shawn Casey. The large woman was eating peanuts, and she recognized me, and she went to say something . . . but one of the peanuts got lodged in her throat. Her large neck started to blow up like a balloon. And the next thing I know she's on her back, in the aisle, her skin a deep shade of purplish blue. And I'm watching the stewardess perform an emergency tracheotomy. It was so horrible I had to watch.

The plane made an emergency landing, and the woman survived. Everyone was so impressed with the heroic stewardess that they applauded. I applauded, too. I was thinking, *The next time somebody chokes on my beauty, I'll know how to save their life.*

One afternoon, back in the States, where I remained unfairly underappreciated, I got a call from Calvin. It was strange: I'd misbehaved during the runway show, and I'd made fun of his knee socks, and he *still* wanted to be my best friend. But suddenly it became crystal clear. He was doing a major show in Japan, for Isotan—the big department store. I was a star in

Japan. One of my first big shoots with Mike had been for Suntori liquors. The result—a poster of me, head to toe, in a skintight yellow bathing suit—had become a collector's item. In other words, Calvin needed me.

The minute the chartered plane took off, of course, some-one offered me some drugs. Since we didn't want to risk get-ting busted in Tokyo, we figured we might as well consume everything then and there. I had tons of friends on the flight—among them Iman and Charlie Haughk—and under the influence of the drugs I just let loose and joined the bac-chanal. Some people were doing lines on their pull-out trays, a couple of gay boys were fucking in the bathroom. It was wild. Some were trying on clothes for the show and walking around the plane bare-assed. I was photographing every-thing. One famous model pushed her crotch in my face and

HAVING A LITTLE TOO MUCH FUN
AT A FUNERAL PROCESSION
IN TOKYO.

said "take this" and I did. I have a wonderful photograph of a famous pussy, but that's not for sale either.

Once in Tokyo, all of us managed, miraculously, to pull ourselves together for the first show, but I ran into a little problem on the second day. I was in makeup, getting ready for Round Two, when I saw a bottle of Vitamin C. I thought I felt a cold coming on—my nose was running, though of course it was the cocaine—so I helped myself to a couple.

Turns out they were somebody's Quaaludes, in disguise. And they kicked in, big-time, about a minute before I was due to step onto the runway. One of the assistants saw I was in trouble and propped me up on a stool. Calvin came walking past just as I slid to the floor. I couldn't have timed it better, but what choice did I have? My spine had turned to jelly. Charlie Haughk hurried over and tried to set me back on the stool.

"What the fuck is going on?" Calvin said between clenched teeth. "I told *all* of you—no drugs!" I could understand why he was upset. The cream of Japanese society was on the far side of the curtain. He had a lot riding on the show.

"It was an accident," I mumbled. I could hardly talk. "I didn't know, Calvin. I swear to God."

"Get her out of my sight," he snapped.

"Don't be such a prick, Calvin," I slurred. "I'm here because I'm doing you a favor. I'm more famous in Japan than you'll ever be."

Calvin was steaming. Or maybe I was hallucinating: That certainly looked like real steam coming out of his real ears.

"You will never work with me again, Janice," he said, going red in the face. "You have my solemn promise on that."

Charlie Haughk took me back to my hotel. He was very sweet. I was really out of it and I didn't want to fall asleep in the cab, so I asked him to talk to me. He told me all about living in Brooklyn, in the projects, with his mom. He told me he was a triple black belt. He told me he thought I was the hottest bitch he'd ever seen. Okay, there are nicer ways to tell a girl you like her. But hey, Charlie was a street kid. And at least he was honest.

I didn't sleep with him on that trip. But the trip we took later that year, to China for a Bloomingdale's shoot, was another story. One day we were taking a cab to some tourist attraction. I had my cameras with me—I was honing my skills as a photographer—when we saw a bunch of Chinese guys practicing their martial arts schtick at the edge of a city park. I told the driver to pull over. I didn't speak Chinese, of course, but I noticed that if you say *HEE YAAAAA!* in a really loud voice, it generally gets their attention.

"Why don't you go over there and show me what you've got?" I told Charlie. The fact is, I didn't believe his triple black belt stuff. Or black belt third-degree. Or whatever the hell he called it.

"Come on, Janice," he said. "It's not right."

"What's the matter?" I said. "You afraid?"

I can be such a bitch.

Charlie got out of the cab. I followed. He went over and did a little bowing and scraping and somehow, using hand signals and whatnot, the Chinese guys understood that the pretty American man in the loud Hawaiian shirt wanted to spar a little. They were delighted. Charlie took them on, one at a time, and—without hurting them—showed them (and me) what he was made of.

It made my Little Flower tingle.

I slept with Charlie for a few months. But he was too nice

to me. What good was he if he couldn't help me with my repetition compulsion?

Back in New York, the 1980s were shaping up like one big hangover headache. Rubell and Schrager had hired Roy Cohn, one of the biggest heavyweights in town, to defend them. But it didn't help. They were fined for tax evasion and sentenced to three and a half years in federal prison.

People talked about it for a while, but then we all seemed to move on with our lives. It bothered me. I mean, it's not like they were my best friends or anything. But I'd known Rubell pretty well. And it just seemed so hopelessly sad. It made me feel lonely; the world felt like a colder place.

Later that year, worse news. Wilhelmina was hospitalized with lung cancer. All those goddamn cigarettes had done her in, and she was only forty years old. She had two children, twelve and five. I'd met them once or twice. I felt awful.

I told myself I was going to visit her in the hospital, but I couldn't bring myself to do it. I don't know why. I guess I didn't have the courage.

Gia went. She told me she climbed into the hospital bed and held her, and that Willie assured her she'd be out of bed in no time. And then weeks later she was dead, of course.

I went to the funeral. It was a media event. It's funny how you read about funerals in the paper the next day, and the reporters always point out how many mourners showed up, like it's a competition or something. It was all very unsettling. All these people looking so chic in black. And all they talked about afterward was how it would affect business, and their careers, and what was going to happen to their little lives.

I wasn't much better than they were. I couldn't believe Willie was dead. She was the one who had validated me when I was starting out. Now she was gone. Did that mean *I* was over?

It was all so cheap. And it made me feel cheap because I was part of it.

I needed some drugs. They weren't hard to find, in that crowd.

What was that line from *Alice in Wonderland*? Something about running twice as fast just to stay in place. Well, that's how I felt. I felt like running.

MAKING IT?

~~~~~~

In 1981, Mark Fleischman, a New York City developer, purchased Studio 54 for close to five million dollars. He didn't want the party to stop, and who were we to argue? So we went back, like sheep. There was something tired and forced about it, yes, and it wasn't the same without Rubell's vibe, and once in a while I got the sense that we were all faking it, but it was still a good party. Right?

Well, okay. Not really. But if you tell yourself you're having fun often enough, you begin to believe it. And we *wanted* to believe.

I saw Peter Beard there one night and went by his place a few days later to say hello and ask for his professional advice. Peter Beard, you'll recall, was the photographer who "discovered" Iman, the African warrior. He was also married, briefly, to Cheryl Tiegs. When I walked into his place that afternoon, the first thing I saw was Mike's Suntori poster. Me, seven feet tall, sleek in that skintight yellow bathing suit.

"You know," Peter told me, "when Cheryl first saw that poster, she ran her fingernails down the length of your entire body, like a cat, and said, 'Peter, you take Janice off the wall or I walk.' "

I loved that story.

"So what can I do you for?" Peter asked. It was almost noon; I was on my first glass of wine.

"I was hoping you'd take a look at some pictures I shot in China," I told him. And I brought them out.

Peter was so impressed that I made an appointment with the art director at Bloomingdale's, and *he* was so impressed that they put the photographs on exhibit at their flagship store, on Lexington Avenue and 59th. I was on top of the world. Whenever I was in the neighborhood, I would go by and look at them, out there in the windows for the whole world to see, and eavesdrop on people's conversations.

"Janice Dickinson? The model? She takes pictures, too? I don't believe it."

Don't hate me because I'm beautiful. Hell, don't hate me because I'm talented.

Some time later, I got a call from Bill Cosby's people. They were developing some ideas for television, they said, and Bill had been following my career with interest. He thought I had the right stuff. All I could think was, *Model, photographer, actress. Is there anything this girl can't do?*

Cosby was staying on Fifth Avenue, at the swank Sherry-Netherland Hotel, overlooking Central Park. I was asked to meet him for lunch, and I was so excited about my new acting career that I ran out and spent nine hundred dollars on a new outfit.

I walked into the restaurant and saw him across the room, and he stood and smiled his big Jell-O smile. He took my hand in both his hands, and thanked me for coming. Telly Savalas was with him. Don't ask me why. Savalas stood and shook my hand, too, and gave me that crazy look from *The Dirty Dozen*. If you don't remember the movie, rent it. Savalas is very good in it. He's insane.

We sat and chatted about our busy lives, enjoying that overhasty intimacy that comes with showbiz membership. At one point I reminded Savalas that he'd been one of the judges at the Waldorf-Astoria—a lifetime ago, it seemed—when I made my New York debut. He just grinned and looked at me with those big eyes, like he wanted to ravage and murder me at the same time.

Then Cosby asked about my acting experience. Just getting through the day was acting, I joked, and he and Savalas found this very funny indeed. And then I told him the truth: that I had only acted once in my life, in high school, as Lady Macbeth. But when King Duncan started forgetting his lines, I was forced to turn the play into a comedy. This got a lot of laughs from the audience—and, when it ended, a standing ovation—but the drama teacher wasn't exactly cheering.

Cosby wondered whether I could sing. "Well," I said, "Muddy Waters seems to think so." And I told them the Muddy Waters story.

Both men grinned through the entire lunch. Grinned and stared and drooled. At one point I thought Savalas might ask his buddy Bill to hold me down while he had a go at me, right there on the table. But they were both unfailingly polite. And before I left Cosby asked me to do two things for him. First he wanted me to read *An Actor Prepares,* by Stanislavski. Next, and far more important, he wondered if I would be good enough to give him my home number.

When it was time to say good-bye, he walked me across the lobby, to the door, oblivious to the ogling fans (*his* fans, alas, not mine). "You have *it,* Janice," he said. "It," of course, is that magnetic inner glow thing that really gifted actors are said to possess. I've only seen it up close twice in my life. Once was with Jack Nicholson. He had *it.* The other was with Mick Jagger. He had *it* to spare. But I'm getting ahead of myself.

I spent the following day devouring *An Actor Prepares,* and beginning, unfortunately, to take myself oh-so-seriously. So I was plenty prepared by the time Cosby called. He told me I should buzz Stubie Gardner, his musical supervisor. He was here in Manhattan, standing by for my call. Again he told me how beautiful I was, how powerfully I had affected him, and how much he wanted to see me again. It would have been nice to hear that under any circumstances, but in those post-Mike days all that soft soap was especially welcome.

I called Stubie and arranged to meet him the next evening. When the time came, I found myself standing next to his piano, trying not to betray my nervousness. But when I opened my mouth to sing, I can't honestly say the angels in heaven pulled out their little trumpets. Stubie looked up from his piano bench with one of those silly smiles glued to his face. He was horrified, and hoping against hope that his eyes wouldn't betray him.

Just then Cosby arrived, smoking a big cigar. He marched over and took my hand and literally bowed and kissed it. My Black Prince!

"So," he asked Stubie, "how was she?"

"Great," Stubie said. The silly smile remained in place.

At that moment I had a small epiphany: *This is why there's so much shit on TV and in the movies! Because people always lie to people in power. No one has the courage to tell them the truth!*

"I'm glad to hear that," Cosby said. He stuck that big cigar in his mouth and licked it. I tried not to read too much into that cigar. Maybe it's true that sometimes a cigar is just a cigar. Cosby turned to look at Stubie and said with great gravity: "Because I'm thinking about having her open for me in Vegas."

An assistant poked his head inside. "Mr. Cosby," he said. "Your wife is on the line." Cosby looked at the assistant as if he wanted to kill him. This was no time to be bothered with the fact that he was married. He turned and took both my hands in his, smiled sweetly, said he'd call me later. Then went off to deal with his wife.

I turned to look at Stubie. "What do you think?" I asked.

WITH PETER
BEARD IN HIS
STUDIO, 1984.

"I think he likes you," he said.

"Really?" I said. I felt like a five-year-old, hungry for approval.

"Really," Stubie said. He was still smiling that stupid smile, only now it looked like it was starting to hurt.

I left the studio and hurried off. It was pouring out, and I was late for dinner with Debbie, so I charmed some middle-aged man into sharing a cab with me. He was very nice. He talked about his wife and kids all the way uptown, then asked if he could see me some time. I told him he should be ashamed of himself and got out and hurried through the rain to Debbie's building. She and Edward Tricome had parted, now she'd found a nice little flat in a quaint old building on the East Side. She was an Uptown Girl all the way.

I told her the whole Cosby story. "I think he wants to sleep with me," I said.

"Of course he wants to sleep with you," she said. "You can't sing."

Debbie could be blunt like that. And as self-absorbed as the next model. Suddenly we were talking about her brilliant career. She was worried; she didn't have her next gig lined up. Guy Bourdin was having an open casting for a lingerie catalog for Bloomingdale's. I figured we should go together.

"Are you interested?" I asked.

"Are you kidding!?" she said. "Where do I sign up?"

The phone rang. It was Alexis. She sounded depressed, so I told her to come to town for a lingerie shoot. I don't know what I was thinking, except that I was always worried about Alexis. I'm sure guilt had something to do with it: I had this crazy image of her living in a commune without electricity or running water, selling beaded necklaces by the side of a rural highway. And I felt she deserved better.

"But I'm not a model," Alexis protested.

"No," I said, "but you have a perfect ass."

When I got off the phone, Debbie looked crushed. "More perfect than mine?" she asked.

"No, Debbie," I said with a tired sigh. "You have a perfect ass, too."

The phone rang again. I thought it would be Alexis, but it was Julio Iglesias. Yes, *that* Julio Iglesias. Debbie had a taste for the exotic, as it were.

Alexis arrived a few days later—Cosby never called, by the way—and we did the lingerie shoot with Guy Bourdin.

"You have a perfect ass," he told Alexis at one point, and I swear Debbie looked like she was going to burst into tears.

Alexis stayed at my place for a while, until one day in the supermarket on the corner she met this crazy Italian guy named Gianni. He was a commercial photographer, known for his beer ads. He talked about beer incessantly.

"SHAPE UP OR YOU'RE OUTTA HERE!" TOUGH LOVE FROM ALEXIS IN NEW YORK CITY.

Now I know that if I ever need to make a tepid glass of beer look all luscious and foamy, all I have to do is add a little salt. Fascinating, huh? Well, Alexis thought so. She moved in with him. The next thing you know she's working as a photographer's rep, repping him and this Polish friend of his, making money and being good at her job and enjoying life. Six months later she goes to City Hall and marries the guy, a complete stranger. But who was I to judge? She was in love. And I had both my sisters back. And for a while we were like a real family. The three Dickinson girls, visiting each other and meeting for dinner and just hanging out, with their three perfect asses all in a row. Family: It had eluded me my whole life, until now.

That summer I rented another house in Southampton, a comfortable distance from the old place. It was more modest, but certainly big enough for me and my friends and family. I was still spending money like crazy. I'd gone to see an accountant who tried to get me to start thinking about the future, but every word out of his mouth—*IRA, SEP, zero-coupon bonds*—just flew over my head. I liked words like *lobster* and *champagne* and *caviar;* that was my portfolio. I figured I'd keep investing in the basics. So I acted like a rich person, like I had too much money to worry about money. And I just kept being *of the moment* and living *in* the moment.

So one night at the Southampton house I'm deeply *in the moment*—coked out of my head, drinking champagne from the bottle because I'd just broken the glass and didn't have the energy to walk into the kitchen for another. And Gianni is sitting there, across from me, so stoned he's cross-eyed. And Alexis is asleep in one of the bedrooms.

And Gianni does another line of coke and totters a little, like he's about to keel over. And I say, "Are you okay?"

And he looks at me for the longest time, looks at me like he doesn't know who the fuck I am; and he begins to shake his head from side to side. I think he's going to cry. And he says, "My life is a fucking mess. I married a stupid American girl for a green card."

It was like a slap in the face. Sobered me right up. I said, "Excuse me? Do you know who you're *talking* to, asshole? Do you know where the fuck you are?"

And Gianni looks at me and claps his hand over his mouth like something out of a cartoon. *Did I say that out loud?* And now he's mumbling to himself in Italian, mumbling and praying.

And I throw the bottle of champagne, and he ducks and it hits the wall and smashes, and I get up and go into Alexis's room and wake her up.

"What? What?" she says. She's disoriented, scared.

And I tell her what her fucking husband just told me. "I don't want that motherfucker in my house another minute," I say. And she gets up without a word and goes out to the living room, with her little sister Janice at her heels, and says, "Gianni, is this true?"

And he's trying to explain, in Italian, invoking the Holy Virgin and a slew of other characters from the Bible, and Alexis picks up an ashtray and hurls it at him and he runs out of the house. And that was the last time I saw the motherfucker. Running down the street, barefoot, at three in the morning, and out of our lives forever.

When I got back to work the following week, Monique Pillard asked me into her office.

"How are you?" she asked. Monique was everyone's surrogate mother. But bookers are like that. They get over-involved in the lives of their girls. They insist on knowing everything.

"You don't want to know," I said.

Monique's table was always cluttered with containers of Chinese food. She speared a shrimp. She was very deft with the chopsticks. I noticed her chubby fingers.

"I need a favor from you," she said.

"What?"

"Gia's in trouble. I want you to look after her."

I called Gia, and we hooked up for drinks later that night at Trader Vic's. By this point she'd made the leap from snorting coke to snorting heroin, and it was fucking her up something awful. The previous week, at Avedon's, she spent three hours with Way and Ara getting ready for a cover shoot. Avedon took one picture, and Gia announced that she had to pee. She went to the bathroom and never came back.

"Who told you that?" she asked. She thought it was funny.

"Monique," I replied.

"It's true. I was bored."

"You can't do that, Gia. It'll get around."

"Look at these assholes," she said. She could change subjects at a moment's notice. I looked around the bar. Men were staring at us, drooling. I made eye contact with one guy and I swear he passed out. All the blood must have rushed out of his head, on its way to his penis. One guy actually got the courage to come talk to us, but he didn't get beyond his ballsy introduction: "Here I am. What were your other two wishes?"

Gia hated men. We started talking about the worst pickup lines we'd ever heard.

Gia's favorite was, "Can I borrow a quarter? My mother told me to call home when I met the girl of my dreams."

I liked, "Hi, I'm Gary. And you're going be screaming my name all night long."

Gia came back with, "I'm new in town. Could I have directions to your house?"

We were bowled over with laughter. Gia fell off her stool. Every man in the place was staring at us. Crazy or not, they wanted us bad.

"Some guy grabbed my butt once and asked, 'Is this seat taken?' " Gia said. She decked him. She *loved* decking guys.

I had a guy come up to me at an airport once, very intense, right in my face, and say: "The voices in my head told me to come talk to you." I don't think he was kidding.

"So," she said, finishing her drink. "Monique asked you to keep an eye on me?"

"Something like that," I said.

"Let's go find some coke," she said. And that's exactly what we did.

In the next few months, Gia and I worked on a bunch of shoots together. I tried talking to her, but I don't think it helped. All she ever wanted to talk about was drugs and Sandy Linter. She was obsessed with Sandy Linter, who had gone and fallen in love with Gia and dumped her boyfriend and was trying very hard to have a normal, lesbian relationship. But Gia was too intense on every level. She loved Sandy so much it was killing her. Sandy never loved her back hard enough. Sandy was never committed enough. Sandy didn't *feel* deeply enough.

She was so lost, Gia. She hated herself. She said she liked heroin because it made her hate herself less. And she hated men. *Loathed* them. She told me that men had been trying to fuck her since she was eight years old. Her cousins tried to fuck her. Her neighbors tried. Every derelict who walked into her stepfather's hoagie joint tried to fuck her.

"I can count the number of guys I've fucked on one

hand," she told me. "And then it was only because I needed drugs."

One day, the two of us were over at Chris von Wagonheim's studio. He had very dark sensibilities. He was heavily into S&M. We were vamping for the camera, and things got a little raunchy, and Gia tried to stick her tongue down my throat. I stopped her. I told her she was just missing Sandy. They had the most volatile relationship in the world, and Sandy had just told her—again, maybe for the hundredth time—that she couldn't take it anymore.

"Fuck her," Gia said. "I don't need anybody."

I liked her. She was funny, mouthy, wild, mischievous— and horribly insecure. Remind you of anyone? Insecurity made both of us self-destructive, yes—but Gia took it to a whole new level. She *really* didn't give a shit. I think that was her Achilles' heel, this total not-caring. She'd been *handed* her career. I paved the way for her and a hundred beautiful mutts like her, and she'd never really had to struggle. It had been so easy for her that it didn't mean anything. That was the big difference between us. She didn't give a shit, but I did; I really did. I cared enough to survive.

One time we were doing a shoot for Italian Bazaar. I took a bathroom break and she followed me inside.

"You look tired," she said.

"Thanks a lot," I said. I *was* tired. I'd been on the road for weeks. Crossing time zones. Hurrying through airports. Working working working. And when I wasn't working, I put everything I had into partying. I would wake up some days and not know where I was or even—on really bad mornings, for a moment or two—*who* I was. The lack of sleep and the free-floating jet lag were catching up with me.

"Here," Gia said. She was offering me a snort. Why not? I never stood on ceremony when it came to a little pick-me-up during a shoot.

But the moment I did that first line, I knew something was wrong. It wasn't coke; it was fucking heroin.

When I opened my eyes, all these people were standing over me in a circle, staring down at me. I was flat on my back. Somebody helped me up. "Are you okay?"

"Yes," I said. "I'm sorry. I haven't eaten all day." Sure! Buy that and I've got a bridge for you. "I'm feeling better already."

They wiped the vomit off my chin and helped me change. I made it through the shoot. I was Supermodel, after all. I could do anything!

I didn't say a word to Gia for the rest of shoot. Didn't say a word back in the changing room. Didn't say a word till we reached the street.

"You fucking cunt!" I shouted, and punched her right in the face. Gia laughed. She thought it was funny.

"Hit me again," she said. "I like it."

I hit her again. People had stopped to stare. Gia laughed again. She was loving it. I hit her again until I couldn't hit her anymore, and then we were both laughing like maniacs, in the middle of the street, and drawing a pretty good crowd.

"Say you're sorry," I said.

"Fuck you," she said. "Let's party."

The thing is, you start to feel immortal. Every day, every hour, someone's telling you you're beautiful, wonderful, a goddess. So you begin to believe it. And if you're cursed with an accommodating constitution, as I was, you can party till six A.M. and show up for a shoot two hours later looking like a dew-kissed rose.

Sure, there were times when you showed up late. Or not

looking your best. But the business tolerates an awful lot. Especially when you're on top. On more than one occasion I called a messenger service to go downtown to fetch a gram or two to get me through the day. No one said a word about it. *We need her and she needs this and that's the way it is. A little cocaine never hurt no-bo-dy.*

"You're product, baby," Ara Gallant once told me. "That's all you are. Fashion seems so glamorous, but it's just advertising. And as long as you're selling their shit, they'll do what they have to do to keep you upright and grinning."

You listen to people like Andy Warhol, and learn not to think beyond the *moment.* You learn not to peek around the next corner. And when people say things like "The only thing you have to know about the future is that *everything gets worse,*" you nod and murmur, *Right on.*

Things certainly got worse for Gia. A lot worse. She was mainlining by this point. People started to call her "Sister Morphine" behind her back. She was only working for the drugs now. One summer night she finally fell completely apart and looked at herself in the mirror and went home to her mother to try to get her head straight. She got on methadone, and for a while it actually looked like she was turning her life around. She came back to Manhattan a few months later. Scavullo wanted to shoot her. I think he knew how much trouble she was in and—God bless his generous heart—he was doing what he could to help.

In April 1982 the shoot made the cover of *Cosmo.* Gia looked beautiful, unless you looked real close. If you looked real close, and you knew Gia, you noticed something about her eyes; her eyes looked dead.

The following year she left New York and never came back.

You forget.

Gia *who*?

You compartmentalize.

You learn not to think about anything that might fill you with terror, like your own uncertain future. Like the fact that you're another day older.

You party.

You say, "Hey, I'm just a shallow happy girl."

And you get on with your shallow, happy life.

When Ara Gallant wasn't busy making Avedon's models look beautiful, or taking pictures of his own, he was giving the best parties in town. His best friend, Zoli, of Zoli Models, had some very hot girls on his roster—Apollonia, Pat Cleveland, Angelica Huston, Geena Davis—and together they used the girls as first-class, surefire attractions for celeb-watching party-goers.

Men are so easy! I was sitting in Ara's crowded apartment one night trying to decide who to go home with. Warren Beatty was too good-looking; Dustin Hoffman too short; Robin Williams, the new kid on the block, too frenetic; and Jack Nicholson too much of a wolf. But Jack had a great smile, and he was irresistibly funny, and he really, really wanted me. He was surrounded by some of the most gorgeous models in the business, but he behaved as if I were the only woman in the room. So I left with Jack—much to Warren's chagrin—and we went back to the Carlyle, where he had a suite. He ordered champagne and lobster and steak, rare, and he was a wonderful host. He wanted to know all about me, and he was earnest and genuine and attentive and outrageously funny. Yes, most of all he was funny. And I'm a sucker for a man who knows how to make me laugh. So I ask you: What's a girl to do?

You were okay, Jack. Really. And you can take that any

way you want. But you pissed me off a little the next morning.

"I want you to do me a favor," Jack said as I was dressing. I had a shoot with Avedon, and I was hurrying because I was already late. "Don't tell anyone you've got star cum inside you." He wasn't kidding, either. He was lying there naked, propped up on the pillows, grinning that famous grin. I couldn't believe he could be so full of himself.

"I hate to come and go," I said, and I left.

When I got to Avedon's, Ara greeted me at the door. "So," he said. "How was he?" Everyone was waiting to hear. Avedon and Way Bandy and Perry Ellis and the whole damn crew. They were all staring. Ara had obviously opened his big mouth.

"Yes, it's true," I said at the top of my voice. "I've been up all night, fucking Jack Nicholson. And I don't think he'll be getting an Oscar this time out. Now, if you don't mind, can we get to work?"

Jack kept calling and calling, but I avoided him. He was fun, sure, but I felt empty. I wanted more than just that same old daddy-thing. I also felt a little guilty about Angelica Huston, Jack's longtime girlfriend. I'd met her and liked her. So I wondered, Why am I sleeping with her man? Not to mention, why is he sleeping with me? Are all men dogs? Whatever happened to fidelity?

"Why can't I find a nice, decent guy?" I asked my friend Alexandra King, as her fuck-me parrot looked on. "Just a nice guy. That's all I ask. Nice. Decent and nice."

"Your standards are too high," she joked. Then she went on to tell me that she had this theory about why love doesn't work. "It's like this, see: A man meets a girl and thinks, 'Wow, she is hot and mysterious and exotic and a little dangerous. I am *way* turned on by this bitch.' So they jump into bed and start hanging out and before you know it she's less hot and less exotic and not much of a mystery at all. In fact, she's become completely domesticated. And he looks at her and wonders, 'What am I doing with this crashing bore?' "

Alexandra was smart. And her theory made sense. But there was another side to it. I brought my own demons to the party. I thought about putting an ad in the paper. *Girl Seeks Dad. Must be kind and loving and nurturing and willing to deal with both of me: the beautiful self-confident babe and the little fucked-up girl inside.*

There was another man who also called around this time—twice—but I ignored him, too. It was Steven Spielberg. Someone at his office left a message for me at Ford: Mr. Spielberg had met me in a restaurant in Southampton and was interested in having me audition for something called *Raiders of the Lost Ark.* I didn't remember meeting Mr. Spielberg, so I imagine I must have been really drunk at the time. That was starting to happen to me from time to time. Blackouts, they call them. Fugue states. You wake up the next day and your memory is shot through with holes. *Raiders of the Lost Ark,* huh? Audition, huh? He must have been talking to his friend Cosby. No thanks. I'm not that naïve.

But there was a third man who kept calling around the same time, and he was the most persistent of the three. That man was John Casablancas. "You're the only interesting model working nowadays," he gushed. "I have to have you." Yeah yeah. I know. I'm the bee's knees. But I *did* think about it. And I started thinking real hard the day Monique Pillard left Eileen Ford and went to work for him.

The thing is, I had a lot of anger in me in those days. I hadn't yet figured out, of course, that it was all connected to my miserable childhood (boo hoo!), so it festered and manifested itself in strange and unexpected ways. At that point, not having a man in my life to be angry with, I was angry at a woman. Specifically, Eileen Ford. And the way I saw it, I had every right to be. She had been so dismissive of me when we first met, and now she was making money on me hand over fist. (Of course, if I'd been smart, I'd have seen that my anger had a lot more to do with my father than it did with her, with the fact that he had made me feel worthless and ugly; but I wasn't smart in those days, at least not about my crazy emotions.) So I decided to punish Eileen. I went over to see John Casablancas. And I told

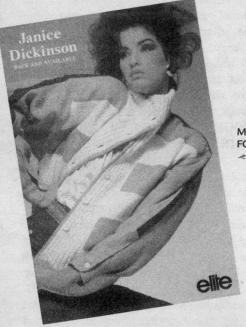

MY COMP CARD
FOR ELITE.

him he could have me, but that he'd have to cut his commission to five percent. Because if I came, others would follow.

"You're crazy," Casablancas said.

"Then what do you need me for?" I said, standing to leave.

"Okay," he said when I reached the door. "You win. I'll take the five percent."

I walked back. Sat. Reached for the phone on his desk.

"It's Janice," I barked into the receiver. "I need to speak to her. *Now.*"

A moment later, Eileen was on the phone. "Hello?" she said. "Janice?"

"That's right," I said. "It's me. Big-lipped Janice."

"How are you, dear?"

"I'm leaving you," I said. "I'm going to Elite. I don't like you, I've *never* liked you. The only good thing about you is Monique Pillard, and she's here, so I don't know what the hell I've been waiting for."

And I hung up. Casablancas was smiling at me. Shaking his head. "You're crazy," he said.

"You have no idea," I said.

My life didn't change all that dramatically. I was still Janice, and everybody still wanted me. Virginia Slims, Suntori liquors, Revlon. But none of these gigs had anything to do with Casablancas. At the end of the day, even with the reduced commissions, Casablancas got the better end of the deal. I knew everyone and I introduced him to everyone, and when I wasn't available there was always another girl in his stable. So, yeah, in retrospect—he was a smart businessman, very smart. There was only one slight problem: I didn't have Eileen Ford to kick around anymore, and I needed *someone* to kick around. So I began to notice men again.

I noticed Warren Beatty a lot. It was hard not to. He was editing *Reds* at some place in Manhattan, and I ran into him at dinner one night, and he called me over and said he'd like to see me. He was with some pale, mousy little man who didn't say anything, just stared at me with his mouth open. I think he was a writer.

"Why do you want to see me?" I asked. "Did I get a good review from your friend Jack?"

Warren laughed. "No," he said. "I just want to see you."

"Well, you're seeing me now," I said, doing my best Mae West.

Warren laughed again and asked me to join him and the drab little writer, but I couldn't do it. I was on my way to Studio 54. I invited him to come along, but he said he didn't party; didn't like that scene. It was true. I found out later that both his parents had been heavy drinkers, and that Warren himself decided early in life that he'd never drink or do drugs. He never did, as far as I know.

So I went to Studio 54 and hooked up with a model called Minka, and I told her that Warren was after me. She said she didn't trust good-looking men. She wanted to be the pretty one in the relationship. I noticed her eyeing an ugly guy at the bar; his arms were covered with tattoos. I guess that was more her speed.

"I'm thinking of getting a tattoo," she said.

"Why would you want to do that?" I asked. This was long before every other suburban housewife in America was out there getting a tattoo.

"Janice!"

I turned to find Diana Vreeland making her way over. She was the doyenne at *Vogue*. I loved her. She was so theatrical, with perfect blood-red fingernails that clicked and slashed when she talked. "How are you, darling?" she said.

"Minka is thinking of getting a tattoo," I said above the din.

"A tattoo!?" She flung her head back and threw her eyes open in horror. "Oh no, dear! No no no! Never mar your body with ink!" And then she saw Liza Minnelli and hurried away.

"There you go," I said, turning to face Minka. And I mimicked Diana's highbrow lilt: "No no no, dear. Never mar your body with ink!"

My sister Debbie showed up; we were both at Elite now. And then Iman arrived, followed by Andie McDowell and Apollonia. And I was looking at all of these beautiful girls and I had a crazy thought.

"John, it's me, Janice. Janice the Great." It was morning. I was in my red bedroom, in my new apartment on West 74th Street, across from the Dakota, calling Casablancas. It occurred to me that my walls were the same color as Diana Vreeland's fingernails.

"How are you, Janice?"

"I'm still the best thing that ever happened to you."

"I know," he said.

"Say, 'Yes you are, dear. Whatever you want, dear.' "

"Yes you are, dear. Whatever you want, dear."

"I want to shoot a Christmas calendar for Elite."

"Huh?"

A few weeks later, I got all of them together in a studio: Beverly Johnson, Iman, Andie, Debbie, Rita, and half a dozen other Elite girls, along with Casablancas himself. I put Johnny in a Santa Claus outfit; the girls— well, I had them in next to nothing. There was more pink Cristal than there were chateaux in the Loire Valley. The walls were buzzing. And the music was cranked up so loud that one of the lights exploded. But the end result was amazing. The calendar was a huge hit. I wish I still had a copy. People were coming up to me for weeks afterward, going on and on about how the pictures leapt off the page.

"It's not enough for them to leap off the page," I told one of my admirers. I was at another one of Ara's legendary parties. "I want them to grab you by the throat and wrestle you to the ground."

There really was no stopping me. I could walk, talk, snort coke, *and* take pictures.

Warren beckoned from across the room. He was with Bitten Knudsen, a gorgeous blond model, very hot in the seventies. I went over. "Do I know you?" I said.

He laughed and waved me into the empty seat next to him. "So," he said once he had me where he wanted me, "how bad are you?"

"Excuse me?"

"All this press you girls are getting. They make you sound like monsters."

It was true. In 1981, *New York* magazine did a piece on "The Spoiled Supermodels." And the *New York Daily News* ran a long series on "The Dark Side of Modeling." It was your basic fluff: We used drugs. We were demanding. We did unspeakable things in the back rooms of Studio 54.

"They didn't get it right at all," I said. "We're *much* worse than that."

Warren and Bitten ended up coming back to my place. Bitten and I did a few lines and drank a little cognac, and Warren promptly fell asleep on the couch. After Bitten finally left, I went over and woke Warren up. He was incredibly handsome. He wasn't one of those people who have to get up in the morning and fix their faces.

"What's happening?" he said.

"You have to go."

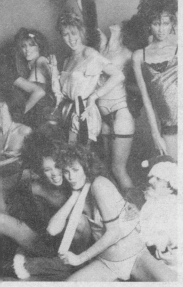

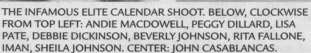

THE INFAMOUS ELITE CALENDAR SHOOT. BELOW, CLOCKWISE FROM TOP LEFT: ANDIE MACDOWELL, PEGGY DILLARD, LISA PATE, DEBBIE DICKINSON, BEVERLY JOHNSON, RITA FALLONE, IMAN, SHEILA JOHNSON. CENTER: JOHN CASABLANCAS.

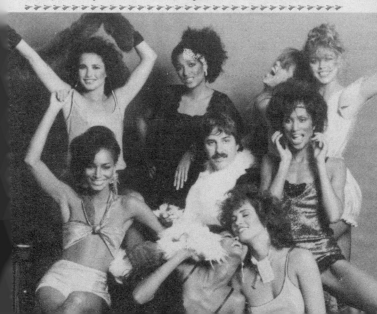

"Where's Bitten?"

"She left."

"Good," he said. "I want to stay here."

"You can't," I said.

"Why not?"

"Come on," I said. And I walked him downstairs and flagged a cab.

"Why won't you let me stay with you?" he asked. Clearly he wasn't used to rejection.

"Because you're much too good-looking," I said, "and I'll probably go and fall in love with you."

The cab pulled up. "But I *want* you to fall in love with me," he said.

I got the door for him and eased him into his seat. "Me and everybody else," I said.

"Janice—"

I shut the door. "Take this man back to the Carlyle Hotel," I told the driver. "And don't stop anywhere. He's dangerous." The cab sped off and I went back to my apartment, feeling quite proud of myself. I'd been a good girl.

The next night, Warren invited me to dinner. He said Bitten was coming, too. I went over to the Carlyle and he asked me up and he was waiting for me at the door to his suite. He was on the phone, and he put a finger to his lips, urging me to be quiet. I looked around. His suite was even nicer than Jack Nicholson's; it was bigger and had a piano. I guess those two were always competing. Probably still are.

I tried not to listen to Warren's conversation—he was talking to Diane Keaton, one of the women in his life—but I could tell he gave good phone. I could imagine Diane on the other end, feeling deeply loved. Then the second line rang and he had to ask her to hold and it was the *other* woman in his life, Mary Tyler Moore. He made *her* feel deeply loved, too. I half-listened as he juggled both of them for a few minutes. Then, finally, at long last, he was rid of them and turned to look at me. God, he was pretty.

"Janice, Janice," he said. He rubbed his hands together like a man about to sit down to a good meal. "You look beautiful, Janice."

"That was quite the performance," I said.

"Excuse me?"

"The way you juggled those two calls. I swear, just standing here, I could feel the love coming off you in waves."

"You're funny," he said.

"Where's Bitten?" I asked.

"She's meeting us at the restaurant. Can I offer you a drink?"

BITTEN KNUDSEN AT A CATALOG SHOOT.

"No," I said. "It's hard enough to resist you sober."

He liked that. He laughed and got his coat and we went downstairs and walked to the restaurant. Bitten really was waiting for us. She was very sweet. She ate quickly and left early. I wondered if Warren had asked her along just to make me feel safe.

"Why don't you walk me back to my hotel," he said after dinner.

"No, thanks," I said, hailing a cab.

He kissed me on the cheek—he wanted more, but I turned my head—and I got in the cab and waved ta-ta as it pulled away. I loved the expression on his face: stunned disbelief. He'd perfected that look in *Bonnie and Clyde*.

I called Debbie when I got home. "Guess what I didn't do tonight?" I said.

"What?"

"Sleep with Warren Beatty."

"Where's he staying?" she asked. Don't worry, she was just kidding. Debbie was funny, too.

Warren called and called and called. I kept putting him off. At the end of the week I had to fly to the Caribbean to do a shoot for *Elle*. (Oh, the drudgery.) But I spent the entire shoot thinking about him.

When I landed back in New York, I found myself standing in the baggage-claim area, waiting for my things, *still* thinking about that man. I walked over to a pay phone and called the Carlyle. He was in.

"Where are you?" he asked.

"At JFK," I said. "I just landed. You sure nobody's there? You're not juggling calls again, are you?"

"Why don't you come over?"

"Bitten's not there? Can it really be—Warren is all alone?"

"I won't be if you come over," he said, laughing. So I did.

He sat down and played the piano for me—what a delight—then ordered room service. We ate by candlelight. He asked me about me. Hung on my every word. Made me feel like the center of the universe.

Of course I slept with him. I'd been wanting to since the first time I'd laid eyes on him. He was great, if you must know. He knew where everything was and what to do with it. But of course he'd had lots of practice. I tried not to think about just how much.

I woke up a few hours later, at around three in the morning. Warren wasn't in bed. I looked across the room and found him admiring himself in the mirror.

"What are you doing?" I asked in a sleepy voice.

"Nothing," he said. But he couldn't take his eyes off himself. He ran his hands through his hair, staring at his reflection in the mirror. I went back to sleep. In the morning, when I woke up, he was standing there again, playing with his hair, mussing it; trying to get it just right—going for that just-been-fucked look. I guess he thought he was pretty, too.

I saw Warren for the next eight months. I never let myself fall in love with him, but it was fun. He let me be a little girl. And he was a nice daddy. He made me feel loved and important. I knew he was making half a dozen other women feel the same way at the same time—sometimes on the same day, even—but it didn't matter. I needed lots of nurturing, and I was getting it from Warren Beatty.

The only thing that bothered me was that he never let me photograph him. You'd think he'd love having his picture taken, vain as he was. And he did. But he had to control that, too. I'm sure if Irving Penn had asked him, he would have jumped. But I was just Janice. He needed to be sure he looked perfect. He would have looked perfect in a fucking Polaroid, but that wasn't enough for Warren. He wanted to look flawless.

I like Warren. I wonder how he feels about getting older. I wonder if he gazes at himself as often as he used to then, or whether he's had sheets draped over all the mirrors.

THE MUSIC MAN

The month after things with Warren petered out (I use the phrase advisedly), I flew to Los Angeles to do a catalog job for Macy's. It was fun; I was working with Rene Russo, whom I adore. She's probably one of the shiest people I've ever met, and she said working in front of the camera was sheer torture. She didn't know who to be when a photographer told her to be herself.

"I'm taking acting classes," she told me. "It's so much easier."

"You must be kidding?" I said.

"No," she said. "It's *acting*. I find it so much easier to be another person."

Made all the sense in the world.

The real reason I was so jazzed about being in L.A., however, had nothing to do with the Macy's shoot. I was jazzed because Peppo della Schiavva had caught wind of my talents as a photographer. Peppo was the Italian publisher who ran most of the fashion magazines in Italy. *Bazaar. Men's Bazaar. Cosmo.* He'd asked me to shoot a line of bikinis for him. And who was I to say no? It was my first paying gig on the other side of the camera, and, believe me, I was thrilled to death.

I asked Rene if she could do it, but she had a scheduling conflict. So I tracked down my old pal Bitten, Warren's little friend. Then I found a local hair and makeup girl and the three of us drove up to Malibu in a rented car. I was distracted the whole way out, trying to remember everything I'd ever learned about photography. I kept making these imaginary lists in my head—things to do and not to do—and the fucking lists were getting so long they were making me dizzy.

But when we got to the beach, I forgot all about the lists. I just stepped up to the plate and *felt* my way through the shoot. I found I had a good grasp of what would work and what wouldn't, and the list simply floated out of my head.

We shot for five hours, at a beautiful sandy beach a mile or two north of Malibu. As the day wore on, I became increasingly confident. My best shots—the ones that ended up in print—came toward the end of the day. I remember driving back to L.A. thinking, *I'm a photographer!*

It was pretty late by the time I returned to my room at the Beverly Hills Hotel. I showered and ordered room service, thinking about making it an early night. I had another shoot the next day—for Perry Ellis—and I was tired. But I was also wired from working. So I called my friends Elmer Valentine and Lou Adler, who owned two hot clubs on Sunset Strip, the Roxy and On the Rox. Lou was at the latter. He told me to come by.

I put on my micromini, slipped into my platform shoes, and got back into my rental car and drove over. Lou took me into his office and popped some champagne, and we chatted until he got a call to go deal with a problem at the other club. I left his office, buzzed on champagne, and worked my way over to the bar. I didn't see anyone I knew, but I saw a lot of people I recognized. Ryan O'Neal and Farrah Fawcett were there. I remember thinking, *People on the West Coast don't know how to dress.* I saw James

Taylor. He was sitting at the bar, crying. I'd read in *People* magazine that Carly Simon had just dumped him.

The song ended. Tina Turner came on, cranking hard. She was impossible to resist. I waltzed out onto the dance floor and shut my eyes and started to boogie. I love dancing with my eyes closed. I can just get down and imagine that I'm there with someone I love. But I sensed someone in my face. And I knew I wasn't imagining it. And I wasn't in love with anyone at the moment. So I opened my eyes.

Mick Jagger was dancing with me. I thought, *That champagne Lou gave me—what the hell was it laced with?* So I closed my eyes, ignored the apparition, and kept dancing. But it wouldn't quit. And it felt powerful. I opened my eyes again, and Mick was still in my face. He was no apparition, and he was grinning.

"Who the fuck are you, then?" he said. "I know you."

"You wish," I said.

He was pure energy. We danced—cleared the floor— and everyone was staring at us. For a moment there, I went back to thinking that Lou really *had* laced the champagne. But he hadn't.

When the music ended, the actual Mick Jagger took me by the actual hand and told me we were going back to the Sunset Marquis. His entourage followed us into the street. That's the kind of power he had. He moved, and his disciples dropped whatever they were doing and stayed close.

"*You're* going back to the Sunset Marquis," I said, turning to give the valet my parking stub. "I'm going to the Beverly Hills Hotel. I have to work in the morning."

"*Work?* Gorgeous girl like you shouldn't have to work."

"I *like* to work," I said. "It keeps me sane."

"I know I know you," he repeated, squinting his eyes and trying to place me.

I offered him my hand. "Janice Dickinson," I said.

"Mick Jagger," he said.

"No!" I said. "Really? You're not putting me on now, are you?"

He laughed. "What are you doing tomorrow night?" he asked.

"Nothing," I said. "I was planning on flying home to New York."

"Well, don't," he said. And he climbed into his limo and disappeared.

Sonofabitch. On the one hand, I was proud of myself. I turned down Mick Jagger. On the other, I felt he could have tried a little harder.

I got back from the Perry Ellis shoot the next afternoon to find my hotel room filled with pink roses. "Someone will be picking you up at seven," the card said. Mick Jagger, a man of few words?

I called Patti Hansen, who was dating Keith Richards, and told her about meeting Mick. "He's *very* fucking hot," I said, stating the obvious. "What's the story with Jerry?" Jerry Hall, that is.

"She's been busting his balls to get married," she said. "But they're not married, are they?"

"No. I guess not."

"You're a big girl, Janice. And Mick's a big boy. Do what you have to do."

It was getting late and I showered and looked for something to wear. Models *never* have anything to wear. I found some striped leggings and a baggy silk shirt and a purple suede sash, and I looked in the full-length mirror and thought, *Shit! I look like Captain Hook!*

But it was seven already—too late to change. So I hurried out to the hotel entrance just as a long black limousine pulled up. There was Angelica Huston, stepping out and coming over to hug me; we'd met in New York a few times, at Studio 54 and on the social circuit. Jack Nicholson followed her out and approached with that Cheshire cat smile. "Jack," she said, "this is Janice—Janice Dickinson. I'm not sure you've met."

Jack shook my hand warmly. "Janice. Big fan here. Nice to meet you." What an actor! I felt like slapping him. I felt like turning to Angelica and saying, "Oh, Jack and I already know each other. We fucked in New York." (And Angelica, if you're reading this, I am so sorry!)

Instead, I smiled and looked Jack dead in the eye. "It's really nice to meet you, too."

Turns out we were sharing a limo. We'd all been comped tickets to the Stones concert. En route, Jack nodded his head attentively and made small talk, asking me about my career. I played right along, Little Miss Innocent, and I found it disarmingly easy. Maybe I had a natural aptitude for acting. The next time Steven Spielberg called, I remember thinking, I should pull myself together and go see the man.

When we got to the amphitheater, we were taken in through the back. Mick was waiting for us in his dressing room. The moment we walked though the door he took my head between his hands, put his big lips on my big lips, and gave me a loud smack. Our mouths were like two oversized electrical hookups, made for each other.

"You call that a kiss?" I asked. I grabbed his shaggy head, jammed my tongue down his throat, and pinned him to the wall. When I finally let him come up for air, he looked at me, impressed. "That was a promising start, Janice. Very promising."

"I've never kissed anyone with bigger lips than mine," I said.

But suddenly it was showtime, and Mick had to run off. We went to find our seats, and I ran into Lou Adler and his partner, Elmer. "You bastards," I said. "I met Jagger at your club last night. He wants to fuck me."

"You lucky girl," Lou said.

And Elmer said, "Do *you* want to fuck *him*?"

"I don't know," I said. Liar.

"Don't be an idiot," Lou said. "Sleep with the man. You'll have stories for your grandchildren."

So I did. We went back to the Sunset Marquis after the concert, Mick and I, and we fucked all night. The man was indefatigable. (I love that word.) He was pure energy—kind of spooky, to tell you the truth. I woke up the next day feeling like I'd been through a war. And I wasn't sure I'd won, either. And then I got my goddamn period, which put a damper on the morning festivities.

Mick had to leave early in the afternoon. He had a business meeting. That's what he told me, anyway. Maybe he was just looking for a girl who wasn't bleeding. He comped me two tickets for that night's concert, too—I could pick them up at the door, he said—then set four hundred dollars on the night table next to my side of the bed. "Here you go," he said. "Buy yourself a pretty frock."

Oh, man! How could he? But he was gone before I knew it.

For the next six months, Mick became my new daddy. He was away much of the time, just like the rat bastard. And he wasn't particularly nice to me when he was around, which definitely made me feel right at home. But he had a lot of energy in bed. And that made up for a great deal.

"I love you," he told me once. "You're built just like a little boy."

"You're sick," I said.

"Yes, I am," he said. And he was off again.

The thing is, he was Mick Jagger. He could have had

anyone, and he did. But he wanted me. *Wanted* me. And I was still hungry for that. That meant I couldn't be so bad, right? I mean, *Hello?* Do we detect a pattern here? Jack Nicholson, Warren Beatty, Mick Jagger. Not exactly settling for second best, was I?

Yeah—okay. I know. I see it *now.* But I'm not alone in this. We're all looking for validation. We all want to be wanted. Some of us are just more desperate than others.

By the end of those six months, though, I found I liked Keith better than Mick. Not that way, of course—Keith was with Patti, and she was a friend of mine. But he was more fun to be around. He was probably nicer to me than he was to Patti.

"Why is Mick so mean to me?" I asked Keith one drunken night. He and Patti and I were hanging out at their place, on 5th Avenue and 16th Street.

"Men are always mean to the women they sleep with," he said.

"Are you mean to Patti?" I asked.

"No," he said. "But don't let that get out. I've got a reputation to worry about."

We drank some more, did some more coke, and before I knew it we were singing.

"You've got a nice voice, Janice," Keith said. He was obviously out of his mind.

"Sure," I said.

"No, really," he insisted, sliding off the couch to the floor. "Talent like that—you shouldn't let it go to waste."

Didn't I say somewhere that we believe what we want to believe? Well, I wanted to believe. And that's how it happened. Two months later I'm in a recording studio, preparing a demo. Keith was on one guitar. Ron Wood on another. John Oates of Hall & Oates was on a third. Some session guy was on drums, looking frankly overwhelmed to be playing with those three. And then there was me, little me, doing my own inimitable version of "In the Boom Boom Room." They all thought I was great. John Belushi showed up in the middle of the session, and *he* said I was great. Who was I to question the judgment of these brilliant, distinguished gentlemen—paragons of honesty and refined good taste?

After we wrapped for the day, Belushi asked me what I was doing later. I thought he was going to ask me to sleep with him.

"Nothing," I said, wary.

"Why don't you come by the studio," he said. "Watch us tape the show."

So I went. Hung out, laughed at Belushi and Dan Aykroyd and Bill Murray, who has always struck me as one of the spookiest funny men alive. There's something indescribably dark about him.

"How are you, Bill?" I asked.

Bill looked at me in that special way he has, like he can see clear through to your soul. "Janice," he said, "there are certain portions of my mind which are best left undisturbed."

Aykroyd came over to say hello. We'd met before. He'd been trying to set me up with his brother, Peter. "Did my brother call you?" he asked.

"No," I said.

"He's shy," he said. "I'll tell him again."

"I'll be waiting by the phone," I said.

"I'd call you myself," he said. "but I'm happily married. However, I would be thrilled if you mailed me some nude pictures of yourself. But please send them here, to the studio. I'd hate for my wife to find them. She'd probably fall in love with you and leave me."

Then the taping was over and Belushi came by and asked if I'd drive to Memphis with him.

"Why?" I asked.

"I want to dance on Elvis's grave."

"Gee, I don't know," I said. "Aren't there any local dead guys you want to dance on?"

"I bet you'd go if I was Mick Jagger," he said, all pouty. But he was just horsing around. He was always saying, "You know Mick Jagger. You fucked Mick Jagger! My God, Mick Jagger! If he asked *me* to sleep with him, I'd probably say yes."

"Okay," I said. "You're on. Let's go to Memphis."

"Great," he said. "But we have to stop in Atlantic City first."

"Why?" I asked.

"Janice," he said, "you ask a lot of questions. That's okay when you're four years old and everything in the world is new and strange, but—at your age—it's very unbecoming."

I don't know whether there was any method to his madness, but he certainly had a strange sense of style. First, we went to Rent-a-Wreck for a car. I have no idea why he wanted a heap when he could have afforded a limo, and I knew better than to ask. Then we stopped at a 7-Eleven for two cases of Bud Tall Boys. It *had* to be Bud Tall Boys. Belushi almost fell apart when he heard they were out, but an enterprising clerk found two cases in back—and got an autograph for his efforts.

"Do you know who this is?" he said, putting his arm around my shoulders.

"No sir," the clerk said. He was holding on to the autograph as if his life depended on it.

"This is Janice Dickinson," Belushi said. "She's seen Mick Jagger naked."

We went out to the car and got in. Then he noticed the pay phone, and he just sat there and stared.

"What's wrong?" I asked.

"You think I should call Darlanne?" Darlanne Fluegel was an actress who'd been in *Conan the Barbarian*. I guess John had a thing for women in loincloths.

"John, you're married."

"Says who!?" he snarled, pouting again. He backed out fast, tires squealing, and we raced over to Tower Records. It was all an act, of course. He was in fine spirits. He filled a shopping cart with tunes and paid for them with Aykroyd's credit card. I knew better than to ask about that, too.

"This is the fucking life!" John said as we pulled away. All the windows were open, and the music was blaring. "By the time we get to Atlantic City, I want to know everything about you, Janice. And don't leave anything out, because if you do, I'll know." I laughed. "I'm not joking," he said. "By the time this trip is over I want to know you better than I know the side of my hand."

"The *side* of your hand?"

"Yeah. Everybody says the back of their hand, but I don't know the back of my hand all that well. The side of my hand—well, I'm on intimate terms with the side of my hand."

You know that old joke, "But enough about me; what do you think of me?" Well, Belushi was the exact opposite. He refused to talk about himself. All the way to Atlantic City, he pelted me with questions. The more personal, the better. And he seemed genuinely interested. He considered every answer carefully.

"You know, Janice," he said toward the end of the ride. "I'm not a therapist, though I've played one on TV. And stop me if I'm out of line. But I think you're pretty fucked up about men."

"No! *Me?* How can you say a thing like that?"

He looked over at me and smiled that old John Belushi smile. He'd had a few Tall Boys by then and was feeling very little pain. "You ever read any Sigmund Freud?"

"Just the Cliff Notes," I said.

"Well, Freud had this theory, see. And I'll try to keep it simple—seeing how you're a model and all. But it goes something like this. Most of us have something in our past—our distant past, like with our parents, say—that didn't work out too good. And what we do, see, is we spend the rest of our lives playing that same fucking tune over and over again, with more and more people, in one relationship after another, thinking we might just get it right some day. You follow?"

"Yeah," I said. "Every idiot understands the repetition compulsion."

He looked at me in disbelief. "You *have* read Freud!"

"Not really. I went to see a shrink years ago. We talked about all that, but I didn't really understand it. Maybe you can explain it to me."

He took a beat, reached for another Tall Boy. "Okay," he said, popping the can. "But, like, you know—stop me if I'm being an asshole."

"Don't worry," I said. "I will."

"Promise?" he asked.

"I promise."

He had a sip of beer and launched in. "This shit with your father, Janice. What a fucking monster. Telling you you'd never amount to anything. Don't you see what it's doing to you?"

"What?"

"You keep falling for guys who make you feel like you don't amount to anything."

"I do?"

"Yeah. And you think, 'I'm going to show this bastard

that I'm a great girl. I'm going to show him how wonderful I am.' And of course that'll never work, see? Because it isn't about any of those assholes. It's about *you;* it's about what happened to you. They're just assholes. Unfortunately, they're the assholes you happen to be attracted to, because they remind you of your father. That's why you need to work on the dynamic, babe. That's why I'm here, Janice. Tonight. With you. To tell you that your life would be a lot easier if you were attracted to nice homely fat guys—guys like me."

I couldn't say anything.

"Are you okay?" he asked.

I nodded.

"This love shit. Pretty hard to figure out, isn't it?"

I nodded again. Joking aside, I was pretty floored by what he'd just said.

"Why don't you roll another joint?" he suggested. I rolled another joint. Or *half* a joint. It was the last of the pot. The exit for Atlantic City was just ahead. He took it. I lit the joint and passed it to him without taking a hit. I still didn't like pot. It made me hungry and paranoid. Not a pretty picture, especially in brightly lit fast-food joints.

"By the way, what I just told you—don't lose any sleep over it," he said. He was still holding the smoke in his lungs. "Everyone I know is deeply fucked up." He exhaled loudly. "Like with me there are things about myself I understand so well, but I can't do a damn thing about them. Because that's *one* part of me—the intellectual part. John Belushi the Thinker. But the other part, the emotional part of me—well, that John's a fucking train wreck. And those two guys are constantly at war."

"So I'm two Janices?" I asked. "Is that it?"

"Yeah," he said. "And tonight I'm gonna fuck them both."

* * *

The reason we stopped in Atlantic City was to see Frank Gorshin, a comedian friend of John's. We were already late, and as we were hurrying through the casino someone recognized John and he was mobbed by fans. He was pretty gracious about it. He signed autographs and cracked jokes and kept telling everyone that he loved Atlantic City. "They've got the best hookers in the world here," he told them now, putting his arm around me. "Look at this girl. Where else in the world can you get a girl like this for a hundred bucks? I will be doing things with this girl in about an hour that are still illegal in the southern part of this country. So—synchronize your watches, *amigos*—at ten sharp I want all of you to close your eyes and picture me and this girl, naked and grunting."

Gorshin was just wrapping the first half of his second set. We went backstage and John introduced me and we chatted a while, but Gorshin had to go back out, and we told him we'd come by after the show. John wanted to watch the show, but he really needed to get stoned again, and he was out of pot.

"Do you know anyone in Atlantic City?" he asked me.

"No," I said.

So we went out to the casino and he cupped his hands over his mouth, right there near the blackjack tables, and hollered at the top of his voice, "ANYONE HERE GOT ANY POT!?"

It got people's attention. Some people snickered.

"You there, sir," John said. He was pointing at this skinny long-haired guy at one of the blackjack tables. "You look like a pothead from way back. You got anything?" The guy shook his head. "So you're not a pothead. You're a card-counter; you just look like a pothead to confuse the pit boss. Anybody else got any pot? Anybody at all?"

We had quite an audience at this point. A man in a suit approached. "Can I help you, sir?" he asked John.

"If you've got pot on you, yes you can. Absolutely."

"I'm Detective Bensink," the man said. "I'm with vice."

"That's very funny," John said.

"Would you please come with me, Mr. Belushi."

"He was just kidding!" I piped up. "We're practicing a sketch for the show."

"That's right," John said, catching on. "It's called, *Got any pot?* I'd be happy to walk you through it."

"That won't be necessary," he said. And we followed him outside, though none too happily.

"Where are you parked?" he asked.

John pointed at the wreck across the lot. "I have some dynamite shit at home," the detective said. "I'll pull round. Just follow me. My wife is a big fan."

His wife practically fainted when John walked through the door. She couldn't believe it. John Belushi! In her home! They pulled out the Polaroid and I took some pictures and John signed autographs for assorted nieces and nephews.

Then we got to the stash. Tons of stuff. *Shoe boxes* full of it. They had bags of *sinsemilla* that rivaled anything John had smoked in a year. "Here, take some," the detective was foisting it on us an hour later, as we went on our way. "Really. I insist. There's plenty more in the Evidence Room. And thanks for making my wife's day. It's her birthday tomorrow. Now I don't have to buy her anything."

We were too stoned to go to Memphis, so we drove back to New York, getting in at the crack of dawn. He dropped me at my place. "Thanks," I said. "I mean it."

"It was a good time," he said, looking solemn. "And it hurts. Because I know that's all I am to you. A *good time*." He couldn't stop with the jokes.

"Yeah," I said. "You're a good time. But I'm actually thinking about what we talked about last night."

"Refresh my memory," he said.

"You've inspired me." I said. "I'm breaking things off with Jagger."

"Really?"

"Yes," I said. "Really."

"Great," he said. "Give Jagger my number. Tell him I'm available. Tell him I'll do anything. Anything at all. You want to hear me squeal like a pig?"

I stopped returning Jagger's calls. He stopped calling. Easy as that.

And I never saw Belushi again. A few months later, on March 5, 1982, he was dead. He never got to dance on Elvis's grave.

One summer night, not long after I ended things with Mick, I found myself sitting at the bar at Heartbreak, an after-hours club in downtown Manhattan. I'd spent the better part of the day getting in and out of various outfits for *Cosmo;* now I was tired and on my way home. But suddenly I felt unimaginably lonely, lonely and pensive, and I didn't want to sit in my red bedroom by myself, thinking about the Meaning of Life. Thinking had never gotten me anywhere. It had never gotten anyone anywhere, as far as I could tell.

So I walked into Heartbreak and made my way to the bar and heads turned to follow my progression across the room. And of course I immediately felt better. So I've got my shallow side. Sue me.

I ordered a drink and saw someone I recognized at the end of the bar.

"Hey, Peter," I said. "How you doing?"

"I'm not Peter," he said.

He was joking, of course. It was Peter Aykroyd, Dan's brother. "Why are you so afraid to call me?" I asked.

"I'm not afraid to call you," he said. "Give me your number and I'll call you."

"You're funny," I said. "Can you dance?"

We danced. He was a good dancer. He had a nice, kissable mouth. For a young guy, I mean. And me—well, I had a thing for fatherly types. We went back to the bar and he bought me a drink. I thanked him, calling him Peter again, and again he insisted his name wasn't Peter.

"What do you want me to call you?" I said.

"My friends call me Bruno," he said. He was very nice.

The next day was Saturday. He told me he was playing softball with his buddies, in Central Park, and said I should come by and watch. I went. I didn't have a life.

At the bottom of the ninth, with the game tied and the bases empty, Bruno knocked a ball deep into left field and ran for all he was worth. It didn't look like he was going to make it, so he dove for home plate. He made it, but he tore up his left arm. Several girls offered to take him home and tend to his injuries. Bruno picked one. Then he saw me there.

"Hi, Peter," I said.

"Hey, Janice—I didn't think you'd make it," he said.

"I got lost on my way over," I said.

"What are you doing tonight?" he asked. "I tend bar at Café Central. Come by and I'll prove to you that I'm not Peter. I'm *better* than Peter."

The little nurse at his side was tugging at his good arm. She was getting jealous.

"Okay," I said.

I went to Café Central just before closing time. Christopher Walken was sitting at the bar. He looked at me like he wanted to fuck me. *Join the club, motherfucker.* The waiters were starting to clean up. Peter, aka Bruno, was tallying the day's take. He was wearing a tight black T-shirt and looked very buff.

"Sorry, miss," he said, smiling. "We're closed."

"I know a little place not far from here that's open all night," I said.

I took him back to my apartment. He was impressed. "What do you do?" he asked.

"A little modeling," I said.

He spent the night. It was nice. An age-appropriate man. I almost felt a little maternal.

In the morning, he snuck out to fetch breakfast. It wasn't exactly Paris—no buttery croissants, no fresh strawberries, no fine cheeses—but a warm blueberry muffin will always do in a pinch.

"So who are you?" I asked.

His friends called him Bruno, like he said, but his name was Bruce Willis. He was from New Jersey, but he'd picked up the acting bug at Montclair State College. He was determined to make it. He was busy chasing parts in small, off-Broadway productions. A real *mensch.* A Jersey guy, a guy from the 'hood. He was such a cliché that I couldn't help liking him. We started seeing a lot of each other. I liked his friends, too. They were totally unpretentious, which was virtually unheard of in my world. I liked the fact that he was nice to everyone. Customers, famous and infamous; waiters; busboys. He was especially nice to the busboys. "You see that kid?" he told me one night, pointing at a scrawny little guy who was busy clearing tables. "If he takes twenty bucks home at the end of the night, he sends eighteen of it to his parents, back in Puerto Rico. Look at him. *Christ.* Don't you think he deserves better?"

Who knew bartenders had such depth?

Of course, that didn't do much for his career. In the eight months we were together, all he ever got was one gig. It was on a soap opera. He was going to play a house painter. He had two lines. "Will that be high-gloss or semi-gloss?" And, "I'll start first thing in the morning." He walked around the apartment for three days, practicing his lines, varying his inflection. "Will *that* be high-gloss or semi-gloss? *I'll* start first thing in the morning. I'll *start* first thing in *the* morning. First thing in the morning, I'll start. Will that be high-gloss *or* semi-gloss?"

I liked Bruno. He was sweet. But he was no actor.

Me, on the other hand, I was going to be a singer. I really thought I was going places. I hung out with Keith and Ron and spent a lot of time in recording sessions, and everyone around me seemed to think I had a gift. I was seriously thinking about a career change. I was starting to find modeling quite irritating, if you must know, and I couldn't seem to make it through a session without a hit or two of coke.

Monique Pillard got some complaints about me. As I said, as long as you're making money for them, they don't give a shit. And they'll keep you in drugs if that's what it takes. But Monique gave a shit. She'd been a fan from Day One.

"You're turning into Gia," she said.

"Oh come on!" I said. "I was a few minutes late. Big deal."

"You couldn't hold your head up," she said.

"That's not true!"

Fuck it. I wasn't going to listen to her. I was on to bigger and better things. I was about to make my feature film debut, in James Toback's *Exposed*. I didn't need her shit. Of course, to be completely honest, the reason I hadn't been able to hold my head up at that memorable shoot was on account of my big movie debut. . . .

I'd had a call about James Toback a few weeks earlier. He wanted me in his film—it had to be me—and wondered if I'd meet with him. I was reluctant, to be honest. Especially when it turned out he was holding court in a hotel room. But I went—hope springs eternal. And he ushered me into his shabby suite—a big bear of a man, unwashed, with pink, sweaty skin and greasy hair—and offered me a seat and said, "You are the greatest." *Good start.* "I love your work. You are my favorite model working today." Jesus, he was beginning to sound like John Casablancas. I was ready to sign with him. But finally he got around to his movie, *Exposed.* He began to describe it. He claimed it was a love story, though you sure couldn't tell from listening to him. Nastassja Kinski was in it, he said; so was Harvey Keitel.

I said yes. Simple as that. And, on the night in question, I found myself at a SoHo restaurant, closed for the shoot, with Nastassja and Harvey and Rudolf Nureyev and two fellow models—Nancy Donahue and Hilary English. But no script. We were just supposed to chat, be ourselves. (Rene Russo would have loved that!) And we chatted and got drunk on good wine, and kept talking and shooting and drinking till the sun came up. So, yeah, Monique—I couldn't hold my head up the next day. *Mea* fucking *maxima culpa.*

Monique was pissed. Understandably, justifiably. And she moved on. She started mothering Cindy Crawford, who'd found her way to Elite at age seventeen, through their *Look of the Year* contest. She hadn't won the contest, but she was a very smart girl. She was all about business. She knew she'd been blessed with superior looks—and she knew how to convert them to legal tender. I guess Cindy was the first of a smart new breed: the Model As Businesswoman. I wish she'd been around to tutor me.

I can say that now, of course. But I'm sure at the time I must have been a *tad* jealous. I was still on top of the world, sure, but younger girls like Cindy Crawford and Christy Turlington were very much *of the moment*. My moment hadn't passed—not yet, anyway—but I was suddenly interested in exploring new possibilities. Photography. Music. Film. And anything else that piqued my interest.

That's when I got a call from Mark Fleischman, the guy who'd taken over Studio 54. He'd heard I was singing and wanted to know if I'd consider making my debut at the club. It was for a good cause, he said: the Alvin Ailey Dance Company was strapped for cash, and he wanted to help.

I was flattered. I said I'd think about it. It *was* for a good cause. *Two* good causes, actually—Alvin Ailey and *moi*.

In the weeks ahead, I was feeling pretty good about myself. I spent time in the studio with Keith and Ron and John Oates, and there was actually talk about a recording contract. Everyone had me convinced I was a brilliant singer. When I wasn't at the recording studio laying down tracks, I was in the shower belting out tunes, or on the dance floor, shucking and jiving and singing at the top of my voice. I know, I know. If I saw myself now, out there on the dance floor, wailing, I'd slap me, too. But back then there was no stopping me. Everyone fed my confidence.

So I went to see Fleischman and told him, sure, I'd do the show. He decided we'd invite everyone who was anyone, and we'd charge thirty-five dollars in advance, and another thirty at the door.

I asked Scavullo to do the invitations, and they were perfect. Mick Jagger called when he got his. "Who the fuck do you think you are, then?" he said. "I'm Mick Jagger, and *I* don't even get what you're getting."

He was just goofing, of course. "I'm Janice Dickinson," I said. "And it's a fucking benefit." I was goofing, too.

Two days before the show, I went to see Harry King and asked him to chop off my long hair. "Are you sure you want to do this?" he asked. He thought the pressure of my professional debut had gone to my head, and not in a good way.

"Yes," I said. "I'm sure."

He chopped. It looked fucking great. But everyone I saw in the next forty-eight hours thought I'd lost my mind. I looked like a boy—and this was before androgyny was all the rage. They thought I was nuts; I thought I was ahead of my time.

I went over to the club the afternoon before my big debut to make sure everything was ready. The florists were there. Mark wanted thousands of fresh rose petals to rain down on me as I came out on stage. And who was I to argue? He also had T-shirts made up with my name emblazoned across the front. *Janice!* They were great.

The DJ tested the sound system, using a tape of me singing "Outlaws," the Ron Wood song. It was part of my demo—I'd laid it the previous week with Ron and Keith—and that was the first song I'd be singing that night, in a matter of hours. I sounded fucking great.

"Everybody's coming!" Mark said. He was incredibly excited. "And all the major record labels are sending scouts."

I went home and got decked out in a Halston-designed rose-petal pink leotard and a little pink tutu. I looked like Peter Pan on a bad day. Mark sent a limo around to fetch me. The club was full by the time I arrived; people were being turned away at the door.

I walked through and grinned my alligator grin for the photographers: They were out in full force. There were searchlights lighting up the New York skyline. It was like the fucking Academy Awards.

Friends and fans mobbed me when I got inside, but Mark dragged me away. He took me out back and sat me down and told me not to be nervous.

"I'm not nervous," I said. "You're making me nervous. You're hyperventilating."

He said the house was packed. Liz Taylor had just walked in with Halston. Robert De Niro was there. All the girls from Elite.

And suddenly—it's showtime, folks! Mark walks on stage. I hear him say a few words about the Alvin *Ailing* Dance Company, hear him thanking everyone for coming, thanking them for their friendship and support, and then he's calling my name. I did two quick toots of some dynamite Peruvian flake, then stepped through the curtain and onto the stage. . . .

It is raining rose petals and everyone is clapping and hooting and hollering. The noise is deafening. It goes on and on: a roar of approbation.

I look down at the crowd and see everyone I know. I see Mick and Keith and Patti and Iman and Stephanie and Warhol and Calvin and Diana Vreeland and half the photographers I've ever worked with. Jesus. *Everyone.* Charlie Haughk is there with his cop father. Charlie waves. Bob Menna is there, a fellow model, a sweet guy. He waves, too. He's excited for me. He points at a passing waiter. All the waiters are running around in *Janice* T-shirts. It's all about me. Everything is about me. They're all there because of me. *Life* is about me.

Yes. I am feeling the love in the room.

Suddenly it hits me. *This is it. This is the moment. It's really happening.* And it takes me back to that fateful night in 1969, at the Doors concert in Coconut Grove. And it occurs to me that Jim Morrison is long dead, and that it's *me* up there now—me, Janice, just as I'd always hoped. This is my moment. I am an angel, bathed in angelic light, and it's raining rose petals.

I am adored, goddamn it. I am adored.

And as I look down at all those smiling faces, I see one face that is smiling more brightly than all the rest of them. It is my father's face. And of course I think I must be hallucinating. That must have been some pretty powerful toot back there. So I blink and I look again and it *is* my father. In a tuxedo. And my mother is with him. And Debbie is next to them, with her Indonesian millionaire boyfriend. And she's grinning. And suddenly I get it. She flew them in. She and her boyfriend. Wasn't that a nice surprise?

And just then they cue the music and I'm standing there with the microphone in my hand, and I goddamn freeze. . . . *You'll never amount to anything.*

I feel myself going weak at the knees. I lean against the mike stand for support. *You'll never amount to anything. . . .*

Nobody's clapping now. They're all staring. And the room is spinning.

And suddenly I hear my voice on the sound system, even though I know I'm not singing. And it hits me. Of course! It's the tape. The DJ saw me freeze up and he's playing the tape. *Maybe I can lip-sync my way through this.* And I try. God knows I try. But I can't even catch up to myself. So it's Janice lyp-syncing to Janice, about three or four beats back. And I can't fucking catch up.

I stumble over my own words. I try to prance across the stage. I try to smile. And my smile is about as convincing as their smiles. They're all looking up at me with those Stubie Gardner smiles: "You stink, but I'll be the last to tell you."

Somehow I make it through the song, and everyone applauds, politely, out of duty or embarrassment. And I disappear backstage and inhale a massive amount of coke in record time. Then Mark comes by to tell me how well I did: I'm a hit, a star. Everything is a blur now. He's leading me out, into the crowd. Everyone is fawning. "You were wonderful!" "A triumph!" "Big things are in store for you, Janice!" Only I know they're all fucking lying to me. I've never been more humiliated in my life.

And then Debbie's there, at my side. And I look at her like I'm going to kill her, and growl, "Get me the fuck out of here." And she hustles me out to the Indonesian's limo and takes me to his big house in Scarsdale, and I don't say a word the whole way there. I am catatonic. I will not talk to her or the Indonesian. She is saying, "I'm sorry. I thought it would be nice, having Mom and Dad here. I'm really sorry, Janice. Really."

Not a word. I just stare out the window, seeing nothing, trying not to think, not to feel.

We reach Scarsdale and I get out of the limo and find my way to one of the guest rooms and crash and I don't open my eyes till the next afternoon. I stumble into the kitchen. One of the servants brings me coffee. I ask the limo driver to take me home.

I get back to my apartment and the phone is ringing. It's Mark Fleischman. "You saved Alvin Ailey! You raised seventy-five thousand dollars for the company. You were great." I mumble my thanks and hang up.

The phone rings again. It's Jerry Hall. "Have you seen the papers?" she says, then quotes from one of the more scathing reviews . . . "Nice try, Janice. Stick to modeling."

"Thank you for sharing that," I say, numb with shame.

"Stay the fuck away from Mick," she warns me. "I have a gun in my purse. And I know how to use it."

My mother calls, but I hang up on her. I get into bed and stop answering the phone. An hour later, the buzzer sounds. It's Charlie Haughk. I tell him to go away. Debbie comes by. She has her own key. I don't even have the energy to be angry with her. And was it really her fault? Maybe she thinks we had normal parents. She didn't go through what I went through, what Alexis went through.

"How you doin'?" she says.

"I'm fine," I say. I just want her to go away.

"I just, you know—I thought it would be a nice thing to do," she stammers. "Daddy's not doing so well. And I thought, you know, it would be nice for him to see you up there, in front of all your friends."

JERRY HALL

"What's wrong with him?" I ask. Not that I'm interested.

"I don't know," she says. "Mom says he forgets things. He's confused a lot."

"I don't blame him for forgetting things," I say. "I'd try to forget, too, if I'd done what he did. No wonder he's confused."

"No. It's like, sometimes he doesn't even recognize her. It sounds really spooky."

"Can you leave now?" I say. I reach for my Peruvian flake and don't even bother to look for my Tiffany mirror. I dump a little on my nail and snort it up.

"I'm really sorry," she says, and leaves.

At some point I fall asleep. I don't know how long I'm unconscious but I wake up to find Monique Pillard standing at the foot of my bed. She has this look on her face like she's at a funeral.

"Hello, Janice," she says.

"What are you doing here?" I am disoriented. I am confused. I remember what Debbie said about Dad and wonder whether his forgetfulness is hereditary. "How did you get in?"

"Some of your friends are here," she says. "Why don't you wash your face and come outside? I brought you something to eat. I'll make coffee."

What the fuck is going on?

I wash my face and throw on a pair of sweatpants and walk into the living room. Debbie is there with Monique and Charlie Haughk and Charles Senior. My model friend Bob Menna is there. They're all looking at me like I'm dead or something.

"Why is everybody staring at me? What the hell is going on here?"

"Janice," Charlie says. "Listen to me. Sit down. We need to talk."

I sit down. I think I'm losing my mind.

"We've been very worried about you," Monique says. She looks over at Charles Senior.

"Janice," he says, "I know we don't know each other very well, but my son has always had a soft spot for you. And I can see why. I like you immensely myself. That's why I'm here. That's why we're all here."

I look over at Debbie. She won't even meet my eyes.

"I see people like you on the street of this city every day," Charles Sr. is saying. "It's my job as a cop. You're killing yourself, Janice. You are going to be mainlining before long. And you're going to end up dead."

Just then, I remember what my father told me many years ago. *Some day you'll be on your knees begging guys to suck them off for a few bucks.* I start to cry. Buckets of tears. Rivers of tears.

I am nothing. I am less than nothing.

REHABBING
AT THE REHAB

The next thing I knew I was en route to St. Mary's, a rehab facility in Minneapolis. Charlie Haughk flew out with me. I sat in the plane, looking out the window, saying nothing. Sat in the back of the cab with Charlie next to me, still saying nothing. Sat in the waiting room, still numb, still silent, until the woman who ran the facility came by and told Charlie it was time to go. Charlie stood up. I stood up, too. He hugged me. I don't remember hugging him back.

I followed the woman down the corridor, toward my room. The place was like cell block C. Cold, austere. I could see the leafless trees outside, the ground covered in hard snow. I was miserable. I lay in bed that first night, in the dark, thinking that the abyss was all around me. If I fell off the bed I would fall for hours and hours, fall for eternity. And there was no coming back. I listened to my breathing until I fell asleep.

For the next twenty-eight days, life as I knew it came to an end. St. Mary's was about taking stock, about admitting that you were a major fuckup. But that was supposed to make you feel good. Once you've acknowledged that you have a problem, they tell you, you can start working on the solution.

I didn't feel good. I didn't like the nurses. I didn't like

the doctors. I didn't
like the psychiatrists.
I didn't like my "new
friends" in Group, as
they called it. I didn't feel
like talking or sharing. They
were a bunch of fucking losers. I
couldn't possibly have anything in common with them. I
mean, look: Mick Jagger sent me this huge basket of pâté
and caviar. And these red roses?—they're from Bill Cosby.
Look at all these cards and letters. From all over the world.
Here's one from Paris. Here's one from Kenya. Do you
even know where Kenya *is,* motherfucker?

"You have a lot of anger in you, Janice," one of the
shrinks told me.

No fucking kidding!

By the end of the week, I had even more anger in me.
My friends in Group didn't like it. "Who the fuck do you
think you are?" one of the girls asked me.

"I'm a fucking supermodel, that's who I am! I've been
on the fucking cover of *Vogue.* I sucked Warren Beatty's
cock. Who the fuck are you?"

"Nobody. But I'm right here, bitch. With you. And I
didn't have to suck Warren Beatty's cock to get here."

She had a point.

"Eat," the doctor said. "You're too thin."

I ate macaroni and cheese and thought about La Tour
D'Argent in Paris and went back to my room and stuck my

finger down my throat. I sat in front of the window like a zombie, watching it snow. I told everyone to go fuck themselves and their fucking Serenity Prayer.

"Bite your tongue," one of the nurses told me. She had a big crucifix around her neck. It was so big she could have put a real guy on it. I hated her. She reminded me of my mother.

"I don't want to bite my tongue," I said. "I want to take a bite out of life."

Thirty-five thousand dollars for twenty-eight days. I could think of a lot nicer places to spend my time and money.

Bob Menna came to take me back to Manhattan. On the way to the airport, he tried to amuse me with stories about some of our fellow models.

"Everyone misses you," he said.

But it wasn't true.

Or maybe it was true, and I was just in Self-destruct Mode again. I was angrier than I'd ever been. I was ashamed. I kept imagining people were still talking about my fiasco at Studio 54. Or maybe I wasn't imagining it.

I was back in New York, *home*. So fucking happy to be out of rehab. I'd forgotten how good good cocaine could be. And champagne—I loved the way the bubbles tickled the roof of my mouth. I snorted too much and drank too much and misbehaved.

No, that's a lie. I didn't "misbehave." I was a total bitch. I showed up late and shouted at assistants, made everyone jump and a few people cry. I was the Nightmare Diva. I was abusive. I was good at it, too. After all, I'd picked up a few pointers along the way. I was Janice the Rat Bastard.

Monique called. "It's getting harder and harder to book you," she said.

"Don't tell me it's hard to book me. I'm Janice Fucking Dickinson. Do your fucking job."

"People don't trust you anymore," she said. "You're throwing it all away. You have *never* looked more beautiful, and you are throwing it all away."

She was right. It got harder and harder to book me.

Then Bill King called. He was doing a shoot for the Italians and wanted me to come in. I did, and started mouthing off the moment I stepped into his studio. Bill grabbed me by the upper arm and took me out back.

"Don't fuck with me, Janice," he said. He was one of those gay guys who could get tough and ugly if he needed to. And I guess he felt he needed to. "Pull yourself together. You're beautiful. I love the short hair. You look like a boy."

"That's what Mick Jagger liked about me. I suppose you want to fuck me, too."

Bill laughed. We were on firmer ground now. "You okay?" he said. I nodded. "You are going to get your ass out there and do what I tell you, and we are going to make some art today."

We made some art. Me and five male models. By the time the shoot was over, we were all naked. One of them looked just like me. The cheekbones, the nose, the short hair—everything. It was uncanny. It was like looking into a mirror.

I took him back to my place and we started making love, but just as things were getting hot I got out of bed and asked him to leave.

"What is it?" he said. "What's wrong?"

"Nothing," I said. "Everything."

I had to get away. I called a travel agent and booked a flight to Bali. I was on it the next day. One small carry-on and a lifetime of baggage. I checked into the

Auberoi Hotel. No drugs. No drinks before sunset. No men.

I stayed to myself. I read bad "beach" books that the other guests had left behind, mindless summer reading. And I sat in the sun, baking.

On the third day, someone came out to the pool to tell me there was an urgent call for me. It was Debbie. She was the only one who knew where I was.

"Monique called," she said. "Avedon wants you to call him. And Bill Cosby is looking for you."

"What do they want?"

"I don't know," she said. "But Cosby left a number in Lake Tahoe. And he said it was really, really important."

I called Avedon first. He was in New York.

"Janice," he said. "How are you?"

"Don't ask," I said.

"I have a story for you," he said. "I think you might enjoy it."

"Shoot," I said.

So he told me how he'd been deep in the heart of Texas—scouting locations for a spread on death-row inmates, of all things! And how he'd gone into the cell of the meanest, craziest motherfucker in the whole place— maybe the meanest man in the entire penal system—and found a picture of me taped to the wall next to the motherfucker's cot. Avedon described the picture. It had been taken by Hiro, a great Japanese photographer who had once been an Avedon protégé, and years ago it had appeared on the cover of Italian *Vogue*.

"Do you remember the image?" Avedon asked.

How could I not? Hiro had made me look like a demure little Sardinian girl, the epitome of Holy Innocence, all wrapped in cashmere, looking lost and lonely and huggable.

"Yeah," I said. "I remember the picture." I remembered the day we shot it, too. I remembered going over to Hiro's studio on Central Park West; remembered Hiro's brown hair and brown eyes and soft, inviting smile; remembered the way he talked to me about my "inner glow"—how he said he could actually *see* it, that glow, clear and blinding and beautiful.

"I thought that shot was an odd choice for a death-row inmate," Avedon said. The line was crackling with static.

"Yes," I said. But I didn't think it was odd at all. Hiro had captured my essence, in the days when I still had an essence. That guy on death row—maybe he wasn't such a crazy motherfucker after all. He didn't want to look at some cheesy pinup. He wanted to look at something innocent and holy—something that might be waiting for him on the other side.

Avedon was still talking. "I asked the guy, 'Why this picture? Why this particular girl out of all the girls in all the magazines?' And you know what he said? He said, 'I don't know, man. Look at her. *Why this girl?* Because this girl is some kinda chick, man.' You like that, Janice? That's what he said. *Some kinda chick.*"

"Yeah," I said. "I like it." I thanked him for calling and hung up.

Then I called Bill. Mr. *Jell-O*. Mr. *I'll-call-you*. And as the line rang at the other end it struck me that I had no reason to be angry. He'd sent roses to St. Mary's. A nice card, too.

"Hey, Bill, it's me. Janice."

"Janice! Janice, where'd you disappear to?"

"I'm in Bali."

"Bali!?"

"Yes, I'm taking a vacation. A vacation from myself." Of course those vacations never work; you get there and it's beautiful and serene but you're still stuck with your fucked-up self.

"Well, get your ass to Tahoe," he said. "You can connect through L.A."

"Why? What's in Tahoe?"

"I'm doing a show here. I want you to open for me."

I thought he must be kidding. I'd bombed at Studio 54. "I can't sing," I said.

"You're wrong," he said. "Who hits a home run their first time out? Almost nobody."

He had a point, right? *Right?* And he didn't even know why I'd freaked. Nobody did.

I was on the next flight to Los Angeles. I had an hour to kill before my connecting flight to Tahoe, so I went into one of those tacky airport bars and had a drink. Or two. Or three.

I almost missed my connecting flight. They were just about to close the gate but held it for me when they saw me wobbling in their general direction. Everyone was very sweet to me. The pilots. The flight attendants. The other passengers. Or maybe it was just the liquor. I suddenly had one of my brilliant flashes: *No wonder people drink! It's not about making themselves feel good. It's because it makes everyone else in the world seem so nice.*

I ordered two more drinks during the short flight. After an epiphany of that magnitude, I deserved them.

After we landed in Tahoe, I floated my way through the terminal, found a cab, and smiled all the way to the hotel. I smiled at the doorman, the clerks, the bellboy who escorted me to my room. I called Cosby. He was one floor up. He told me to come up; we had dinner reservations at eight. I hopped in the shower and went up.

Cosby answered the door in nothing but a white towel. He was fresh from the shower, too; his black skin was glistening. He hugged me, a little too enthusiastically; told me how much he'd missed me, and how nice it was to see me. I believed him. Liquor does that to a girl.

"God, you're beautiful."

He kissed me, full on the lips, then went off to dress and we went downstairs, to dinner, where Cosby spent the next two hours talking about himself. It was *An Evening with Bill Cosby. A Tribute to Bill Cosby.*

And suddenly I remembered something Andy Warhol once told me. It was his definition of an actor. He said, "An actor is a person whose eyes glaze over when the conversation is no longer about them."

And I thought, Well, then, *Bill Cosby is an actor's actor.*

After dinner he asked me back to his room, and I went. But I stopped myself at the door. "I'm exhausted," I said, begging off. His eyebrows went a little funny.

"Exhausted?" he asked, and it was clear he was trying hard to keep his temper in check. "After all I've done for you, that's what I get? *I'm exhausted.*"

"Well, gee, Bill," I stammered. "If I had known it was going to be like this—"

He waved both hands in front of my face, silencing me. Then he gave me the dirtiest, meanest look in the world, stepped into his suite, and slammed the door in my face. *Men.*

Back in my room, I found a tiny bottle of Courvoisier in the minibar, poured it into a plastic cup, and began pondering some of the Big Questions: *What the fuck am I doing in Tahoe? What the fuck am I doing with my life?* I dug through my bag for my bottle of Vitamin C and popped two Quaaludes and drifted off to sleep.

In the morning I checked out, took a cab to the airport, and got on the first flight to New York. I didn't even call Cosby. What was I going to do—yell at him? Thank him for the opportunity? Try to explain?

I started to panic before the plane even landed, and the panic only grew worse as the cab got closer and closer to New York. Usually, as we crossed the bridge and the Manhattan skyline came into view, I would get that old feeling. *Here I am, where I belong.* But that day all I felt was terror. I didn't want to be in New York. I didn't want to be anywhere. I was uncomfortable in my own skin.

I got to the apartment and tore it apart looking for drugs. I was completely out of Quaaludes, and there was barely enough coke dust to numb my gums. I looked through the mail. There was a letter from Paris. I opened it. It was from Pam Adams, my old childhood friend from Hollywood, Florida—a friend who'd disappeared from my life so many years ago. The handwriting looked shaky. "Dear Janice," she wrote. "I can't believe how famous you are. You have never looked more beautiful. I have thought many times about writing you, but I'm sort of in awe. Do you even remember me? I miss you. I am in trouble. I am in Paris. I know it's a lot to ask, but could you lend me a little money? I really need help . . . Love, Pam."

That was it. That was the whole letter. I assumed Pam wanted money for drugs. I didn't know what to do.

Then the phone rang.

"Hello?"

"I told you we were going to make art." It was Bill King, the photographer who had done the shoot for the Italians.

"How do I look?" That's what I said. I couldn't help myself. That's what models always say.

"You look amazing," Bill said. "Peppo just saw the proofs. He wants to talk to you." Peppo was the Italian publisher who'd given me my first paying break as a photographer, a lifetime ago, back in Malibu. Peppo loved me.

"Peppo wants to talk to me?"

"Got a pen? Here's his number."

It was a number in Milan. I dialed and got through. Peppo was just leaving the office, but the secretary said he was eager to talk to me so she asked me to hold and ran after him. He was on the phone a moment later.

"Janice!" he said. "Janice Janice Janice!"

"Peppo," I said. "Peppo Peppo Peppo."

"I love you," he said.

"I'm glad somebody does."

"No, you don't understand. You are so beautiful. Have you seen the proofs?"

"Not yet."

"Janice—you've done it again."

"What have I done?"

"You are showing us the way."

"Peppo, you're dreaming. What 'way'? I can't find my *own* way."

He started waxing poetic about the future of fashion and androgyny and the melding of the sexes, and my beautiful short hair, and my perfect eyes and perfect lips and perfect bones and absent tits.

"What are you trying to tell me, Peppo?" I said, interrupting.

"I need you, Janice. Will you please come to Milan for a while? *Please?* I will get on my knees if it helps."

"Gee, I don't know," I said.

I was en route the next day. I have never needed to be needed as much as I needed it that day. Sometimes I think Peppo's call—and Bill King's photographs—saved my life.

THE GOOD NUN

There was a limo waiting for me at the airport in Milan. The driver was exceedingly polite. He took me to the Hotel Grand. I *felt* grand. I had fallen in love with Italy years earlier—with the food, the art, the architecture, the rolling hills—and I was back.

Peppo took me out to dinner that first night, and by the following day he had me working. And it didn't stop. I was running from one end of the city to the other, from one job to the next, wildly popular and desperately wanted.

They pushed the androgyny. It was new and fresh and *shockant*. One day—I guess they were feeling particularly brazen—they paired me up with a stunning Yugoslavian girl for a Bulgari shoot. We were both nude, except for the jewels. Huge glittering rocks and huge emerald bracelets and huge pendants hanging between my nonbreasts. The little Yugoslav was getting very hot and bothered, and I yawned and thought, *They all want me. Men. Women. Barnyard animals.*

I kept promising myself that I'd find a nice little apartment and settle in and make a real home, but I was too busy working and too happy at the Grand. The staff were so wonderful. They all knew me: It was *Signorina* this, *Signorina* that, *Signorina* the other. I felt important. I felt I mattered. I felt loved.

I became close friends with Daniela Moreira, who wrote about fashion for several Italian publications and was married to a fabulously wealthy textile manufacturer. I often dined at her house, or joined her and her friends at the best local restaurants. I didn't have a moment to myself. It was wonderful. I was too busy to think, too busy for introspection.

I stayed away from cocaine, but I still drank. I fell in love with Italian wine. I became a bit of a connoisseur. I could tell what *side* of the hill the grapes were from. (Well, not really, but that sounded pretty impressive, didn't it?) Daniela took me and a group of friends to Tuscany for the weekend, and we drank our way through several vineyards. One of her friends was an Italian film director. He kept accosting me—in dark hallways, in corridors, by the ruins of a once-magnificent castle—to tell me he wanted me, that he couldn't get me out of his mind. He did it with such passion I felt like I was in the middle of an Italian movie—a bad one, maybe even one of his.

"But you're married," I said with theatrical aplomb.

"Not always," he said.

It was a funny answer. But I turned him down. I turned down Alberto Grimaldi, too. And he was a fucking prince! Alberto said he thought he was falling in love with me. I told him to get in line. But I was only joking. I told his sister, Princess Caroline, that she should find a nice girl for Alberto before he got himself in trouble.

"He's attracted to trouble," she said.

"So am I," I said.

He kept calling. It was like a comedy routine. "Janice, why don't you like me?"

"I like you, I like you," I said. "But not now."

"When, then?"

"I'll let you know."

"I'll wait."

How absolutely regal.

One night I went back to my hotel to find messages from that Italian director, Prince Albert (again!), and Peter Beard, Cheryl Tiegs's old beau. I called Peter, who was in Rome.

"Janice, you bitch," he said. "Where the hell have you been?"

"Hiding," I said.

"Nobody can find you."

"That's sort of the point, isn't it?" I said.

"I tracked you down through Italian *Bazaar*. Are you living in Milan?"

"I guess so," I said. "I'm not sure. It just sort of happened."

"You look fantastic. You're everywhere—all over Europe. You look delectable. You look like a little boy."

"Tell me something," I said. "Do all heterosexual men hunger for little boys?"

Peter laughed so hard he almost choked.

"Are you all right?" I asked.

"Tell me you'll go to Kenya with me and I'll be all right," he said.

"What's in Kenya?"

"An assignment for American *Playboy*. It's perfect for you. And the money's very good indeed."

"Is it slutty?" I ask him.

"Janice, darling—you couldn't be slutty if you tried!"

That was the right thing to say. The following week I was on my way to Kenya.

Peter met me at the airport, took me back to the hotel, and introduced me to the two dowdy women from *Playboy*'s Chicago office. They'd brought duffel bags full of accessories. Fuck-me pants. Undies with zippers. Cowboy hats. See-through bras—as if I needed a bra. And I said, "Ladies, this cheap shit doesn't work for me."

And one of them said, "I'm sorry. This is what you're going to wear, sweetheart."

"Yeah? We'll see about that, *sweetheart*."

So I went to see Peter, to whine about the outfits, and he agreed that the outfits were tacky in the extreme. And the two of us spent the rest of the morning in the local markets, buying incredibly beautiful African wraps. They have the most amazing fabrics in Kenya. *Maasai, shuka, kikoy.* And that's what he shot me in. Then he asked me if I minded extending the shoot. He had a ranch at the base of Mount Kenya, right next to the place where Karen Blixen wrote *Out of Africa,* and he wanted me to see it. So we flew out in one of those lumbering prop planes and landed on this dirt strip, where a Jeep was waiting for us on the tarmac. Peter hopped behind the wheel—very macho—and we drove on the rutted dirt roads to his ranch. It was pure, unspoiled wilderness. The place consisted of nothing but three huge tents in the middle of nowhere. The trees were so graceful they made me feel like weeping.

"It's nice, isn't it?" Peter asked me.

"Nice? *Nice?* Are you out of your fucking mind? It's paradise."

There were servants everywhere, and they cooked us dinner out in this big open pit. Venison, I think it was. We ate and drank champagne and watched the sun set, and I felt like Meryl Streep. But I couldn't remember any lines from *Out of Africa.* The only Meryl Streep line I could remember was, "A dingo ate my baby!"

We finished our champagne and turned in: me in one tent, Peter in another. And in the middle of the night I woke to hear the most frightful growling and I screamed at the top of my voice: "Peter! Peter, goddamn it! Get in here!"

A few moments later, I heard him coming. And I heard that sound again and I leapt into his arms, terrified. And he began to laugh. "What are you afraid of? It's just a couple of big cats, fucking," he said. And I said I didn't care. I wanted him to stay with me, in my tent. And he slipped into my cot and held me. And it felt nice.

In the morning, Peter grabbed his equipment and we drove to a nearby village that was popular with the tourists. They had a collection of crocodiles there that were goddamn prehistoric. Some of them were up to sixteen feet long. Real monsters. Peter had the croc-wranglers anesthesize six of the biggest ones and tie their snouts together with transparent fishing line, then asked the men to pile the beasts on top of each other.

"What the hell are you doing?" I asked.

"I want you on top of that pile," he said.

"Oh no," I said. "No fucking way. You're crazy."

"Here, Janice. Have a beer." Seemed like a good idea.

And of course by this time the tourists were out in full force, snapping away with their Instamatics. And, while the natives got busy building a pile of crocodiles, I fortified myself with beer.

Finally, it was the moment of truth. Peter helped me out of my wrap, and the men in the crowd ooohhed and aaahhed with delight. I was wearing the skimpiest little thong, and a tiny little top that barely covered my tiny little nontits. And I was a little drunk, to be honest. I don't see how I could have done it sober.

Two of the wranglers helped me across this stagnant little pond, toward the pile of crocs. I was terrified. For good reason. I put my hand on one of them and I could feel its skin move and flutter and recoil against my palm.

"Come on," Peter bellowed. "Hurry, before they wake."

I began to climb. I could hear them purring like cats, asleep but not asleep enough for me. I could feel their low, guttural grunting; I could hear their wheezy breath.

But I was on top now. I'd made it. My bare feet hurt against their hard, leathery skin, but I didn't care. The crowd was cheering; Peter was snapping away. And there I was, vamping and posing and kicking my legs like a crazy, drunken ballerina. And suddenly it occurred to me: *Janice. You are fucking nuts. You are a crazy person. You should be locked up.*

I got back to Milan and picked up where I left off. Work is great, the ultimate escape. I flew to Rome, Berlin, Prague. Then back to Milan, with barely time to catch my breath before it was off to Santo Domingo. This was a biggie. The legendary Horst P. Horst would be taking my picture. He'd been working for *Vogue* since the early 1930s. Horst P. Horst, Dear Reader, had shot Marlene Dietrich.

"Tell me about Marlene," I said during a break.

"She was very sensitive about her wrinkles," he said. "She made me put the light below her face, here, like this, and, presto!—the wrinkles disappeared."

I asked him about Maria Callas. "Horrible," he said, his face darkening. "Absolutely horrible. I was lucky to escape with my life!"

Next assignment was Normandie, with another great: George Hurrell. I met him on the infamous beach, surrounded by assistants. He was wearing a silly little safari hat, a vest with hundreds of pockets, and khakis with white knee socks. He looked like a caricature of himself.

"This is where our boys kicked their asses," he said by way of introduction. He was referring to World War II, of course. The sand below our feet had once run thick with blood. Then he smiled at me and patted his camera. "You see this camera? I shot Marilyn Monroe with this camera."

I don't even remember the shoot. I vaguely remember the wind and the crashing surf, and the hair and makeup people fluttering about like nervous birds. Mostly I remember this strange feeling of dread, a feeling I couldn't for the life of me understand. That was George *Hurrell* on the far side of the lens. It didn't get much better than this. So why did I feel like I was standing on a precipice, looking down into the abyss?

Back in Milan, I couldn't shake the feeling. It was as if some dark, evil demon was following me around. I could sense its lurking presence everywhere.

I tried taking long walks through the city, but that didn't help, either. I would notice couples arm in arm or kissing at cafés, clearly very much in love. I had no one to kiss, and I wanted to be in love. Most of all I began noticing children. I suddenly found myself aching for a family of my own. I wanted the whole Norman Rockwell nine yards. Twenty happy people around a Thanksgiving table. Laughing, eating, loving, being a family; a *real* family. The kind of family I'd never had. The kind that was held together by love, not fear.

One afternoon I got back from one of my walks to find a note from a friend in Manhattan telling me that Way Bandy had died of AIDS. Then I heard that Ara Gallant had blown his brains out in car. Then Gia died; AIDS again. I was frozen, stymied, stunned. I loved my friends. I didn't know what to do.

Debbie called from New York and started listing the names of people who were dead or dying. I went numb. I couldn't listen. I didn't want to hear more. Bill King. Rubell. Perry Ellis. There was even a rumor that Capote had died of AIDS.

"Janice? Janice, are you there?" she asked.

"No," I said. "I'm not here." And I hung up.

But the calls kept coming, and I'd get off the phone, numb, and open my address book and X out another name. It was devastating. And impossible to escape: One afternoon in Florence, wrapping up a shoot, the photographer asked if I'd be willing to come back the following week for another session. He wanted to pair me up with Joe McDonald, one of the original Zoli models, a wonderful human being. "You're too late," I said. Joe had died the previous week.

I was afraid to be with people, and afraid to be alone. Peppo called me, worried. Daniela called me. Alberto called me. My director friend called and sent flowers and told me how much he wanted me.

Sex. Christ. Who knew it could be fatal? I thought about the men I'd been with. Yeah, there'd been a few, maybe more than a few, maybe too many, but I was nowhere near as promiscuous as people imagined. Then I heard that sex wasn't just about your partner anymore, but about every partner your partner had ever had. I thought about Warren Beatty. I thought about Mick Jagger. Jesus. Was I in trouble?

I felt like running away, but I didn't know what I was running from or where I'd go. I filled every minute of every hour. I went to visit the Vatican, and found it frightening. All that ostentatious display of wealth and power— was that what Catholicism was about? I went again and again to the Duomo, the most magnificent gothic cathedral in the world. One afternoon I found myself on the Duomo's rooftop, looking out over Milan, crying. I went to see Da Vinci's *Last Supper* at Sante Maria delle Grazie. I went to the art gallery at the Brera Palace. I visited the Sforza Castle, on the outskirts of the city, and felt the demon's presence more intensely than ever.

I remember that particular afternoon as if it were only yesterday. I was frightened and tired and it was late, so I left the castle and took a cab back to the city. I was supposed to be at Daniela's place at seven. She was having a few friends over for drinks and then we were all going out to dinner. She had begged me to come. She wouldn't take no for an answer.

The traffic was horrendous. The cab's air conditioner was broken. I was sweating, trapped. I couldn't stop thinking about Way and Ara and Gia and all the others; people I knew and loved, dying before their time. I was sad and frightened and felt like screaming. I took a few deep breaths and reminded myself that my life was *good*. I was alive, for God's sake. I was at the top of my game. I had more offers than I could handle. I had just done back-to-back shoots with Horst and Hurrell. So why was I feeling such dread? I should have been on my knees, thanking God in total gratitude.

By the time the cab reached Milan, it was too late to go to the hotel and change and return to Daniela's. Her place was closer than the hotel, so I went directly there.

"Janice! Darling! How are you? Thank you for coming!" Daniela was very theatrical. Her hands flew this way and that and her voice rose and fell with operatic fervor.

"I need to borrow your shower and some clean clothes," I said.

"But of course!"

"Is everybody here already?"

"Almost, but take your time. The champagne's on ice."

She took me back to the master bedroom. I got out of my sweaty clothes and into the shower, and I stood there under the hot water, leaning against the tiled wall for support. Suddenly I began to cry. Huge, wracking sobs, as if I were opening the door to some bottomless void inside me. Maybe that was the abyss I'd been looking at, me—Janice. I was a beautiful, empty shell. There was nothing inside.

What did it all mean? What the fuck did it mean? Good wine and friends and laughter and fancy dinners and hard work are all well and good, but suddenly they aren't enough. It occurred to me that I was like a drug addict. These amusing diversions no longer had the kick they used to have, didn't numb me the way they used to numb me, didn't provide the escape I longed for. . . . You always need a bigger hit, a little more and a little more and more and more and more.

Interesting, I thought. That's what Lewis Carroll must have meant in *Alice in Wonderland*. What was it the Queen told Alice? "It takes all the running you can do to keep in the same place. If you want to get somewhere else, you must run at least twice as fast as that."

So there I was in the shower, at Daniela's place, the hot water beating against me, and I couldn't stop sobbing. I didn't know who I was or what I was doing with my life or whether I was ever going to get it right. And then I heard a man say, "*Scusi,* is everything okay?"

And I stopped sobbing long enough to say, "I'll live." Which of course sounded ridiculous.

And he said in his broken English, "I am sorry. I do not mean for to pry. I am hearing crying, and I just see if for maybe I can help."

I drew the curtain back a bit. A big teddy bear of a man was standing there, peering at me through Clark Kent glasses. He had thin, gray hair and smooth skin and round, soft-edged shoulders.

"I am Alberto," he said. "I can help maybe, yes?"

"I'm depressed and lonely and more lost than I've ever been in my life," I said.

And he said, "You are so gorgeous! You must not be depressed! And I will not let you be lonely."

"Come here," I said. I threw my naked arms around him and pulled him into the shower and got him sopping wet. But he didn't seem to mind. He held me close and tight and patted me on the back and made me feel like I was the best little girl in the whole wide world.

So of course I moved in with the poor guy. My new daddy, a very rich new daddy. An international soda magnate. A very wealthy man indeed.

For a while, it was a real honeymoon. We went sailing. We went to Tuscany for long weekends. We stayed at his family's villa in Elba. We summered in Sardinia. We went to Saint Moritz in the winter and skied with Princess Caroline and her family.

And everywhere we went there were children. From rosy-cheeked babies to mischievous adolescents.

"Alberto," I said. "I want a child."

"No," he said. No *bambini* for him. Absolutely no interest in *bambini.*

So the honeymoon started to wind down. We fought. The Ultimate Daddy was denying me the one thing I really wanted. So what did I do? I got pregnant, of course. And Alberto went ballistic.

"You are not having this child," he said. "I don't even know if it's mine."

I couldn't believe he could say that to me. "You bastard!" I shouted. "How dare you!?"

"I will arrange for an abortion," he said.

"If you don't want to have a child with me, if you don't think I'm good enough to have your baby, then say so. But goddamn you—don't tell me I'm cheating on you, because I've *never* cheated on you!"

He took a beat. "I don't want this child."

I fell apart. I couldn't get out of bed for days. Alberto carried on as if nothing was wrong. He went to dinner, visited friends, traveled. I stayed in his big opulent place, alone and frightened. I didn't want to lose him. I felt the evil demon's lurking presence. I agreed to the abortion.

Afterward, I was crippled by depression. Alberto tried to cheer me up, but as the days turned into weeks he got tired of trying. He began to ignore me. He behaved as if I'd outlived my usefulness. We had reached that stage where we both knew it was over, but neither of us had the energy—or, in my case, the courage—to do anything about it.

One night we were out to dinner with a few people, including that Italian film director and his beautiful wife, a celebrated actress. The director was across the table from me, and he could see that I was in a foul mood. I kept pestering Alberto, and he began to treat me like a child. "What do you want?" he snapped. "You sit there and whine and demand my attention, and when I ask what you want you don't know."

"I want you to pay attention to me. That's all."

"I'm supposed to just look at you?"

"You can talk to me," I suggested. "Or try smiling with your eyes."

"What do you want to talk about?"

"I don't know. Anything."

"Let me know when you figure it out," he said, popped his cigar back in his mouth, and turned his back.

Suddenly I felt something jabbing my knee. I looked down. It was a foot. The director's foot. He had taken off his shoe and was holding a slip of paper between his toes. I took the slip of paper, discreetly, and unfolded it next to my plate. "Meet me in the bathroom," it said. I crumpled up the paper and tried not to look at him, then I got up and made my way to the bathroom. Alberto didn't even notice. The director got up a few moments later and met me in the corridor, near the rest rooms.

"I want you," he said.

"Take a number," I said.

"No, I'm serious. I need to see you. What are you doing tomorrow?"

"I'm going to Rome tomorrow. I'm doing a shoot for Italian *Vogue.*"

"Rome is perfect! I know a marvelous little church in Rome. Nobody knows about it." Then he went on to tell me that I should meet him there at noon sharp, as the bells were tolling. And that he wanted me to dress like a nun.

"You're crazy," I said.

"Don't let me down," he said.

I went back to the table and sat down and told Alberto I wanted to leave. "So leave," he said. He was having a good time. He blew cigar smoke in the air and reached for his cognac. I got up and went outside. There was a beautiful red Ferrari in front of the restaurant, with the keys in the ignition. I got in and drove away. I looked in the rearview mirror. The poor valet chased me halfway down the block.

I didn't know what I was doing. I half-expected the police to come after me. But I knew Alberto would fix it. Money fixes everything. (Well, almost everything.) I turned toward home, but then changed my mind and made my way to the *autostrada*. I decided I would drive to Rome, and I did. Like a maniac. In high style.

I reached Le Grand Hotel before daybreak and left the Ferrari a block away.

"You are early, Miss Dickinson," the clerk noted.

"Yes," I said. "Is my room ready?"

"Absolutely. I'll have someone show you the way. Any bags?"

"None," I said. "But I need a favor. Could you wake me at ten? And would you be good enough to find me a good costume shop."

"A costume shop?"

"Yes," I said. "A costume shop. You know. To dress up. We Americans do that from time to time."

"I know this!" he said. "It is Halloween already, yes?"

"For some people it is."

They woke me at ten and I had breakfast and took a cab to the costume shop. It was a dank, musky place. The old woman who ran it found an antique nun's outfit in the storage room. It was clean but needed a good pressing. She took care of it. I tried it on. It was a little big and she did what she could on such short notice and I wore it out into the street and flagged down a cab. I gave the driver the name of the church but he didn't know it. We lost our way and went around in circles until an old man told us he knew the church and pointed us in the right direction. I paid the cabdriver and got out and went through the heavy front doors. There was no one there. It was beautiful inside. And deathly still. It was like a cathedral that had been shrunk down to manageable size: grand but small, if you know what I mean. My footfalls echoed on the marble floor. The bells began to toll. I looked at my watch. It was twelve on the button.

At that moment, the heavy doors opened and a priest entered. I looked away, embarrassed, afraid of getting caught. I thought, *If he talks to me, I'll tell him I'm an American nun. If he asks me to explain my vestments, I'll tell him I belong to an old Italian order of nuns who make their home in Brooklyn and believe in having a good time.*

The priest began moving toward me.

"Please," he said. His voice was familiar. I turned. It was my friend the director, also in disguise. With a theatrical sweep of the hand, he indicated the confessional. This looked like it might be fun. I got into my side of the confessional. He got into his. I could see him through the latticework. He slid back the small panel.

"I'm listening, child," he said. He was very serious. He was really into it.

"I've been bad, Father."

"How have you been bad?"

"Oh Father, I've been bad in every way it's possible to be bad. I wouldn't know where to begin. We'd have to go away for a weekend just to get through the first few chapters of my badness."

"Perhaps that can be arranged."

"So you're one of *those* priests," I said.

"Yes," he said. "I want to fuck you."

"Oh heavenly Father!"

He left the confessional and came round to my side and helped me out. I followed him through the empty church to a small alcove in back, and he lifted my robes and fucked me against the cold stone walls.

"You're a dirty slut," he said.

"Yes, I am," I said. (But I make a pretty good nun.)

He drove me back to the hotel after we were done, and as we were pulling up we saw Alberto getting out of a cab. I ducked down and he sped past and parked around the corner. I was still wearing my nun's outfit. I told my priestly friend I would see him later and got out and hurried back to the hotel.

Alberto was still in the lobby. He turned as I came in, and his jaw dropped.

"Janice!"

"Hello, Alberto. What are you doing here?"

I walked across the lobby to the bar. He followed me, still in shock, his mouth still open.

"What is the meaning of this?"

"I'm thinking of joining a convent," I said. I reached the bar and ordered a Bellini. There were few people at the bar at that early hour, but even a blind man would notice a nun at a bar, drinking. They stared. The bartender stared. He set the flute in front of me.

"Janice, I asked you a question." Alberto was in serious daddy mode.

"*Now* you're paying attention to me?" I said, and kicked back the Bellini like a truck driver. I looked out the window: They were towing the Ferrari.

He told me his friend the actress was worried about her husband. "She thinks something is going on with you two."

"Yeah," I said. "I came to Rome dressed like a nun and fucked him in a little church about a mile from here."

"Janice!"

"He was dressed as a priest. With no underwear."

"You are making me very angry," he said.

"Well, I have news for you, Alberto. I don't give a shit." It was over.

By the end of the month, I was gone.

Milan was history.

CITY OF ANGELS

In 1988, at the age of thirty-three, I moved to Los Angeles. I wanted a fresh start. I wanted to reinvent myself. And I'd been told Los Angeles was just the place for it.

I moved in with my flamboyant friend Angelo DiBiaso, a hugely successful hairdresser. He was a big favorite with the rock stars. David Bowie, Duran Duran, even my old pal Mr. Jagger, all availed themselves of his talent. Angelo took me everywhere with him. He showed me the city and introduced me to his friends.

Meanwhile, I buckled down and got to work. Or *tried* to, anyway. I heard about a bathing suit shoot in Maui and really lobbied for it. I didn't get it. Then there was a shoot in Ojai—I could've driven there; it's a lousy hour and a half from L.A.—but I didn't get that, either.

One morning I was flipping through *Playboy*—God only knows what Angelo was doing with a copy of *Playboy*—and came across a spread of Elle McPherson, shot by Herb Ritts. *That should have been me,* I thought. But I knew I was kidding myself. Elle looking fucking great. I wondered if my best days were behind me—in terms of modeling, anyway—and the thought filled me with terror. I signed up for acting classes and yoga, went on long hikes in the surrounding mountains. I tried to fill every minute of every day so that I'd go to bed exhausted, and sleep sweet, dreamless sleep. It worked, sometimes. But the truth is, I was going through withdrawal. I had become addicted to seeing myself in magazines and on billboards and smiling at the world from the sides of buses; addicted to the spotlight. Suddenly I didn't have that any-more, and I felt lost and empty. I needed validation. Don't we all?

One morning, Angelo and I were having breakfast at Hugo's, on Santa Monica Boulevard, when he indicated a man across the restaurant. "That's Simon Fields," he said. "He runs a big production company. They do lots of videos. You should get to know him."

Simon looked up at that very moment. He was paying his bill. Angelo waved. Simon left some money on his table and came over. He smiled at me. He had a big gap between his front teeth, like Alfred E. Newman.

"Hi, Simon," Angelo said. "This is my friend Janice Dickinson."

We exchanged numbers. He was very sweet. He called me the next night and asked me to dinner. He gave me directions to his house and cooked a fantastic meal. I think I fell in love before we got to the main course. Yeah. I know. It's crazy. But that was the pathology. I couldn't be without a man. I didn't know who I was with-out a man. If I wasn't being wanted, loved, ached over, fought with—well, I just plain didn't exist at all.

And Simon fell in love right back (though he probably waited until after dessert). He was wonderful, witty, funny, whip-smart, and immensely talented. He was making videos for MTV: Madonna, Prince, Peter Gabriel, Michael Jackson, Rod Stewart, Paul McCartney. He had energy. He loved life. He was great. He made me feel great. We were great together. *I* was great.

Four months later, lo and behold, I was pregnant.

So I moved in with him, of course. And I started spinning out my future in my head. I was going to have a family, the one I'd always dreamed of. I loved the way my body began to change. I loved the feeling of life growing inside me. I started developing breasts and hips. I stopped drinking and smoking. I wouldn't eat a lousy hot dog because I thought the nitrates might harm my beautiful little baby. Don't get me wrong. It wasn't smooth sailing every day. When those hormones kicked in—*get back, motherfucker!* I was the Devil, disguised as a lovely, glowing, pregnant woman. But I always came back, became the glowing pregnant woman again. I was giddy with happiness. My jaw ached from smiling. I laughed out of context all the time. And I cried a lot. For no reason. For

MY GOOD FRIEND LIONEL GEORGE AND MY BRIDEGROOM, SIMON, AT OUR WEDDING.

PREPARING FOR THE
WEDDING WITH DEBBIE.
I LOVE MY SISTER.

every reason. For the life ahead of me. For the life I was leaving behind. For the life inside me. Those *fucking* hormones. Still, when all is said and done, I felt completely *right* about everything for the first time in my life. This was *it*. This is what it was all about. Motherhood. Children. Family.

On the appointed day, Simon and I were in the hospital together, having our baby. Or trying to, anyway. It was the most painful experience of my life. I was in labor for twenty-three hours. I couldn't stop screaming and cursing. (Think of *The Exorcist*—on crack.) Our son, Nathan, refused to come out. I began to think that some sixth sense was telling him I was going to make a lousy mother. In the end, the nurse was practically sitting on my stomach, and the doctor was down between my legs, with some kind of suction pump. And then—there he was! A little baby boy! In my arms. He was gorgeous. His little lips were searching for my wonderful big new tits. He was crawling around on my belly, groping, mewling, trying to find his way, when, *boom!*—our eyes met and I started to cry. I just lost it. Completely. I had never felt love like that in my life. Right then and there I swore I would give Nathan everything I had been denied. "Thank you," I told Simon, still blubbering. "You've made me the happiest woman in the world." God. Taking him home. What an experience! We'd bought the regulation car seat and everything, like they told us to, and an orderly came to fetch me with a wheelchair. It was hospital policy. I sat down, holding my tiny baby in my arms. Simon walked beside us to the elevator, and down the corridor to the exit. I looked up at him, the good wife. He was beaming his proud-papa beam. People looked and nodded and smiled. *Life is good, motherfucker!* I was so in love! With my child, my husband, the whole fucking world.

We got to the car and strapped the baby in and pulled away, and I began crying in earnest.

"What are you crying about?" Simon said. "This is a great moment. You should be happy."

"I am happy. I've never been happier in my life!"

Motherhood. I was so in love with Nathan. I couldn't stop taking his picture. That's all I did all day. Love him and shoot his picture and glow. I'd glow when I drove him to the market. I'd glow when people stopped me on the street to tell me how beautiful he was. I glowed when he laughed and glowed when he cried and glowed when he shat. It's a fucking miracle I didn't short-circuit from all that glowing.

My mother came to visit. She cooed at Nathan and talked about the Good Lord and his mysterious ways and I didn't hear a word. I was so besotted with Nathan that the world didn't exist. There was only Nathan and me: The rest didn't matter. Certainly my mother and her problems didn't matter. She sat there in our house in Beverly Hills, a house that had once belonged to Liz Taylor, crotcheting a little blanket for Nathan and talking about the rat bastard. *He's very sick,* she said. *His heart is bad,* she said. *He has Alzheimer's.* "Sometimes I come home and he doesn't recognize me and beats me."

Hello! He beats you when he does recognize you. But I bit my tongue and rocked my baby boy.

"Why don't you call him?" she said. "He'd love to hear from you."

"Look at my little Nathan," I said, not hearing her, not wanting to hear her. "Isn't he the most wonderful creature in the world?"

She started filling me in about "our Alexis," who had become addicted to anything even remotely connected to self-help and self-improvement. Yoga. Meditation. EST. Rolfing. Actualization therapy. Deep colonics. God. And about "our Debbie," who'd fallen madly in love with Mohammed Khashoggi, who plied her with rich food and champagne and caviar and surrounded her with fawning servants. They were always on the go. If Mohammed heard that a new restaurant in Cannes had just been awarded three stars in the Michelin guide, they'd hop into his jet and be there in time for dinner.

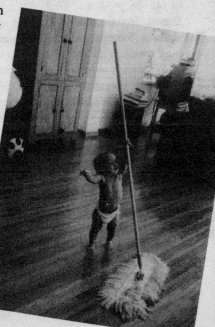

I didn't speak much to either of my sisters in those days. We each had

THE GREAT NATE!

lives of our own, clearly, and we all struggled with the usual sibling rivalries. Debbie had been a great model in her own right, but I think she'd lost patience with me. She stopped returning my calls. And Alexis lived in another world. She was growing vegetables and painting and sculpting with glass, and I was in Hollywood, being a Hollywood wife and mother—though definitely not in that order—and I guess we didn't have a lot in common.

"It's a pity you girls don't talk much anymore," Mom said.

"Well," I said. "I try." But that wasn't true. I didn't try at all. I was just as wrapped up in my shit as they were in theirs.

Finally Mom went home and Simon and I went back to our happy lives. Well, *I* was happy. I can't speak for Simon. But then his father got sick and died. I felt awful about it. Simon had actually loved his father, been close to him. I wished the reaper had taken *my* father instead.

Within six months, I was pregnant again.

"I don't want another child," Simon said. I'd heard that before, and it wasn't getting better with age.

"Why not?"

"I just can't fucking cope right now, Janice. My father is dead and I'm feeling lost and I just fucking can't, okay?"

No, not okay; not really. "Don't make me have an abortion," I begged. "It's going to make me resent you."

"We're not having another baby," he said.

So I had the abortion. And I began to resent him. I knew myself pretty well by that point.

I was unhappy. And very restless. I'd get out of bed in the morning and wouldn't know what to do with myself. I needed something, but I didn't know *what*. And then one day I was climbing out of the bathtub, and I looked in the mirror, and I realized that my big lovely tits were gone.

And I thought, *If I can't have another kid, maybe I should at least buy myself a pair of new tits.* I mean, Christ—I deserved a little something.

So I lined up the best tit-man in town. And weeks later, there I was, ready for my state-of-the-art 36-C rad puppies. Getting wheeled into surgery, already groggy with anesthetic. And I remembered the rat bastard telling me I looked like a boy. And all I could think was, *Just you wait.*

Within weeks I was working again, as both a model and a photographer. I went to Antigua and did a shoot for a Chesterfield cigarettes campaign. I took Nathan and the nanny. It was great. I *could* have it all, after all!

I came back and Billy Baldwin posed for me. I shot Matthew Modine. I shot Dylan McDermott and Randy Quaid. I shot Carre Otis. I shot Beverly Johnson for the cover of *She.* I shot myself, naked, for the cover of *Photo.* It was sensational. I got a call from one of the top photo agencies, Sygma, asking if they could represent me. I said I'd think about it.

I shot a famous actress, who arrived late and proceeded to behave like a complete bitch. "Hey!" I shouted. "I was a bigger bitch than you could ever hope to be. Now shut the fuck up and get to work." Her jaw dropped, but she didn't say a word. The rest of the shoot went beautifully, and we became great friends. (And, no—I won't rat her out; you'll have to guess.)

A week later I got in touch with Natasha Gregson Wagner, Natalie Wood's daughter. I waited for her at a friend's studio, in West Hollywood, and then there she was, coming through the door: tiny, a little pixie, more waiflike than Kate Moss. But *glowing* somehow—a depth there.

Of course she was a little uncomfortable; it was our first meeting. And I found myself seducing her with the camera. I was parent, therapist, best friend. I was doing for Natasha what the best photographers had done for me: convincing her she was the Center of the Civilized Universe. And it was working.

Then, good God, she said, "I brought this little dress with me. I don't know why. I had this crazy urge to bring it, so I did." And she took the dress out of a paper bag, and I looked at it: a plain white dress—*too* plain; a little peasant-style nothing. I didn't know what to say without hurting her feelings. And before I could say anything, she said, "That's the dress my mother wore in *West Side Story*."
Whoa!

In a flash, she's in her little white dress, looking like an angel, and I'm fluttering, fixing, lighting, arranging, rearranging, *nuturing*. Janice is in total control, baby. In The Zone. And then I'm behind the camera, and I look at Natasha and think, *I can see right through to her soul.* And, click! One shot. A perfect shot. And I know I've nailed it. I am *good,* motherfucker. Bad photography is about surface. Good photography—well, it goes to the core, to the source. And I'm there. Natasha and I are there, baby.

That perfect shot ran in *Newsweek*. And Sygma called again—and this time I signed with them. My pictures began appearing in *Esquire, Paris Match, Photo*. The work kept me going. And the money kept me in expensive shoes. Then one day I was at Paris Photo, a studio on La Cienega Boulevard, shooting Naomi Campbell—in the nude—when this buff little guy showed up, unannounced, looking for her. I didn't recognize him, until I took a closer look. It was Sylvester Stallone. I couldn't believe how short he was. I felt like laughing, but I managed to stifle myself.

"What are you grinning about?" he asked.

"Nothing," I said.

"So where's Naomi?" he asked.

"She's changing," I said. "But I'm not done with her yet."

"Well, can I have a lousy minute?" he barked.

"Sure," I said. "If you'll pose for one picture."

He walked across the room and turned to face me and tucked his hand down the front of his pants.

"Anything interesting down there?" I asked him.

"Something you'd like," he said. "Bam ham slam."

"Looks like a dead rat," I said, and snapped his picture.

"It's just resting," he said, and Naomi walked in.

"Who's resting?" she asked.

Sly crossed the room and took her in his big arms and kissed her.

"Yum," she said.

A few days later, Naomi came by the house to see the proofs. She looked great. And Mr. Stallone looked great in that one shot.

"What's he doing with his hand down his pants?" Naomi asked.

"I don't know," I said. "Testing the equipment."

"Let's go show him the pictures," she said.

"What? Now?"

"Sure," she said.

So we went over to his house and showed him, and in

typical actorly fashion he was only interested in the one of him. "Pretty good," he said.

"Pretty good?" I shot back. "You look awesome."

Naomi went to find a drink.

"I want to publish it," I said. "What do you think?"

"We can talk about it over dinner," he said.

"I'm a married woman," I said.

"So what?" he said.

"You must have a little French blood in you," I said.

"Huh?" he said.

"Forget it," I said.

I went back home and resented Simon. I couldn't help it. I'd never been much good at letting go of anger.

I filled the growing emptiness within me by having people over. I had parties at the drop of a hat. Everyone came. Don Simpson and Jerry Bruckheimer. Iman. Naomi. Diane Keaton. A lot of people named Peters. Bernadette Peters. Jon Peters. Corinne Peters. And Peter Peters, one of the world's great dry cleaners.

Sly came to dinner one night, with Naomi. When she was out of earshot he told me the "dead rat" was feeling a little twitchy. I looked hot that night. I was wearing Manolo pumps and a dress that looked like it was spray-painted onto my perfect-again body.

"I thought Naomi was taking care of the rat," I said.

"You're the real deal," he said.

"You're weird," I said, and moved off.

A few days later, I got a letter from Pam Adams's mother, in Florida. Pam was dying of cancer. I took the next flight to Fort Lauderdale and went directly to Hollywood Memorial Hospital, where my mother still worked.

"Pam talked about you often," Mrs. Adams said. She'd always been distant, and distant she remained. "She told me she wrote you from Paris."

"That's right," I said, remembering that short, mysterious note.

"She was fighting the cancer," Mrs. Adams explained. "She had gone to Europe looking for a cure. They had some experimental drugs in Europe that weren't available in the States. But of course they were expensive."

I felt like dying. I'd been right: Pam *had* wanted money for drugs, but not the types of drugs I'd imagined. I wondered why Pam hadn't explained. But what could she have said? "I'm dying. Can you help me?" How do you reach out from such a distant place?

"I wanted to call you while there was still time," Mrs. Adams said.

But there wasn't time. Pam was in a coma. She had developed a particularly aggressive form of melanoma while living in the Caribbean. She'd first noticed it as a little spot on her back, while she was out island-hopping on a sailboat, and she'd ignored it. By the time she went to see a doctor, it was too late.

I couldn't get over the sight of her. She looked beautiful. She was hooked up to all these monitoring devices—her heartbeat

PAM ADAMS IN FLORIDA WHEN WE WERE KIDS.

was slow and steady—and she was done up beautifully. Every hair on her head was lovingly combed, perfectly arranged against the bright white hospital-issue pillow. She was wearing makeup. Her fingernails were perfect. Her hands were laid out flat on either side of her body, looking pale and pink against the bedspread. I cried—I couldn't help it—and Mrs. Adams left the room. I pulled the chair closer to the bed and told Pam I was sorry. I was sorry we'd lost touch. I was sorry I'd never answered her letter. I was sorry she was sick.

"Please don't die," I said. "I want you to meet my little boy, Nathan. He's wonderful. You'll love him. Maybe you could be his godmother." I just talked and talked. About my love life, such as it was; about the ups and downs of my career. I told her about L.A., that Simon and I had plenty of room for her, and that as soon as she was up and about I wanted her to pack her things and fly out. "I'll pick you up at the airport," I said. "You'll move in. It'll be like old times. We'll be kids again."

I sang her a James Taylor song, fighting the tears. We used to love listening to James Taylor. A nurse entered the room as I finished. She said I had to go, visiting hours were over. I could come back the following morning.

But there was no following morning. The following morning she was dead.

RETURN OF THE RAT BASTARD

~~~~~~

I was in a funk for weeks. Paralyzed by depression. At first, Simon didn't know what to do with me, but suddenly he was too busy to worry about it. He got a green light to produce his first feature: *Teenage Mutant Ninja Turtles*. We would be shooting in Wilmington, North Carolina, so he sent someone down to find us a home for the duration.

It was hot in Wilmington. Early summer and already the mosquitoes were out in full force. Simon was stressed and Nathan was a little colicky and we'd bought a little puppy that peed everywhere. You'd look at him and he'd pee. Call his name and he'd pee. "Here boy!" and he'd pee double.

My mother phoned. She wanted to visit. She had never been on a real live movie set. I told her real live movie sets were arguably the most boring places on earth. Nothing happens. People sit around for hours, most of them with their thumbs up their asses, getting ready for a shot. Then they do the shot. And they do it again. And again. From every conceivable angle. And before long you know the lines better than the actors. And you can't get them out of your head.

"A mutant ninja turtle ate my baby!"

I sent her a ticket and went to the airport to get her. She got off the plane. Ray was with her. My jaw dropped. I couldn't believe she'd brought him. I'd only sent one ticket.

"Hi, honey," she said. She was all excited. She had a new crucifix. It was huge. It reminded me of the nurse at St. Mary's. The crucifix was like a weapon. I noticed an ugly bruise on her neck, below her ear, but I didn't say anything. "Say hello to your daddy," she said.

I looked at the rat bastard, and he looked at me. But there was nothing in his eyes. He was a zombie, a shell of his former self. It was still Ray, of course, but he shuffled along as if he'd been lobotomized. He didn't know who I was. He didn't even say hello. There was no one home.

We got to the car. "Give me the keys," Ray said, the first words out of his mouth. I froze. Even his voice had changed. It was flat, but still venomous and angry. "I want to drive."

My mother looked at me and shook her head no.

Ray looked furious, like he was going to come at her, but suddenly he went red in the face and stumbled against the car. She reached into her purse and pulled out a lit-

MY FATHER WITH DEBBIE IN THE BATHROOM OF OUR CHILDHOOD HOME.

tle vial of pills and he grabbed for it like a starving man and swallowed one without water. They were for his heart.

Calmer now, frightened, Ray got into the backseat. Mom got in front with me.

"So how have you been, dear?" she asked me.

"Great," I said. "You?"

"Wonderful," she said.

With the scare over, Ray began grumbling and cursing under his breath. I couldn't make out the words, but he was not a happy camper.

It was late by the time we got to the house. Mom wanted to see Nathan but he was asleep and I didn't want to wake him. He'd been having trouble sleeping lately. I told her she'd see him in the morning.

I offered them something to eat, but Mom said they'd had dinner on the plane and thank you but they were fine. Maybe a glass of milk for Dad's stomach. "Give me the keys," Ray croaked. "I want to drive."

The fucking guy was gone. Mom tried to drag him into the guest room and he punched her right in the face. My mouth fell open. Mom acted like it had never happened and smiled at me and scurried off down the hallway, dragging him along. She shut the guest room door behind them.

Still trying to process what I'd just seen, I went to look in on Nathan. My little towhead was asleep. The nanny had fallen asleep, too. Simon was still on the set. They were on a tight schedule, and it was going later and later every night. I went into the kitchen and poured myself a glass of chardonnay. *The fucking rat bastard was sleeping under my roof.* I couldn't believe it. I walked into the living room and the puppy scurried away, peeing itself.

I heard a noise in the corridor. Mom came out. She'd removed her makeup. She was still a beautiful woman, but

I could see the dark circles under her eyes, and bruises on her face and neck.

"I'm sorry about your father," she said.

"*You're* sorry?" I said. "How much longer are you going to take this? He should be locked up."

"He's just having a bad day."

The puppy came over and nuzzled my hand. There was another noise in the corridor. Ray came out in his boxer shorts. "What are you doing out here?" he hissed at Mom. Then he looked at me. "Who the fuck are you?"

"Ray, dear, please go back to bed," my mother said.

Ray saw the dog. He kicked it hard and it scampered away, whimpering.

"What the fuck did you do that for?" I shouted.

The nanny came out, rubbing the sleep from her eyes. I told her to please go back to Nathan's room and to stay with Nathan and not to come out under any circumstances.

"I want the keys to the car and I want them now!" Ray bellowed.

I went to the phone and called the set, but nobody could find Simon.

"Give me the fucking keys or I'll kill you!" Ray was shouting. "I want to drive."

I called the police. I told them my father was beating my mother.

"Is he beating her now?" the cop asked.

"No," I said. I was trying to be honest.

"Then we can't come," the officer said.

There was a vase next to the phone. I picked it up and threw it against the wall and it smashed. The cop heard it.

"How's that?" I said.

"Is he hitting her?" he asked again.

"He's having a fucking heart attack!" I lied.

An ambulance was there within minutes. They sent two cops along as back up, expecting trouble, I guess. I got the front door for the paramedics, and when Ray saw them he began cursing at the top of his voice. Then one of the cops walked in and he turned into a meek little mouse.

"How're you feeling, sir?" one of the paramedics asked.

Fear got the better of him. "Leave me alone! There's nothing wrong with me!"

They could see they weren't dealing with a well man. They tried to talk him into going to the hospital with them, but eventually had to remove him bodily. When they got him into the ambulance, they had to use restraints to keep him in place.

I called Simon and left word that there was an emergency, and that we were on our way to the hospital. I told Mom to stay in the house; I would deal with this. She gave me his pills and told me not to forget them—his life depended on them.

I followed the ambulance in the car. I remember looking down at the vial of pills . . . then suddenly found myself rolling down the window and tossing them onto the highway. We got to the hospital in Wilmington, but there was no sign of Simon. They wheeled my father in, strapped to the gurney. His eyes were wide and frightened. I loved it.

The doctor asked me what was wrong with him. "He's insane," I said.

"What do you want me to do with him?" he asked.

"Ice him," I said. I was out of my head by this time. It was all coming back. All the years of pain and abuse.

"Excuse me?"

"You heard me. I want this motherfucker dead. Finish him off."

Simon arrived. I didn't see him come in. I leaned over

the gurney and looked into Ray's eyes. And here's what I said: "Die, motherfucker! Die, you fucking pig! I hate you!"

Two orderlies restrained me. A third wheeled the gurney out of sight. "I hate you, you motherfucker! Do the world a favor and die!"

Simon was at my side now. I've never seen him more alarmed. One of the orderlies gave me a tranquilizer, which I took without protest. I calmed down a bit. Simon held both my hands in his, then another nurse came over.

"Does your father have any medical condition we should know about?" she asked.

I looked her in the eye. "Well, you know, he's demented." I said. "And not just from the Alzheimer's."

"He has Alzheimer's?" she asked.

"That's what I've been told," I said. The tranquilizer was beginning to kick in.

"Anything else?"

"No," I lied. "He's healthy as a horse."

Simon drove me back to the house. I was asleep before we got back. He carried me to bed.

It was almost noon when I woke up. My mother was in the kitchen with Simon. They were having coffee. I said good morning and poured myself a cup. We just sat there, not knowing what to say. Then the phone rang. Simon reached for it. It was the hospital. He listened. He said "Uh huh, uh huh" a few times, followed by "I understand, certainly," then "Thank you. I'll call you right back." He hung up and had trouble meeting my eyes.

"What?" I said.

"I have some bad news," he said. "Ray passed away a few minutes ago. He had a heart attack."

I thought I would feel like cheering, but I didn't. I didn't cheer. I didn't say anything. Mom buried her face in her hands and wept.

Debbie and Alexis flew down. We had him cremated right there in Wilmington; it was easier than shipping him back to Florida. I didn't go to the service. Debbie and Alexis and Mom hired a small boat and scattered his ashes at sea.

"It's what your father always wanted," Mom told me when they got back. They were all sitting around looking bereaved. I thought I was in the middle of a nightmare.

"Are you guys out of your fucking minds?" I said. "We should be celebrating. I can't believe you're acting like he was this great guy, like we had this great normal life or something."

Debbie got really pissed. She thought I was way out of line. Then I realized she didn't really know what had gone on in that house of horrors. Alexis knew, but she was a new person now. She had been transformed by self-help. She had worked through it. She'd met a wonderful new man who taught grade school in Long Island, and they were talking about having children. She was moving on with her life.

"I've forgiven him," she said.

"Well, good for you," I said. I stormed out of the house and walked around till long after everyone had gone to bed. I kept hoping a wave of relief would wash over me, but there was no relief. I began to wonder if there ever would be.

BETTER LIVING THROUGH CHEMISTRY

◄◄◄◄◄◄◄◄◄◄◄◄◄◄◄◄◄◄◄◄◄◄◄◄◄◄◄◄◄◄◄

When we got back to L.A., I decided to get serious about therapy. I went to see a shrink in Los Angeles. He told me I'd never processed what had happened to me as a child, and that until I did so I'd just keep looking for men with whom I could reenact the early abuse.

I told him he was crazy. "Why would I want to be abused?" I said. "I want to be loved."

"But you don't think you're lovable," he said.

"I don't?"

"No," he said. "You see yourself as your father saw you. You see yourself as hateful and worthless."

"But these men love me!" I protested. "Simon loves me."

"That may well be," he said. "But you don't believe it. Not deep down. So you test their love. You misbehave. You push and push until they explode at you, the same way your father did."

"Why would I want to make them do a thing like that?" I asked.

"Because it's what you know. It's *familiar*."

"I don't understand this at all."

"It's really quite simple," he went on. "Once you've turned Simon into your father, you try to win him back. In winning him back, you think you're undoing the damage that was done to you as a child. You're saying, 'See, Dad? You were wrong! I'm *not* worthless. I'm good and wonderful and lovable.' Only Simon and these other men aren't your father. The damage you suffered has nothing to do with them. The damage is inside you. Only you can fix it. Not them."

My head was spinning. I left his office with a brutal migraine and a prescription for Ativan, some kind of antianxiety medication. I drove home and tried to think about what he had told me, but it made me anxious. I'd been a lot happier in denial.

Then I got the prescription filled, and I instantly was less anxious. It was great. I didn't feel like thinking anymore.

I went back for a few more sessions, but I wasn't there to explore my sordid history. I was there for the drugs. I asked for stronger drugs, and he gave them to me. He even threw a little Lithium in for good measure.

I began smiling again. It was one of those Hare Krishna smiles. I was walking on a cushion of air.

"What's going on, Janice?" Simon asked me one night. We were on our way to a party. He was concerned about my odd behavior.

"Nothing," I said, smiling broadly. If I were Simon, I would've slapped me. Then again, I must say, in my defense, that the medications were partly to blame.

"Do you realize we haven't had sex in six months?" he said.

"No," I said. "Is that a fact?"

At the party that night, I ran into Greg Gorman, a very happening celebrity photographer. He couldn't believe how good I looked. He thought I was positively glowing. He asked me to come by his studio: He was doing a book of celebrity nudes and wanted me in it.

I showed up at Greg's studio a few days later, dressed like a fuck machine. Liam Neeson was there, half-naked. My Little Flower tingled. No, it didn't tingle. It fucking rocked. Suddenly I realized that I was missing sex, too. Just not with my husband.

"I've been a big fan of yours for years," Liam said. That accent! I thought I'd died and gone to heaven. He mentioned some of my spreads: Penn, Avedon, Hurrell, Horst. Either he'd done his homework or he really *was* a fan.

THE IRRESISTIBLE LIAM NEESON.

"Thank you," I said. I tried to smile demurely. I didn't want him to know how much I wanted him.

"I hear you're quite a photographer yourself," Liam said.

"I can't deny it," I said.

"When are you going to take my picture?"

"What are you doing Saturday?" I said.

We went out to Malibu the following weekend. We walked to the end of a deserted pier and climbed down into the rocks. He took off his shirt and I snapped a few pictures and told him to keep going. He didn't bat an eye. He peeled off his pants and an Evian bottle popped out. I mean, Jesus—the man was hung like a donkey.

"Well, I—uh, I'm speechless," I stammered.

Liam laughed. He put on a little Speedo he'd brought along, and I took a few family-friendly photographs.

"When can I see you again?" he asked, looking at me like I was lunch.

"You can't," I said.

I went home and took a shower and put on a little makeup and dressed provocatively and hugged my son and made a spectacular pasta primavera for Simon. He didn't even notice.

"Why don't you come to bed?" I said, trying to sound sultry.

"I have things to do," he said.

"You were right," I said. "We haven't had sex in six months. Let's do something about it."

"I can't just jump back into it, Janice."

"You think this is easy for me?" I said. "Come on, Simon. Let's give it the old college try."

"I've got to get back to the editing room," he said. And he left. *Bastard.* Fat lot of good it did me, trying to seduce him. After looking in on Nathan and the nanny, I went over to visit my friends Evi and Randy Quaid. Randy opened the door and took one look at my skintight dress and his eyes bugged out of his head. "Now here's a walking argument for infidelity," he said, laughing. I went inside and hugged Evi while Randy went off to make me a drink. I told them that Simon had lost interest in me: We were in the last stage of married sex, where you pass each other in the hallway and say "Fuck you."

I took a sip of my drink. It was a pepper vodka. It was good. I drank it down like water. Suddenly, everything started blurring. It occurred to me that I hadn't eaten all day. Well, I mean, aside from the Ativan, the Lithium, and those two hits of Valium.

The next thing I know, I'm waking up at Cedar's Sinai. Simon is standing next to my hospital bed.

"Holy shit," I said. "What happened?"

"You need to go into rehab," Simon said.

He took me home, still talking about rehab. I would clean myself up, he said. Stop with the pills. Stop with the booze. He and the nanny could handle Nathan until I got out. Everything was going to be fine. He was trying to be nice but I could sense his frustration. We were finished and we both knew it.

I stayed in bed for the next three days, numb. I called my Beverly Hills shrink, who had the pharmacy ship out some Klonopin. He said I'd love it. I set the phone down and it rang. Liam Neeson was on the other end, missing me and wanting me. I told him I'd be right over. I got up and brushed my teeth and ate a little something and showered and went over. He fucked my lights out. I thanked him, though God knows why: I felt like I needed an episiotomy.

Simon was waiting for me when I got home. "Where've you been?" he said.

"What do you care?" I said.

He slammed the front door on his way out, which woke Nathan. I went into his room and held him close and tight. I had Nathan. No one could ever take him away from me. He was mine, and my love for him was clean and pure and true.

Liam called again two days later. He was on his way to New York. Would I meet him there? I left on the red-eye that night. He was staying at the Ritz-Carlton on Central Park South. He was just waking up when I walked in. He ordered breakfast for both of us, and we spent the day in bed.

The phone rang late in the afternoon. It was Simon. To this day I don't know how he found me.

"Who is this?" Liam said, acting dumb. "You're looking for whom?"

But I'd had enough lies for a while. I took the phone.

"What the fuck are you doing, Janice?" Simon asked.

"I'm taking pictures of Liam Neeson for *Movieline*. What the fuck do you care?"

"I care. Please come home."

"What?" I said. "Now you want me? *Now?* Now that it's over, you're asking me to come home!" I hung up. The phone rang again, but I told Liam not to answer it. "Let's go to dinner," I said.

We went to dinner and Liam talked nonstop about Julia Roberts. Julia had dumped him, broken his heart. The only other woman he'd ever loved as intensely was Helen Mirren. He talked about her for a while, too. His voice cracked. I swear to God, I thought he was going to cry into his soup. When we got home, he went into the bathroom. When he came out he was drying his hands with a well-worn, ripped-to-shreds, hand towel with her initials monogrammed in royal blue: J.R.

What the fuck are you doing here? I asked myself.

I took one look at that towel and I knew instantly what it was good for.

I douched with it.

Sorry, Julia.

I flew back to L.A. the next morning. Liam didn't understand. He was going to Cairo to make a movie, and he wanted me to go with him.

"I'm still married," I said.

"I know what you think," I said when I saw Simon. "But nothing happened."

He didn't believe me but he wanted to believe me because neither of us wanted it to end. We had Nathan to think about, and we were both madly in love with Nathan. We were going to make it work for Nathan.

I kept popping pills, looking for the magic formula that would make everything all right—the self-help cocktail that would keep me happy for life. I came close. For a while I regained equilibrium. I was back on my cushion of air, smiling my Hare Krishna smile. Until one morning, that is, when I looked in the mirror and found my mother's face staring back at me. I knew I should stop right then and there, but I couldn't. I loved my little pills. They came in all colors, shapes, and sizes, like Nathan's toys. Two little red pills got me out of bed in the morning, the green and pink ones kept me on my feet all day, and the blue ones made for cozy slumber.

Then Simon's niece came to visit from Windsor. She couldn't have come at a worse time. And she brought a little friend with her. They were eighteen and desperate to meet celebrities, so I took them drinking on Sunset Boulevard. We ended up at Club Rubber. Mickey Rourke owned the place, and he was there. My niece and her little friend were beside themselves with joy. Mickey kept flirting and plying them with alcohol. I was pretty gone myself. At one point, I think he suggested that we all go to the back office and take off our clothes. I knew it was time to leave. I drove the girls home in a drunken stupor. They were sick for two days. On the third day, Simon put them on a plane home. When he got back from the airport, he told me, again, that I needed to go into rehab.

"Fuck you," I said. Then I called a friend to get the name of a female attorney.

"Go into rehab," the attorney said. "This could get ugly."

DIVORCE WARS

I checked into St. John's Hospital, in Santa Monica. They had a twenty-eight-day program that was supposed to be among the best in the country. That's what they'd said about St. Mary's, of course; that's what they said about all of them. Still, I knew I didn't have much choice, so I tried to put a positive spin on it. I decided to think of it as a vacation from Simon. *Yeah,* I said to myself. *That's it! Time off. I'll have fun. I'll make friends. Good friends. Friends that'll be there forever. That's the ticket!*

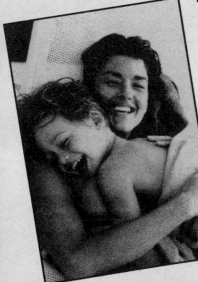

When I got out of the hospital, Simon filed for divorce. I counterfiled, and—as predicted—it got ugly. He wanted sole custody. In the papers, he claimed I was an unfit mother.

WITH NATHAN, 1990.

I wept for days. Then I pulled myself together and fought back. In my response I said I knew I wasn't perfect, but that I loved Nathan more than life itself. I said Nathan knew it, and Simon knew it, and that by and large I'd been a good mother. I also said there was no way in hell I was giving up custody of my son.

After I got out of rehab, I found a small house in Nichols Canyon. I lived for the nights that Nathan slept over and ached for him when he was at Simon's. The divorce got nasty over the usual issues—money, property, charges of infidelity. Simon and I were so full of rage that we couldn't risk seeing each other, so the nanny became the go-between. She brought Nathan over when it was my turn to have him and came to pick him up when it was time to take him back to his father's. I dreaded Nathan's going more than anything I'd dreaded in my life. When I heard her car pulling up out front, I thought I'd fall apart. I would take Nathan in my arms and hold him close, telling him I loved him more than he could imagine. "More than all the stars in the universe," I said. I would cry and ask for a few more minutes, until I couldn't ask for more and she had to take him from me. The anguish was so intense I didn't know how I'd survive it.

On one such unhappy occasion, as I was strapping him into his booster seat, Nathan told me, "I love you more than all the grains of sand in the world."

"Is that all?" I said, doing battle with the lump in my throat.

"No," he said, his little face crinkling up with mischief. "I love you more than all the atoms and molecules in the universe."

Jesus! Where'd he learn to talk that way? I thought of my father. He had produced an angry, fucked-up girl. I had produced a poet.

One night, shortly after the nanny had driven off with Nathan, I found myself at my wit's end. I couldn't sit still. I was tired of crying. I was having trouble breathing. I tried breathing into a paper bag, but that didn't work, either. So I showered, jumped into my car, and met my gay friends at this run-of-the-mill drinking hole over on Melrose. It was nice for a minute not to be gacked out of my gourd in some Motel 6, living the dream. Still, all I wanted was a drink. Then this handsome stud walked right by me, and I was awestruck. I was paralyzed. I fumbled with words, and got Drew Barrymore's mother Jade to ask him to come over. God knows I was too shy. He looked devilishly good in his suit. He walked up and sat next to me and introduced himself. His name was Michael Birnbaum. He worked for Aaron Spelling, the TV producer. We talked for three hours. I was smitten. Every word out of his mouth sounded like poetry.

He called the next day. And the day after that. And on Friday he took me to dinner. Two nights later, on Sunday, we went out again. We ended up dating for almost a year, and despite myself I fell in love with him. He was a nice guy, Michael. *Too* nice. I started thinking about some of the things that first shrink had told me, back in New York. How I was replaying ancient history, re-creating the old hurts in an effort to magically undo the damage—to "fix" it this time around. I thought about what Belushi had said on that crazy drive to Atlantic City: that I always went for guys who made me feel like I didn't amount to anything, because *I* felt like I didn't amount to anything—and because I wanted so much to be told that I was wrong, that I was really wonderful and amazing and incredibly lovable. And I thought about what my Beverly Hills shrink had told me: that I saw myself as my father had seen me, as hateful and worthless, and that as a result I looked for men who made me feel as hateful and worthless and awful as he'd made me feel—as awful as I thought I *deserved* to feel.

It was so complicated. Why was it so complicated? I just wanted to be wanted. Sure, maybe it had something to do with my father. He had never wanted me. But he was dead now. When would I get off the train?

The nanny was on her way over with Nathan. I was taking him to Chuck E. Cheese for lunch, and then we were going to the zoo, which he loved. He was the center of the universe, my little Nathan. It was Nathan who got me through the days and weeks and months.

Michael stepped out of the shower. "God, you look good," he said.

"Yeah, right, I know—I'm a sexy bitch."

WITH MICHAEL BIRNBAUM. A GENTLEMAN AND QUITE A STUD.

Michael laughed. He started getting dressed. "You want me to go to the zoo with you guys?" he asked.

"No," I said. He was a good guy, my Michael. Too good. Too nice. What was I doing with him? I liked trouble.

A few nights later I went out for dinner with Bette Midler and her husband, Martin von Haselberg. They told me they wanted to set me up with a close friend of Martin's, an abstract artist who taught at UCLA. *He* sounded like trouble. I went out with him and we ended up in bed, and I felt awful about it. Nothing to do with the artist, of course. It was this wanting-to-be-wanted bullshit again.

When I got back to my place, Michael was waiting outside with flowers.

"What's the occasion?" I asked.

"I want you to come to Cannes with me," he said. So we went.

He'd booked us on business class. I was disappointed. I wanted better. That's what I told myself, but it wasn't really about that at all. It was much simpler. I was fed up with Michael for being so goddamn nice. How was I going to replay ancient history with someone who insisted on being so good to me?

I felt the presence of that familiar, lurking demon. I'd been married and divorced twice. I'd been in and out of rehab twice. I'd had two abortions. I had a son, but his father and I couldn't even be in the same room together without trying to claw each other's eyes out. I was sitting on a plane next to a man who seemed to love me, but I couldn't love him in return. I felt uncomfortable in my own skin. *Christ! What is this?* I wondered. *I'm too young for a midlife crisis.*

We checked into the Hotel du Cap, then went upstairs and showered and dressed for lunch. I kept looking at

Michael, this kind, wonderful, loving man, and I realized that he wasn't the problem; I was. We passed through the lobby, en route to lunch, and when the elevator doors opened I thought I saw someone I knew near the front desk.

"Give me a minute," I told Michael. "I have to say hello."

It was Sly Stallone, perched on a pair of cowboy boots with three-inch heels and blue jeans so tight it was a wonder he could breathe.

"Hello, Mr. Stallone," I said. He turned to face me. His assistant, Kevin, looked like he was ready to intervene.

"Yo, Janice!" Sly said. He's such a goofball in real life that it's hard to believe he became what he became (well, for a little while, anyway). "What are you doing here?" He looked across the lobby and saw Michael, who half-waved from the distance. "Geez, you're still with him?" Sly said.

"Get me the fuck out of here," I said. "I'm going out of my mind."

"Can it wait till tonight?" he asked.

"If it must," I said.

"My plane leaves at ten. Kevin here will set everything up." Then he gave me a kind of stage handshake, to show Michael that it was all on the up-and-up, and clacked across the lobby in his high heels.

I rejoined Michael. "Jesus," he said. "The fucking guy is *short*."

We went to an early lunch and back to the room and I made love to Michael. It was pretty hot. I felt like Ingrid Bergman in Casablanca. *Fuck me! Fuck me as if for the last time!*

Michael had business throughout the day, so I sat by the pool in my thong. I looked through some fashion magazines. The girls looked so fucking *young,* and suddenly it occurred to me that they *were* young. Some of them hadn't been born when I'd gotten my start. Spooky.

When Michael got back, I broke the bad news. "Sylvester Stallone has agreed to let me take his picture, but I have to fly back with him tonight."

"That's ridiculous," Michael said.

"What can I tell you? He's going back to L.A. They're shooting *Demolition Man* and he wants me on the set."

Michael was crushed. "I can't believe you're doing this," he said.

"Go ahead," I said. "Tell me I'm a cunt."

He wouldn't do it. I realized I really *wanted* him to do it.

Sly sent a car for me. The Warner Brothers plane was waiting on the tarmac, and Kevin took me inside. It was a fucking palace. I'd never been on a sleeper plane. This one had half a dozen actual bedrooms. It was filled with studio executives, the cream of the crop. Sly came over and gave me a big kiss. He was wearing a tuxedo with ruby studs and ruby cuff links. I think he and Liz Taylor had just cohosted some major AIDS fund-raiser. He put his arm around me. "Hey, everybody," he announced in that thuggy voice. "This is Janice Dickinson. Isn't she something?"

Everyone was very polite. We had drinks and caviar, and then the plane took off and we had more drinks and more caviar. But slowly people began to drift off to their rooms. And then it was just me and Sly.

"What are you doing with that Birnbaum character?" he asked.

"What do you know about Birnbaum? He's smart. He' sexy. And he's *nice.*"

"He's no Sly."

"No," I said. "Thank God for that. Where am I sleeping?"

"With me," he said.

"Aren't you being a little presumptuous?"

"All the rooms are taken, babe. It's either me or this chair here, and I think I'm a better bet."

I looked at him. "You have a good face. I wish you'd let me take your picture some time."

"I'll think about it," he said.

"You're pretty full of yourself, aren't you?"

"I can't help it. I look in the mirror in the morning and it's me there and I can't believe it. It's like, 'Holy fuck, I'm Sylvester Stallone. I'm fucking Sly Stallone.' "

"We all have our crosses to bear," I said.

We went into his room. He began taking off his clothes. "Nice cuff links," I said.

"You want one?"

He meant it, too. "No thanks," I said. Then I asked him for a T-shirt. He had one with *Demolition Man* scrawled across the front. I slid out of my clothes and slipped into it.

"Now what?" I said.

"Anything you want, babe."

"How about sleep?"

"Sleep is good."

He offered me a Halcion to help me sleep and took one for himself. He was being a perfect gentleman, and clearly he was serious about sleep. We got under the covers.

"You mind if I hold you?" he asked. He put his arms around me. They were massive—bigger than Christy Turlington's thighs. And there was something about the way he held me. I swear to God, it was *electric*. Maybe this was my fucking soulmate!

"Comfortable?" he asked.

I didn't say a word. I was afraid if I said anything, it would lead to more. I just nodded. He held me tighter. The next thing I knew, I was waking up in Los Angeles. Sly kissed me good-bye outside the terminal. Said he'd be in touch. His assistant, Kevin, drove me back to Nichols Canyon.

I tried not to think about how good I'd felt in Sly's arms. I told myself it never happened.

BAM HAM SLAM

❯❯❯❯❯❯❯❯❯❯❯❯❯❯❯❯❯❯❯❯❯❯❯❯❯❯❯❯❯❯❯❯❯❯❯❯❯

Two days later, I got a call from Kevin. Sly wanted to see me. He was going downtown later that night, to the L.A. Convention Center, to the set of *Demolition Man*. They were blowing up a building, and he thought I might enjoy taking pictures at the scene. So I hadn't really lied to Michael after all. . . .

A few hours later, Kevin came by and drove me and my cameras to a house on Benedict Canyon. It was a rental; Sly was remodeling his new home. "He's waiting for you upstairs," Kevin said.

"Tell him to go fuck himself," I said. "I thought I was going downtown to take pictures."

"You are," Kevin said. He went off and returned with a cranberry vodka. I chugged it and went upstairs, looking for Sly. I was pissed off.

"Yo, babe, in here," he said. I found him in the master bedroom.

"What are we waiting for?" I asked.

"This," he said.

He took me in his big arms and started kissing me. Before I knew it, we were both naked on the bed. It didn't last long, but I *think* I enjoyed it.

"Bam ham slam," he said. He got up and we got dressed and I followed him downstairs. Kevin drove us downtown.

I wasn't sure about what had just happened, or why I'd allowed it to happen. What was wrong with me? I was suddenly filled with self-loathing. In the space of a week, I had slept with three men: the abstract artist, the producer, and the superstar. What the hell was that all about? Who was driving this rig? Yeah, it's nice to be wanted, but not like that. Most men are dogs. They'll take anything that moves. This crazy notion of mine—that a man wanting me actually meant something—was beginning to worry me.

"You're awful quiet, girl," Sly said. "What are you thinking about?"

"Nothing," I said. But I had plenty on my mind. I was wondering how that lurking demon who'd followed me to the Sforza Castle, on the outskirts of Milan, had found his way to Los Angeles.

We arrived at the convention center, and Sly introduced me to his costars, Benjamin Bratt and Sandra Bullock. He told Joel Silver, the producer, to let me do what I had to do. I crept around for much of the night, cameras in hand, taking pictures. Sly pretty much ignored me. They were still shooting at the crack of dawn, and the building was still standing, so I decided to go home. I waited for a break and told Sly I was leaving.

"You'll be hearing from me," he said. And he went back to work.

I got back to Nichols Canyon to find Nathan and the nanny having breakfast. Nathan looked worried. He told me he went to look for me in the middle of the night, and I was gone. He wanted to know where I was.

"I was working," I told him.

I drove him to school. All of seven years old, and he sat in the back of the car like a brave little soldier. "I don't want to have to worry about you, Mom," he said. "Next time you're going to work late, please tell me."

Birnbaum called later in the day and asked me to dinner. He knew something was up. He took me to the St. James Club, on Sunset Boulevard. I told him I'd slept with Stallone. If nothing else, I was trying to be honest. For a few moments, he didn't say anything. He seemed to be having trouble catching his breath. Then he signaled for the waiter and asked for the check.

"I'm sorry," I said.

"So am I," he said.

He was hurt and angry. But he didn't want to shout and he didn't want to cry. He didn't say a word as we left the restaurant. Didn't say a word as we waited for the valet. Didn't say a word as he drove me home.

When we reached my place, he got out and got the door.

"Aren't you going to say anything?" I asked him.

"What do you want me to say?" he said. "I'm in love with you, goddamn it. Why did you have to go and do this to us?"

But he didn't want an answer. He got in his car and drove away. No good-bye. No I'm-here-for-you. No call-me-if-you-need-me. Nothing. Michael was gone. I'd made a mistake and it wasn't the kind of mistake that I could undo with a simple apology. I thought I'd give him time. I gave him time. All the time in the world.

The phone never rang. Michael didn't call. And *Sly* didn't call. What the fuck had I done?

So I tried not to think about Michael. And I tried not to think about Sly. I concentrated on being a good mother, on being the Greatest Mom Ever. And I was getting pretty excited about my photography: The *Demolition Man* pictures looked terrific.

But goddamn it—I couldn't not think about Sly. I had dumped Michael for the Demolition Man, and the Demolition Man wasn't calling. Another week passed. Still no call. And—bad news—no period. Three days later I went for a pregnancy test. It was positive. I drove home in shock. Who was the father? Who did I *want* it to be?

What difference did it make? Nobody was there for me. I was alone. I could feel the abyss under my feet.

The phone was ringing as I came through the door.

"Hello," I said.

"Yo," Sly said. "I miss you."

I fucking melted. I almost wept with relief. Anyone who's been there knows the feeling.

I went over to his house that night. Kevin made dinner for us. We went to the bedroom afterward and made love for hours. He'd improved considerably since our brief debut.

"Bam ham slam," he said afterward.

And I said, "I'm pregnant."

That got his attention. "You're what?"

"I'm pregnant," I repeated.

Sly took a beat. "How do you know it's not Birnbaum's?" Well, I didn't. It could have been the *artist's*, for all I knew. But I didn't think I needed to mention that. What good would that have done either of us?

"It might be Birnbaum's," I said. "But I don't think it is. I think it's yours." I did, too. In all honesty, deep down inside, I felt the child was his.

Sly was a real *mensch* about it. We started spending more time together. He took me golfing. Sailing. Horseback riding. He never mentioned Jennifer Flavin, and I never asked. He introduced me to his friends. One time, at a dinner party, a young producer came over and tried to talk him into doing one more *Rocky*. "I'm done with Rocky," he said. "The only thing I'm fighting these days is arthritis."

We were staying at his place in Malibu. The pregnancy

began to show. He didn't like it. "When a kid goes into a pet store, what do you think he's going to take home with him: the momma dog or the puppies?"

"You're not a kid," I said.

"Every man's a kid on the inside. That's the problem with men."

"You got that right," I said.

"Tell you what," he said. "I'll give you a million bucks to get rid of the baby."

"No," I said. I didn't know whether or not he was serious, but I didn't even have to think about it. I'd already had two abortions.

"What if he's not mine?"

"*She,*" I said.

"It's a girl?"

"That's right. It's a girl."

"How do you know?" he asked.

"I just know. And I know she's yours."

"How?"

"I don't know, Sly. I just feel it, okay? A woman knows."

"A million bucks is a lot of money," he said.

"I don't want your fucking money," I said.

We flew to Miami on a private jet. He was shooting *The Specialist* with Sharon Stone, but the *National Enquirer* was more interested in me. Somehow they got hold of the story: *The Superstar and the Supermodel—And One of Them Looks Pregnant.* It was a huge fucking story. Even the reputable papers called with inquiries.

"You sure you want to have this kid?" Sly said.

"Yes," I said.

We were on our way to lunch, at South Beach, and found a small crowd gathered for some kind of shoot. Sly wanted to take a closer look, and of course I tagged along.

And wouldn't you just know it: It was Helmut Newton, shooting girls in skimpy bathing suits.

"Hi, Helmut," I said. He turned to look, and scowled the moment he saw me. Christ, what a child! Yes, he was Helmut Newton, and, yes, he was a great photographer. But years had passed since that incident in the south of France, and he was still angry. "I guess I missed my chance," I said, and walked off.

Sly hurried to catch up. "What the hell was that all about?" he asked.

"Oh, just another man I pissed off," I volunteered. "And I didn't even sleep with him."

By the time I got back to Los Angeles, my street was crawling with reporters. Some of them actually looked like reporters. Others wore disguises: telephone repairmen, electricians, cable guys. It was like a shoot for *This Old House*.

One of my friends came over. He was sweet. He let me

WAITING FOR SAVVY TO DROP.

cry on his shoulder. I told him I was frightened, that I wanted to be a good mother and just hoping to make a life with Sly. A week later, much of what I'd said showed up in the *National Enquirer.* He'd sold me down the river. I told him I never wanted to see him again, and I never did.

On the big day, I called Sly at home. "Diva's on her way," I said.

"I'll meet you at the hospital," he said. "And Janice, please don't call her 'Diva.' You'll live to regret it."

I told him not to hurry. I had the nanny drive me to the hospital. Nathan was jumping up and down, thrilled at the prospect of a little sister. He kept telling me she could stay in his room for as long as she wanted—and that he'd take care of her.

She came fast. *Too* fast. Sly got to the hospital about five minutes after she popped out and was beside himself with joy. He held her in his big arms, with a stogie hanging out of his mouth, and rocked her and grinned and grinned. He had two sons from a previous marriage, but this was his first little girl. I swear there were tears in his eyes.

"I hope she's mine," he said to me later.

"She is," I assured him.

"We're not calling her 'Diva,' " he said.

"Okay," I said. "How about Savannah?"

We took her back to my place in Nichols Canyon. The

paparazzi followed us all the way home. We got inside. Nathan followed us around like a confused puppy: *So this is what a baby sister looks like?* We put Savannah in her crib. Sly beamed like a proud father.

"We're going to get you back in shape," he said.

"Is that your big concern?" I asked. "Getting me in shape?"

"No," he said. "I'm still wondering whether she's mine." I thought that was a shitty thing to say. The phone rang. Gianni Versace was calling to congratulate me. He also wanted to know whether I'd be ready to go back to work in six weeks; he was having his haute couture show in Paris, and I was the first girl on his list.

"Six weeks?" I said. I looked at Sly. "Sure. I'll be in fighting shape in six weeks."

Within days, Sly was popping me with his vitamin regimen. They'd worked for him and they seemed to be working fine for me. I exercised religiously, and took care of my kids, and thought of my new life with Sly. No, we weren't living together, we weren't man and wife, but it sure looked like it was in the cards. He went with me to visit the pediatrician when it was time for Savannah's one-month checkup. But it wasn't completely selfless: He wanted to make sure she was his, so he'd arranged for a DNA test. I wasn't concerned in the least. I *knew* she was his.

The lab called a few days later. The results were murky, they said. One of the technicians had screwed up and they needed another sample. Somehow, I never got around to giving them their lousy sample. Meanwhile, Sly was concentrating on turning this momma dog into a puppy. He got me into the best shape of my life—him and his vitamins.

The day before I left for Paris, my doorbell rang. The man outside identified himself as a lab technician from some facility in Long Beach, just south of L.A. He said he was there to take samples of Savannah's blood. It pissed me off—Sly hadn't forgotten—but I couldn't exactly send the man on his way. He took her blood, the goddamn vampire, and left with his little vials.

The next evening, I flew to Paris with Savannah and the nanny, for Gianni's show. Nathan went to stay with his father. Sly had some dubbing to do; he couldn't get away till the following day.

I ran into Versace in the hotel lobby. "Whoa!" he exclaimed, his eyes bugging out of his head. "What happened to you?" I didn't look like a model anymore. I was buff, *cut*. I looked like an East German swimmer.

Sly showed up in time for the show the next day. It was a huge hit. People kept coming up to tell me they couldn't believe how good I looked. I had Savannah backstage, and everyone was cooing over her. Some people thought she looked like me; others thought she looked like Sly.

Sly left his seat before the show was over. I had no idea where he'd gone. I went down the runway for one last turn and looked at his empty seat and

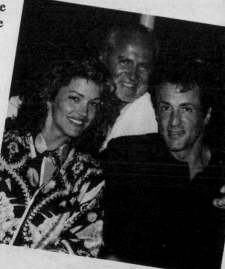

WITH SLY AND
THE LATE GREAT
GIANNI VERSACE.
➤➤➤➤➤➤➤➤➤➤

felt a little hurt. I hurried away before the applause died down and went back to the hotel. He was waiting for me in my room. He did not look happy.

"What's up?" I asked. "Where'd you go?"

"She's not mine."

"Excuse me?"

"Savannah," he said. "She's not mine. I just heard from the lab in Long Beach."

"How is that possible?"

"Send my regards to Mr. Birnbaum," he said. He stood up.

"Sly—"

"We had a good run, Janice. Say nice things about me and I'll say nice things about you."

He walked out. I felt like I'd just been kicked in the solar plexus. The phone rang. I was hoping it was Sly, but it was Versace. He was ready to leave for the postshow party at the Louvre, and he was waiting for me out front.

GALOTTI, PAREE, AND ME. TEE HEE.

I made my way downstairs in a daze, as if I were under water. I was accosted by fans. I signed a few autographs. I even smiled for the paparazzi. I got outside and Versace was standing next to a big white limo. He waved me over, grinning. Some flashbulbs popped. I smiled my alligator smile and climbed into the limo. Versace slipped in next to me and closed the door and the driver pulled away.

"You were marvelous, darling," he said. "You look marvelous."

"I feel marvelous," I said. I was compartmentalizing again. I was getting good at it.

The party was terrific—that's what the newspapers said, anyway. I don't remember it too well. I remember smiling my denial smile, and shaking lots of hands and bussing lots of cheeks, and thanking people for their kind compliments. I remember not answering when I was asked if Sly was coming; I just smiled harder and tried to look model-dumb.

Later in the evening, I found myself on a balcony. I was taking deep breaths, trying to steady myself, but I couldn't seem to get enough air into my lungs.

"You are a stunning woman," I heard someone behind me say. "But you don't look particularly happy."

I turned around. It was Ron Galotti, the publisher of *Vogue*. We'd met before, but only briefly. He had wonderful eyes. "You're right," I said. "I'm not happy."

"Let's blow this popsicle stand," he said, "and you can tell me all about it."

So we went for a walk and I told him everything. I told him about Sly, Savannah, Birnbaum. I told him about Ron Levy, my first husband. I told him about my father. I told him about the lurking demon that had followed me from Milan to Los Angeles and had now made its way to Paris. I talked until the sun came up. And Ron listened. He held me when I needed it and dried my tears every time they flowed. And then he said, "Janice, it's time to face the demon."

He was right, sure; but I didn't want to face the fucking demon; I didn't know where to begin.

HIDE YOUR HEAD
IN THE SAND,
LITTLE GIRL

➤➤➤➤➤➤➤➤➤➤➤➤➤➤➤➤➤➤➤➤➤➤➤➤➤➤➤➤➤➤➤

So I ran away. I took Savannah and the nanny and spent two weeks with friends on a yacht off the coast of France. We stopped at every fashionable port and hit all the best clubs and restaurants, but I felt like shit. On top of everything else, I think I was going through vitamin withdrawal. I was jittery all the time. I ran into Ivana Trump one night. "Dahlink," she said, "vat happened to you? You look so sad!"

"Dahlink," I shot back, "why are you pretending you don't read the tabloids? My life is a mess. Sly just dumped me."

"Men! Vee don't need men, my little pumpkin. Go out and rule the vorld!"

But I couldn't rule the fucking world. I was miserable. I called Nathan from the yacht every day. I told him he was my little man. That I loved him and missed him and that I'd be home soon. He told me that he didn't like pizza anymore; his new favorite food was cheeseburgers. And Ron Galotti called me every day. Sometimes twice a day. His spies found me on the yacht. Why had I run away, he wanted to know. He missed me. He missed my voice. He missed my tears.

I guess I needed to hear that. When I got back to the States, we tried the bicoastal thing for a while. He was tender and attentive and a wonderful lover, but before long I realized I was just repeating the old mistakes. I was still looking to be saved, still looking to be told that I *wasn't* worthless, still looking for someone to undo the damage that had been done a quarter of a century earlier.

"I'm scared," I said.

"We're all scared," he said. "Look at me: I'm just a little street kid who happens to know a little bit about magazines. The Big Questions? I'm as lost as the next guy."

"As lost as me?"

"Well, not *that* lost!" he joked.

Truth in humor. At that moment, it struck me that I was the only one who could change my life. And I got started: The bicoastal thing wasn't working for either of us, so we ended it—amicably. I went home to life with my two kids, my photography, and an occasional modeling gig. And for a while there I thought I was on the right track. *Here I am, Janice. Taking my son to school, preparing mac and cheese for dinner, making rules about TV, and reading my little girl to sleep each night. Here I am, taking pictures, honing my craft; here I am, still modeling, taking acting classes, staying away from drink and drugs.*

There was, of course, one little problem. I still didn't know who Savannah's father was, and there were two possibilities: my friend the abstract artist or Michael Birnbaum. *Please God,* I said to myself, *please let it be Michael.* It wasn't that I didn't like the artist. I liked him fine. But he'd been a one-night stand, a mistake. And Michael? Christ—Michael had really been there for me. Michael had really loved me. Michael and I had actually been *in love* at one time. He had to be the father, right?

But what if it wasn't Michael? I was paralyzed with

worry. My head was spinning with questions. If it wasn't Michael, well—maybe that would be for the best. After all, the artist and I didn't have a relationship. He wouldn't want anything to do with her. But then Savannah wouldn't have a father. Of course, if it *was* Michael, there was always a chance that he might not want to be her father. Then again, if he *did,* how was that going to work?

I called the artist—it was less emotionally demanding—and told him the story. He didn't say much on the phone. I could picture him sitting in his house, in near shock, hearing what he was hearing and not wanting to hear it. I mean, God, I don't think he ever expected to hear from me again. Then I dropped the bomb:

"How would you feel about taking a DNA test?" I asked.

"Well, I, uh . . . " He had a hard time getting the words out. But at the end of the day he was a perfect gentleman. He agreed, and for the next few days we waited. I was a nervous, miserable wreck—but no doubt he was more so. Then the tests came back: He wasn't the father. I was immensely relieved, and so was he—trust me. Then I thought about the task at hand—calling Michael, whom I hadn't seen since I'd told him about Sly—and relief went out the fucking window.

I'd been through a bitter, hellacious custody battle with Simon Fields. I didn't want to go through that again. *Ever.* I wasn't going to lose my little girl. So I decided I simply wouldn't tell Michael. End of story.

But it wasn't, of course.

At night, I would wake up drenched in sweat, thinking someone was in the room with me. Was it my father's ghost? Was it the lurking demon? I started sleeping with the lights on. Or not sleeping at all. I began to lose my sense of time. I was up at four one morning, making mac and cheese for breakfast. I hollered for Nathan. *Time to get up. Move move move!* I took Savannah out of her crib and marched into the kitchen and plopped her into the high chair.

The nanny walked into the kitchen, rubbing the sleep from her eyes. "I think you should talk to someone," she said. I looked over at Savannah, who lay slumped in her high chair, asleep again. Nathan was awake but miserable. "Can I go back to bed, Mom?" he asked. "*Please?*"

I looked over at the nanny, mortified. This is what my life had become: I was so alone that the only person who could see I was in serious trouble was the nanny.

I went to visit my Beverly Hills shrink. He told me I looked beautiful and wrote me two prescriptions. "There're all sorts of wonderful new things on the market," he said.

"That's great," I said. "Because I don't want to feel anything."

"That's what we're here for," he said.

As predicted, the new drugs were pretty wonderful.

"Hi, Mom," I'd say, calling Florida now and then to see how she was doing.

"Hi, honey," she'd say.

"How are you?" I'd say.

"Fine," she'd say. "You?"

"Fine," I'd say. "You?"

It was like a comedy routine gone wrong. I'd become my mother. All I needed now was a man just like the man who'd married Dear Old Mom.

Then Sly called. "Yo, it's me," he said. "How you doin'?"

"Go fuck yourself," I said.

"I want you," he said.

"You had your chance," I said.

The house on Nichols Canyon started feeling claustrophobic. I called a realtor, who found us a new home off Beverly Glen. He asked me if I was seeing anyone; he had a friend who was newly single. He thought I'd like him.

"Set it up," I said.

The friend's name was Albert Gersten. He came by and picked me up and took me to a trendy little place in Beverly Hills. I liked him right away. He had ice-blue eyes and thinning hair and lots of energy. He was loud and confident and cocky—and more so because he liked to drink, as I did.

After dinner, he took me to the Gate, a club he owned on La Cienega. It was a bit second-rate, but I didn't mind. There were a lot of sleazy-looking characters hanging around looking for a good time. Shannon Doherty was there. She broke a beer bottle over her boyfriend's head. It was very entertaining.

Albert got louder and crazier. He laughed. He liked my sense of humor. He took me home as dawn was breaking, and we kissed a bit in the Ferrari. I wouldn't let him into the house.

"Why not?" he asked.

"I'm not that easy," I said.

In the days and weeks ahead, he began to romance me in earnest. He took me to his place in Malibu. He took me to Las Vegas on a private jet. He was very rich, clearly. His family had made a fortune in real estate. But it wasn't just about money. He said all the right things. He told me he was in love with me, that he wanted to adopt Savannah, that together our life would be better than anything I'd ever dreamed of.

Yes, Dear Reader, I slept with him—and savored the feeling of being held again. But something about the feeling scared me. He scared me a little, too, to be honest. During the day he was the sweetest guy in the world. But sometimes, after a few shots of chilled Patron tequila, like many people who drink, he turned into another person—

I called my shrink, looking for refills, but he was out of town. There was a message on his machine providing the name of a backup shrink in the event of an emergency. I called the backup shrink, but he refused to give me pills over the phone. I went to see him. He was young and good-looking and very smart. We talked for the full hour. I went back the next day and the day after that.

"Janice," he said. "This has to stop. You're giving them all the power."

"Who? What power?"

"It's all well and good to be swept off your feet and fall in love," he said. "It feels great, yes. And it's wonderful. But what happens when it ends?"

"I don't know," I said. "I just know I hate it. It's fucking horrible."

"That's because you don't like yourself."

"Don't I?"

"You tell me," he said.

He was right. I didn't like myself. There had been times lately when I looked at my reflection in the mirror and found my adolescent self staring back at me, her eyes red from crying. I was seeing her more and more lately, and it scared me. I got the feeling that she wanted something from me—that she wanted the adult me to tell her she was a good little girl. But I didn't know where to begin.

"What about that refill?" I said.

"It's not as hard as you think, Janice," he said. His voice was low, gentle. "You're alive. You're smart. You have your health. You've survived. That's a miracle in and of itself— the fact that you survived the abuse. That right there is something you can be very proud of. Why don't we start with that?"

"Fuck this," I said. "I don't need this deep bullshit. I'm just a shallow, happy girl. I want my fucking drugs."

"I think you've had enough drugs," he said.

"You're not the only shrink in town."

He took a beat. "Janice, listen to me," he said. "If you judge yourself solely through other people's eyes, you're going to get into a lot of trouble. A man tells you he loves you, you feel good. He stops loving you, you feel rotten. You get a high-profile modeling gig, you feel good. You don't get it because they like Cindy Crawford better, you feel like shit."

"That was cruel," I said.

"No," he said. "It was honest. You're giving everyone else the power. Men. Work. Your ex-husband. Your current boyfriend. Your children even. You've got to take the power back. You're the only one in the world who should stand in judgment of Janice Dickinson. You know the difference between right and wrong, between good and bad. Take responsibility for yourself and your actions and your life. Grow up. You'll be a lot happier."

"I like me just fine," I said, standing. "It's you I don't like." I turned and stormed out.

By the time I reached the lobby, I felt as lost and alone as I'd ever felt in my life. I looked at my watch. It wasn't quite four o'clock yet, but what the hell. I took myself drinking. I made the rounds of all the best bars in town. I made pit stops on Melrose Avenue, Sunset Boulevard, Rodeo Drive.

At about three in the morning, I'm driving along, trying to find my way home, when a deafening wail pierces my brain. I ignore it. I think it's in my head. I've burst a fucking blood vessel or something, no biggie. Only it's not in my head. It's coming from the police car behind me. I pull over, scraping the tires against the curb. I cut the engine. I leave my hands on the steering wheel like you know to do if you live in Southern California, and I focus on the rearview mirror. *Okay, there he is. He's getting out now. Here he comes. Here he is.* Only it's not a he; it's a she.

"Can I see your driver's license and registration, please?" she says.

I look dead at her. She's kind of cute. Her pants are really tight. And that big gun—the things we could do with that gun. For a moment there I wonder what my life would have been like if I'd been a lesbian. But of course I'm not a lesbian. I'm a gay man.

"Did I do something wrong, officer?" I say. I'm slurring. I feel like an idiot. She tells me to step out of the car and puts me through the motions. One foot in front of the other; turn around and try it again, tip of the finger to the tip of the nose. *What nose? Oh, that nose! Why didn't you say so in the first place!*

She drove me to the Beverly Hills jail. If you have to spend a night in jail, people, this is the place to do it. They offered me coffee and warm blankets; I think one of them was cashmere. *Did I hear someone say croissants?* The male police officers were very friendly. They kept coming by to ask me if I was sure I didn't want to make a phone call. Yes, I told them. I was sure. Who was I going to call at this hour? Albert? How could I let him see me in this condition?

I stumbled out of jail at eight o'clock the next morning. The first thing I saw was my old friend Esme, the model. She'd just pulled up to a day care center directly across the street from the precinct. I thought I was hallucinating. She saw me and her jaw dropped.

"Janice?" she mumbled. I nodded. *Yeah, it's me. In the flesh.* She made a little motion with an upraised finger—*I'll be right back!*—and hustled the kids along to keep them from witnessing this living horror. I couldn't blame her. I had so much mascara running down my face I looked like Alice Cooper.

I didn't wait for her to come back. I walked to the corner, where I'd been told I'd find a cab, and hopped into the first one in line.

"Where to?" the driver asked.

"What difference does it make?" I said.

Two weeks later, on a Saturday night, Albert Gersten came to my house and fell to his knees and handed me a twenty-three-carat diamond ring. I said yes. The newspapers got wind of it. Everyone called, mostly to congratulate me.

"Why the fuck are you marrying that loser?" Sly said.

MY WEDDING TO ALBERT GERSTEN. LEFT TO RIGHT: FREDERIQUE, DEBBIE, ME, ALBERT, ALEXIS, MITCH (ALEXIS'S HUSBAND).

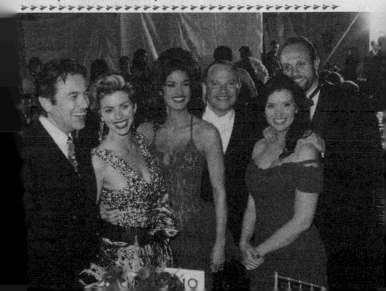

"Everyone's a loser except you, right, Sly?"

"You're making a big mistake," he said.

"You were my last big mistake," I said, hanging up.

Albert and I were married on Valentine's Day, 1995, at the Gate. Karl Lagerfeld made my wedding dress. It was an old-fashioned Moulin Rouge number, scarlet red, with a corset so tight I could hardly breathe. It was just as well. If I'd been able to breathe—if a tiny bit of oxygen had been able to reach my brain—I might have had the good sense to run away.

Sly called just before the ceremony. He begged me, again, not to go through with it. "Just say the word and I'll land a fucking chopper on the roof right the fuck now," he said.

"Earth to Rambo," I said. "I'm getting married. Do you copy?"

I hung up. For a moment there, I kind of hoped he would show up with a chopper. But after a few lines of coke and three-quarters of a bottle of champagne I decided to go through with it. I walked down the makeshift aisle in front of two thousand guests. Governor Gray Davis married us. I don't remember much else. Everyone seemed to be having a good time. Alexis and Debbie were there. And I'd invited my mother, but she couldn't make it. She was struggling, quietly, with cancer.

Albert and I went to St. Bart's for our honeymoon. On the first night we hooked up with a few of Albert's friends for dinner, and drank voluminous amounts of champagne. Albert didn't even like champagne—tequila was his drink—but he bought it because he enjoyed showing off.

After dinner we went to some hot club called the Parrot. That got me thinking about Alexandra King's parrot, the one that said *Fuck me Fuck me Fuck me*. That made me sad. Now I was thinking about my first marriage, to Ron

Levy. I wondered what had happened to him. I wasn't sure I wanted to know.

"What's wrong?" Albert asked.

"Nothing," I said.

"Try to look a little happier," he said.

"I'm happy," I said. And we had a few more drinks. When they started getting ready to close, Albert wanted to drag everyone back to the hotel, but no one was game— thank God. The valet returned with the mini-moke, a convertible Jeep.

"I'll drive," I said. We were both pretty wasted, but he was in worse shape than me.

"Don't be ridiculous," he said.

He gave me one of his Albert Gersten shut-the-fuck-up looks. So I shut the fuck up and got in the car and he pulled out, tires squealing. It was a very curvy road. He had the brights on, but they didn't seem very bright to me. I couldn't see more than fifteen or twenty yards ahead, and the road was coming fast.

"Please slow down," I begged.

"What were you thinking about back there? Do you regret having married me?"

"No, I do not regret having married you. But I'd like to live long enough to enjoy it."

He gunned the engine. We were really whipping around the curves now. My mouth felt dry.

"Albert, please," I said. But that was all I said. He lost control of the car around the next curve, and we sailed through a retaining wall and plummeted over the side.

I'm dead, I thought. *Please God don't let me die. I have two kids who need me.*

We were moving awfully fast, crashing over rocks and through brush and small trees. I could hear glass shattering and one of the tires blowing—loud as a gunshot—and then the windshield popped and everything went dark. When I came to, not long afterward, we were still upright, with the right front side of the car a few feet off the ground and the right tire audibly spinning. I could smell gasoline.

I should have seen it coming. Third time to the altar, and I can't even get out of the honeymoon without a car wreck. Story of my life.

"Albert?" I said. He was moaning. I looked over at him. His face was covered in blood. "Albert, are you okay?" He didn't answer. I popped my seatbelt. I wiggled my toes. It was probably a silly thing to do, but I wanted to make sure I wasn't paralyzed. I opened my door and got out and went around to Albert's side and opened his door. "Can you walk?" I asked. He just moaned. I reached in and removed his seatbelt and dragged him out of the car. He was useless. He tried to walk up the pitched hill, with me half-carrying him, but we still had to stop and rest every thirty seconds. Finally, exhausted, we reached the side of the road. It was deathly still. I looked over at Albert's face. He looked awful. He seemed to be in shock. "You're fine," I said. "You're going to be fine."

I heard the distant whine of a motorcycle and got to my feet and stood in the middle of the road. I waved my arms, and the motorcycle slowed down and stopped. The driver cut the engine. He looked wide-eyed and frightened. "Please get help," I said. "My husband is badly hurt." He raced off. I went back to the side of the road and sat beside Albert and held him in my arms and tried to comfort him. I think I fell asleep for a while. The sirens woke me. I could barely keep my eyes open en route to the hospital, but all the way there I held Albert's hand. "You're going to be fine," I said. "Everything is going to be fine."

It took a hundred stitches to patch him together, and when the doctors were done he looked a little bit like

Frankenstein. Then again, as the doctors pointed out, we were both lucky to be alive.

We stayed in St. Bart's till Albert was well enough to fly. When we finally got back to L.A., Albert sat around for a week, staring at the walls and feeling sorry for himself. But then he couldn't take it anymore. He started going out to the club and drinking again, showing off his scars like some returning goddamn war hero.

But I didn't go to the clubs with him anymore. I was tired of that scene. Instead, I stayed at his place in Malibu, with Savannah and the nanny, and tried not to think of the mess I'd made of my life. I tried not to think about the failed marriages and the abortions and the ongoing battles with Simon, who was determined to punish me by asking the courts to grant him sole custody of Nathan. Of course,

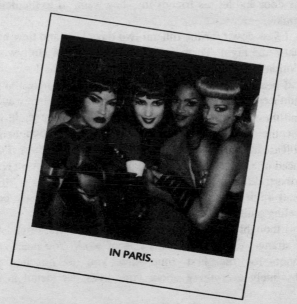

IN PARIS.

it all gnawed away at me no matter how hard I tried to ignore it, but there's nothing like a few drinks and bad sitcoms to ease the pain. You feel so much better about yourself as the liquor warms your belly and works its way toward the extremities. And everything on TV sounds so wonderfully witty when you're drunk. I giggled myself into exhaustion, drank and giggled my way to sleep.

Late one night, when I was watching Letterman, the phone rang. It was Debbie, calling to tell me that Mom had just passed away. I didn't know what to say, so I didn't say anything. Debbie got pissed and hung up. I sat there, numb, until I heard cars pulling up outside. Albert was home. He'd brought a bunch of hangers-on from the club—something he did almost every night.

"My mother died," I said.

"Gee," he said. "I'm sorry, honey." Then he went to get the door and let his friends in. They went off to the den to drink.

I flew down for the funeral two days later and flew back that same night. There was nothing for me in Hollywood, Florida, anymore. And it occurs to me now, as I say that, that there had never been anything for me there. Albert didn't come. When I got home, there was a letter waiting for me on the kitchen table. It was already open. It was from Stephanie Seymour: an engraved invitation to her bridal shower in Paris. She was about to marry Peter Brandt, a successful entrepreneur. Axl was history, of course. But we all had a little history, right?

"I think we should go," Albert said. He must have been feeling guilty. "We'll go and have a good time."

I thought about Stephanie and all the others. Friendship is strange, especially in this line of work. You meet on a shoot—for the first time—and you tell each other absolutely everything about your lives. No detail is too intimate. But then the shoot's over and you go back to your lives, as if you'd shared nothing, nothing at all, and find yourself feeling more alone than ever. I felt horribly alone at that moment. I missed the girls; I missed the sisterhood; I missed modeling. . . .

So we went to Paris. And we tried to have fun. We went to restaurants and clubs and I drank too much and I did too many drugs. Finally, it was time for Stephanie's party. I left Albert to his own devices and took a cab to the Bristol Hotel. Donatella Versace and Naomi Campbell, the hosts, had booked the penthouse suite, with its huge deck and lush gardens. Claudia Schiffer and Shalom Harlow and Amber Valetta were there. Donatella and Naomi made little speeches, and there were jokes about second marriages. Stephanie opened her gifts. We kept oohing and aahing over them. Sexy lingerie. Purses. A necklace or two. Stephanie began to cry. "I'm going to make it work this time," she said. "I need this to work. I really love this guy. It's not like last time."

We went to the Barfly afterward. We piled out of the limo—one girl more beautiful than the next—and into the nightclub. Heads snapped round: The men must have thought they'd died and gone to Party Model Heaven. We stayed in our little girls-only corner and got shit-faced, and I ended up on the table, doing a little bump-and-grind number for everyone in the place. It was an X-rated version of my adolescent dance at the Orange Bowl so many years ago, a lifetime ago. Men started throwing money at us. And the girls were laughing and grabbing the big bills and stuffing them between their tits. But suddenly I wasn't feeling very good. Naomi helped me off the table and led me to the bathroom, where I promptly threw up. And I realized it had nothing to do with the champagne or the cognac or the cocaine. I was sick over *me;* I was sick about *me;* I hated myself at that moment. I had just turned forty, and I'd made a fucking mess of my life.

"Are you all right?" Stephanie asked me. She'd come into the bathroom to see if she could help. I was still facing the bowl, like a goddamn bulimic.

"I'm fine," I said. "I just drank too much."

On the flight home, I couldn't even look at Albert. I had decided I was going to tell him everything—we were prisoners on the plane, a captive audience: why not just come clean?—but of course I told him nothing. I practiced, sure. In my head. In my head I told him it was over. In my head I gave him the ring back. In my head I told him we'd made a huge mistake and apologized for my part in it and suggested that we just move on with our lives and pretend it never happened. I explained that I had a great deal of work to do on myself, and that I wanted to get started before it was too late. It was bizarre, like one of those fantasy sequences in a movie. You think it's really happening until suddenly you hear that voice on the PA system—"Good evening, ladies and gentlemen. We're beginning our descent into the Los Angeles area"—and you turn to look at the person next to you and it hits you like a ton of bricks. *Jesus. This is me. This is my goddamn life.* That's when Albert turned to face me and smiled his sweet smile and said, "I love you, babe." And I smiled sweetly back and said, "I love you, too."

On the ride home, in the limo, I told myself I'd talk to him in the morning, when both of us were rested. Come clean. But I didn't talk to him the next morning, or the morning after that. I drank and watched sitcoms for what felt like weeks on end, and one night he came home in a frenzy and asked me who I was fucking.

"I'm not fucking anyone," I said.

"Liar!" he bellowed.

I asked him to keep his voice down; I was worried he'd wake Savannah. He grabbed my arm and we started pushing each other.

"Who are you fucking?" he asked again.

"No one," I said. I was crying by this time. He was yelling, and scaring the shit out of me. I mean, I'd never seen Albert like this.

"All right," he said. His teeth were clenched. His eyes were red with fury. He crossed to his desk and found a pad and paper and returned to my side and threw them at me. The pen fell to the floor.

"Pick it up," he said.

"Albert—"

"Pick the fucking pen up right fucking now!"

I reached for the pen. It was shaking in my hand. I couldn't stop shaking.

"Okay," he said. "I want you to write down the name of every man you ever fucked."

"Albert, that's crazy."

"What's the matter? Can't you remember? Are there too many to count, slut?"

"I can remember," I said. Tears were streaming down my cheeks. "But I don't want to remember. I've made my share of mistakes. Is that what you want to hear? I'm ashamed. I admit it."

"I don't see you writing," he said.

"I'm not doing this, Albert. You're crazy." I stood up and tried to leave, but he grabbed me and pulled me onto the couch, then sat next to me.

"Albert, please . . ." I started writing. I wrote every male name that popped into my head. I made up names. I wrote down the names of men I'd never slept with. I wrote and wrote and filled two pages with names: Colonel Sanders. Helmut Kohl. Don Knotts.

"Is that all?" Albert said.

"Yes," I said.

"I don't see Warren Beatty," he said.

I pointed out Warren Beatty's name.

"Where's Jack Nicholson?" he barked.

"There," I said. "A little farther up."

He looked. He seemed satisfied. "If I find out you left anyone out . . ."

"I didn't leave anyone out, Albert."

"I'm going to study this list carefully," he said.

"Can I go to bed now?" I asked.

He didn't answer. He went over to the desk, with the list, and switched on the Tizio lamp and sat down to read it. I went to bed. I popped two sleeping pills and drifted off, wondering how it had come to this. But I knew how it had come to this. I knew who was to blame. *I* was to blame. The big question was whether I was going to do anything about it.

ON MY OWN

❥❥❥❥❥❥❥❥❥❥❥❥❥❥❥❥❥❥❥❥❥❥❥❥❥❥❥❥❥❥❥

In the morning, Albert acted as if nothing had happened. I found him in the kitchen, staring into his coffee.

"Hey," he said.

"I'm leaving you," I said.

"What?"

"You heard me," I said.

"Why?" he said.

"Why? *Why?* Because you're fucking insane," I said. "That's why."

"I don't know what you're talking about," he said.

My jaw dropped. "You don't?" I asked.

"No," he said.

The minute he left the house, I packed what I could into a small bag, grabbed Savannah, and drove us to the Westwood Marquis. I cried as I checked in. I cried in the elevator. I cried when the doorman showed me the view.

Word got out fast, and people called. Everyone was very concerned about me, at least in principle, but only my gay friends really came through. Every last one of them offered me his home. All the others offered me the usual: "I'm here if you need me." "Let me know if there's anything I can do for you." "Let's have dinner Tuesday." It reminded me of that great cartoon in *The New Yorker*, of some executive standing at his desk, on the phone, saying, "No, Thursday's out. How's never? Is never good for you?"

Sly came by the hotel, unannounced and uninvited. He stood in front of me, shaking his head in disbelief. "I can't believe it," he said. I noticed he was staring at the engagement ring. "How many carats is that fucking thing?"

"Twenty-three," I said. I looked down at the ring, too. I made a mental note to myself to return it. In due time, of course.

Savannah woke up and began to cry. Sly looked over at her and suddenly he was in a foul mood. "Call me," he said. He split; I went off to change a diaper. I would've cried, but I was all cried out. I was dehydrated from crying. I remember thinking, *That can't be good for my skin.*

The next day I got a call from Jon Peters, the producer. He had a guest house in Beverly Hills that was bigger than any house I'd ever lived in. He asked me to bring Savannah over and move in. I packed up my things and my little girl and drove over to Jon's estate.

Jon Peters was very, very rich. He'd made a few bucks off *Batman,* and a couple hundred million more when he and his partner, Peter Guber, sold their production company to the Japanese geniuses at Sony Pictures. People said it was payback for Pearl Harbor. They gave them a lot of turkeys. But who hits a home run every time at bat?

The house—the *guest* house—was magnificent. The main house—well, I can't find words to describe it. Robin Leach could've lived a thousand lifestyles within those art-drenched walls.

Albert kept driving up to the forbidding front gates in his jet-black Ferrari, day after day, sometimes two and three times a day. He told the private security guards that I wanted to see him, that he had an appointment. He was insistent and belligerent. Finally, the guards asked him not to show his face again. If he did, they told him, life was going to get unpretty. Of course, the language they used was rather more descriptive.

So instead, Albert called and called, at all hours of the day and night, and I threatened to go to the police if he kept it up.

"Would you just tell me what I've done?" he wailed.

"You know what you've done," I said, and I hung up.

He kept on calling. He'd cry and cry, and even resorted to cursing me. "I was the best thing that ever happened to you," he said. "You're nothing without me!"

Jon Peters was a good friend and a perfect gentleman. Savannah played with his children. He had me over for dinner parties. Barbra Streisand was a frequent guest. I met Kevin Costner there. Will Smith. John Cusack. Mike Ovitz. I met more A-list talent in the next four months than I'd met in all the years prior and all the years since.

I took pictures of Jon and of his kids and he flipped over them and asked why I wasn't cashing in on my talent. So I called Sygma, the photo agency, and told them I wanted to get serious. I went out and took pictures and made money and lived life. And I still got occasional calls for

WITH JON PETERS IN 1994. HE HAS ALWAYS PROTECTED ME.

modeling jobs. They were generally jobs for a woman of a "certain age." I didn't ask for the jobs, but I took them. I was making ends meet, yes, but I was a long way from summer rentals in Southampton and platinum Rolexes. Still, who needed that? What I needed now was balance, forward movement; *peace*. Of course I didn't know where to find those things. I thought, briefly, about opening a small boutique: "Self-esteem? That'll be on Aisle Three, right next to Self-love." Ha ha.

My search led me, finally, to the bookstores. I began to haunt the self-help sections, floating among the shelves like a wounded ghost, always on the lookout for the latest Big Promise. I kept running into the same people over and over again—people who were as lost as I was. We would nod politely as we squeezed past each other in the aisles, too self-conscious to make eye contact. We were ashamed, I guess. We felt bad for being damaged, for being needy.

I was voracious. Insatiable. I was reading morning, noon, and night. But I wasn't finding what I was looking for. All the books told me the same thing. *Life is hard,* they said. I know life is hard, motherfucker. I'm just looking for a little basic happiness. "Oh? *Happiness? Basic* happiness? That's on Aisle Seven, just before Drooling Euphoria."

The phone rang one night. Two A.M. It was John Cusack. "I hear you're rowdy," he said.

"You hear wrong," I said.

"Come on," he said. "Come out and party."

I hung up on him. Every few weeks he'd call and ask me out and make me laugh. He sounded lonely. He sounded like he'd been drinking. I knew what that was like. Eventually, he stopped calling. But years later I ran into him on a plane en route to New York, and, well—what can I say? Shit happens.

* * *

In late August I found a house in Bel-Air, thanked Jon for his hospitality, and moved into my new digs. I didn't have a man in my life, but I had gay men in my life—thank God—and plenty of good friends. I discovered something important about friendship: It may be less exciting and less fulfilling than a passionate romance, but it's also less demanding, and less noisy. You can have a friend and still have a life. I'm sure you can have a man and have a life, too, I just didn't know how to do it, and I didn't feel like taking any chances. I felt "cured" of men. I wanted to believe I was cured. And I had my kids to keep me warm.

So I became a full-time mother. The morning rush to school, the box lunches, the play dates, the PTA meetings, the karate-computer-ballet-music-art classes—my kids consumed me. This was all deliberate, of course: the rapture of losing myself in them, of getting caught up in their little dramas. I'd had enough dramas of my own.

SAVANNAH GIVING ME A FACE.

I will be a better parent than my parents ever were, I promised myself, over and over. Of course, that wouldn't be too hard. A rabid dog would have been a better parent than my father. But I really meant it. I really truly wanted to be a good mother. After all, there's something miraculous about kids, all kids. There's such fragility there. Such hope. Such dependence. One day I watched Savannah go off to kindergarten with her little lunch box: She looked like a tiny businesswoman going off to her tiny job.

Nathan spent half his time at his father's house, the other half with me. He was angry about the divorce, and I couldn't blame him. I told him I was sorry we'd made such a mess of things, but that that didn't change how we felt about him, and that we both loved him so much we wanted to share him for the rest of our lives. He listened, but he was still angry. He could get angry about a cloudy day, a ripped shirt, soggy fries. I was patient with him, most of the time. But I lost it occasionally, and whenever I raised my voice and saw how much it frightened him, I was filled with remorse and self-loathing. *I will never again scream at him,* I told myself. *Never ever.* But of course I broke the promise now and then, and felt worse about it every time.

Guilt, the way it wears you down. I let him play Game-boy for hours and hours, and he spent way too much time on the computer, and I never made him eat his veggies. Pasta and cheeseburgers were all he ever wanted. I would have made him pheasant under glass if I thought he might eat it, but I didn't know how. I wasn't much of a cook, to be honest. Another shortcoming. Great! I guess I wasn't much good as a mother, after all. Maybe I wasn't much good, period.

That pithy little maxim my father had drummed into my head came pounding back like a migraine: *You'll never amount to anything.*

Once again I felt the presence of the lurking demon. I didn't know what to do about it. *He isn't real,* I assured myself. *It's just your imagination.* I could feel myself slipping into the abyss. I was terrified. I felt more alone than I'd ever felt in my life. I reached for my Filofax, desperate for help, and went through each name in my address book. There must have been four hundred of them—my *close, personal* friends. But by the time I got to the Zs I decided I couldn't call a single one. What would I tell them? *Well, like, you know, there's this fucking demon in my closet. He has a face like a goddamn gargoyle. And he follows me everywhere I go.* And what could they do? Arrange another intervention? Lock me up in a nuthouse?

WITH THE GALLANT TONY PECK, JULY 2000.

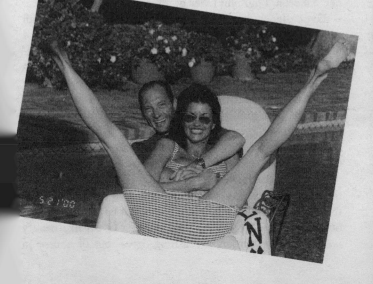

Then I began to rationalize my crazy thinking. I couldn't tell them what was going on because they didn't want to hear it. They didn't want to listen to my heavy shit. Life was all about surface. My friends liked me—if at all—because I was Crazy Janice. I was a good time.

But the truth ran deeper. I was afraid of the bogeyman because no one had ever been there to help me face him, to hold my hand and tell me everything was going to be all right. There was no lifeguard on duty. Never had been.

My phone rang. I was almost afraid to answer it.

"Hello?" I said.

"Want to grab a bite to eat?" It was my friend Tony Peck, Gregory's son and Cheryl Tiegs's ex-husband. He swung by to get me and we drove through Beverly Hills to dinner. I put the demon out of my mind, relegating him to the backseat. The streets were ablaze with Christmas decorations. The night was clear and crisp.

"What a beautiful night," I said, but to my ears I sounded like a moron. I thought I was going out of my mind.

Over dinner I smiled and laughed and gossiped and went on and on about my two wonderful kids. I guess I went on about them a little too long, though, because suddenly I noticed that Tony had lost interest. He wasn't even looking at me. He was looking at something across the room. Curious, I turned to look for myself. It was a beautiful woman. A girl, really. She couldn't have been more than twenty-one. I looked back at Tony. I was shattered. But the pain gave way, instantly, to anger.

"What?" he said. *Now* he was paying attention.

Okay, motherfucker. Fine. I know. I'm a long way from the girl I was twenty-odd years ago. In those days, I was the cliché. I would walk into a room and things would flat-out *change*. In those days, I did my best to act like beauty was a horrible burden, a crashing bore—but of course in those days I could afford to behave like that. In those days beauty worked for me. It worked for me in spades. Beauty opened all the doors; it got me things I didn't even know I wanted, and things I certainly didn't deserve. And now? What now? Who was I now? A pleasant diversion? Or was I even that much? After all, in this town, a town full of beautiful women, well—maybe I wasn't all that pleasant or all that diverting.

"So, Tony," I said, barely able to contain myself. "Have I lost my looks?"

"What?"

"No, no. Please. Be honest with me. I can take it."

"Jesus, Janice—"

"Fuck this," I snapped. I got to my feet and stormed out. Poor, innocent Tony. He followed me out to the street, wondering what he'd done wrong. The valet went off to fetch Tony's car, and Tony kept apologizing—God knows why!—and still I ignored him. When we reached my house I got out and slammed the door and went inside without so much as a good-bye. Then I fell apart.

What the hell was happening to me? I looked at myself in the mirror. Was it over? No, goddamn it! Heads still turned when I walked into a room; men still wanted me. Or did they? I needed to be wanted. I couldn't go on without being wanted. And I couldn't stop thinking about that little bitch at the restaurant. *I used to be that woman,* I thought. *I used to be the one who turned heads.*

Now . . . Christ . . . I was becoming invisible.

I went to look in on Savannah. She was fast asleep. She looked like a little angel. I could see so much of my former self in her little face. She was . . . she was almost seven years old. And it hit me like a car wreck: That was almost the same age I'd been when the rat bastard had done what he'd done. A loud, involuntary whelp of pain burst loose from deep inside me. Savannah stirred and turned on her side, but didn't wake. I hurried out of her room, shaking with rage and terror.

Twenty milligrams of Ambien put me out for the night, and I slept the sleep of the dead. Sweet, dreamless sleep. At seven A.M. Savannah burst into my room and crawled under the covers next to me.

"Is it almost Christmas yet?" she asked, snuggling close.

"Almost," I said.

"I can't wait," she said.

"What do you want from Santa Claus?" I asked her.

"A daddy," she said.

"Well, you know, honey, that's a tough one," I said. "But I'll ask."

"You keep saying you're going to tell me who my father is," she went on. "I really really really want to know."

I could feel my throat swelling with emotion. "Like I said, Sav, I'll see what I can do."

The whole morning, as I got her ready for school, I tried to keep it together: smiling like a lunatic, humming as I buttered her toast, laughing out of context.

"What's wrong, Mom?" she asked.

"Nothing," I said. "What could possibly be wrong?"

I drove her to school, got her settled in, got back in my car, and cranked up the music and went home. I pulled into the driveway, singing away at the top of my voice—*squawking*—and walked into my empty house and literally fell to the kitchen floor in tears. But I wasn't just crying; this went well beyond crying. These were loud, keening howls. I was experiencing pain like I'd never experienced it before. I couldn't stop. I was crying so hard I couldn't breathe. I counted to ten. I counted to ten again. I told myself I would stop crying the *next* time I counted to ten, but I couldn't manage it. I struggled to my feet, crossed the kitchen, and reached into the back of the cupboard for my bottle. As I poured myself a stiff drink, I looked at the kitchen clock. It wasn't even nine A.M.

I got back in my car and drove to West Hollywood, scored a couple of grams of coke, and raced home. The phone was ringing as I walked inside and I reached for it without thinking. It was Tony Peck.

"Leave me alone," I said, and hung up.

He kept calling. I grabbed my bottle of vodka and my coke, then went up to my room and did a couple of lines and drank the vodka straight from the bottle. The phone kept ringing. I tried to disconnect it, but I couldn't figure it out, so I yanked the wires right out of the wall. I had another snort, another hit of booze. I could hear the phone ringing downstairs. I didn't want to hear the phone, or any other goddamn thing. So I locked myself in the walk-in closet, and sat there among my designer dresses and designer shoes and designer fucking underwear and got drunk and buzzed and weepy. I was trying not to think. I was tired of thinking. Thinking had never done a goddamn thing for me. But I couldn't help it. I couldn't stop thinking about Savannah, and about what she needed in her life, and about what I had needed at her age and seemed, apparently, to need still. *A kid needs love, goddamn it. It's that fucking simple. Why can't I even get that right?*

I don't know how much time passed. It was pitch dark in the closet. The cocaine was gone. The vodka bottle was almost empty. I was thinking about crawling into my bedroom and calling the corner store and asking them to deliver a couple of quarts, when suddenly the closet door burst open and I saw the fucking monster standing there, silhouetted against the frame. *Oh my God*, I thought. *He's here! He's come for me!*

But it wasn't the monster. It was Tony Peck.

"Jesus Christ, Janice," he said. "What are you doing to yourself?" He picked me up, as if I were a child, and carried me into the bathroom. He stripped me and sat me in the tub and turned on the shower, then went downstairs to make a gallon of strong coffee.

Two hours later we were in his car, pulling up to a little café on Sunset Boulevard. It was across the street from the Chateau Marmont, where my friend John Belushi had died. We went into the café, which had been cleared of tables, and sat near the back, on stiff, metal folding chairs that had been laid out in neat rows. A middle-aged woman was telling her sad story to several dozen attentive listeners. It was a pretty compelling story. Marriage, drinking, divorce, remarriage, more drinking, another divorce, some whoring around, still more drinking . . .

I signed up. They gave me some twelve-step literature. They paired me up with a young woman who looked like she'd lived too hard for too long. I promised to call if I felt like having a drink. Tony dropped me at home. I poured myself a stiff drink, to brace myself for what was coming, then did what I'd been instructed to do: dumped every last ounce of alcohol in the house.

That first night was hell—and it was only the beginning. I went to see my doctor the next morning. He gave me a little Valium and warned me not to overdo it. I took some Valium: I felt like washing it down with a drink. So I called my female "buddy"; kept calling; called at all hours of the day and night. I called Tony Peck. I called numbers at random and tried to engage strangers in conversation. (I felt so fucking alone—and so fucking scared.) I went over to see my neighbor and asked for a drink, and he was kind enough to say no—even when I started screaming at him like a crazy woman.

And then, good God—it got better. I woke up one morning and I had this strange feeling that today was going to be easier. And it was. Don't get me wrong—it was no walk in the park. But I managed. Without falling apart.

"I think I'm finding my way back," I told Tony.

"Good," he said. "I knew you would."

I went off to shoot Sharon Stone. "You seem different, Janice," she said as I fiddled with my camera. We had met before—a lifetime ago, when she was a nobody and had come to pose for Mike Reinhardt; then later, on the set of *The Specialist*, along with my not-so-good old buddy Sly.

"Different bad or different good?" I asked.

"Different good," she said.

I felt like hugging her, but I didn't. I just took my pictures and packed up my gear and headed home.

Christmas came and went. I made it through without a drink, and Savannah made it through without a daddy. She got other presents—too many, of course, because I felt so guilty—and she seemed to like most of them.

BICEPS BY YOU-KNOW-WHO. HOLLYWOOD, CALIFORNIA, 1994.

Early in January we went to the mall to return the ones she didn't want. We were coming off the escalator when I saw Michael Birnbaum moving toward us. My heart leapt into my throat. We hadn't seen each other in close to seven years. He froze. I froze.

"Hello, Michael," I said.

"Hello," he said. He looked down at Savannah—anything to avoid meeting my eyes—and smiled at her. "And who might you be?" he asked.

"Savannah," she said.

"Savannah," he repeated. "What a beautiful name."

He looked back up at me. Like everyone else in the world, he'd read the tabloids during my very public breakup with Stallone, so he knew that Savannah was the child in question—the child who didn't belong to Sly. I wondered if *he'd* ever wondered whether she was his, but then I realized he had no reason to wonder. The papers had made me look like a total slut. I'd had one very bad week, certainly—three men in three days; not my finest hour—but, contrary to popular opinion, I didn't fuck everything that moved.

Jesus. The way Michael was looking at me. I wanted to grab him by the lapels and pin him to the wall and say, "You dumb bastard! She's your daughter! Look at her, goddamn it! The same coloring, the same long limbs, the same cheekbones! A blind person can see the resemblance!"

And that's exactly what I did—in my mind. Another exciting Hollywood fantasy sequence: passersby stopping to stare. Savannah sobbing. Michael taking her in his arms and blubbering like a baby.

But I decided not to make a scene.

"It was nice to see you after all these years," Michael said.

"It was nice to see you, too," I said, calm as can be.

"Call me sometime," he said. "I'm listed." Then he looked down at Savannah. "Nice to meet you, Savannah."

"Can we go now?" Savannah said, and Michael laughed that nice laugh of his and went on his way.

I had a drink when I got home. Just a little one, from the small bottle of vodka I picked up at the corner store. It tasted fucking great. But I only had one. And then another little one before bed. Just a teeny weeny one.

The next day I didn't have a drink at all. But I knew where the bottle was. My twelve-step buddy called, wanting to know why she hadn't heard from me. "Not hearing from me is supposed to be a good thing, right?" I said. She laughed and told me she was there if I needed her. Tony Peck called. We chatted a bit. He said I sounded different. "Different good or different bad?" I asked.

"Not good or bad," he said. "Just different." But I could tell he was concerned.

I had a little tiny drink the next day. Just one—honest. And two very tiny drinks the day after that. Then I began to lose count. I went to the corner store for more booze. I went so often that the clerks were reaching for the bottle before I reached the counter. I started hiding bottles everywhere. I felt like I was starring in my own version of *Days of Wine and Roses*. I got very drunk one night and found myself having an imaginary conversation with Jack Lemmon, who was nominated for an Academy Award for his role in that amazing movie. "I'm proud of you, Jack," I slurred. "You came out of it all right."

And Jack got a dirty little gleam in his eye and said, "You're a good-looking girl, Janice."

And I said, "I'll drink to that!" And I did.

Savannah walked into the room in the middle of one of these little fantasies. "Who're you talking to, Mom?" she asked.

"Nobody," I said, slurring. "I had the TV on."

"Why are you talking funny?"

"Funny? Who's talking funny? The only talking we're going to do around here is serious talking. So I'm going to ask you again, seriously, are you sure you don't want to go to Disneyland for your birthday? We can take five of your best friends."

"No," she said. "I told you. I want to go to The Time Machine." The Time Machine was some arcade-type place on Ventura Boulevard. We'd been there often, just to pass the time, and Savannah loved it. But I wanted to give her something special.

"How about the zoo?" I asked. "Or the Santa Monica Pier? We can have it at the carousel at the Pier. You can bring your whole class."

"No," she said. "I want to go to The Time Machine."

The next day, after I packed her off to school, I popped two Advil, washed them down with cognac, and dug up Michael Birnbaum's listed number and called him.

"Hi, Michael," I said. "It's me."

"Wow," he said.

"You asked me to call."

"So I did," he said.

"How would you like to go to your daughter's seventh birthday party? It's a couple of weeks from now. We're having it at The Time Machine, on Ventura Boulevard. It should be fun." He didn't say anything. "Michael?" Still nothing, but I could hear him breathing on the other end. "Michael?"

"What did you just say?" he asked. He couldn't disguise the shock in his voice. He sounded depleted. He sounded, in fact, like he'd been punched in the gut.

"I'm sorry," I said. I began to cry. "I wanted to tell you but I didn't know how to tell you. Simon tried to take

Nathan away from me. I didn't want to go through that again. I don't want to lose my daughter."

"That little girl—the little girl at the mall last month? She's *mine*?" Michael was still in shock.

"I guess I could have found a better way of breaking it to you. I'm sorry. I just—what was I going to say? Will you come to her birthday? Please?"

"Give me your number," he said. "I need a few minutes."

I gave him my number and he hung up without saying good-bye. I waited for him to call back. He didn't call back. I had another drink. The phone rang. I thought it was Michael, but it was Tony Peck.

"You sound like you've been drinking," Tony said.

"No," I said. "I'm stuffed up. I think I feel a cold coming on."

"You want me to believe that?" he asked.

"Yes," I said.

"Okay," he said. "I'll believe it."

"Can we talk later?" I said.

"I'm here," he said.

I hung up and had another drink. Savannah came home. We swung by Simon's house, and I picked up Nathan and took them both to California Pizza Kitchen for dinner. I wanted desperately to order a glass of wine, but I restrained myself. I ate everything they wouldn't eat: Pizza. Pasta. All the bread and butter. The remains of two ice-cream sundaes. When I took Nathan back to his father's place, I hugged him so hard his bones practically cracked.

"You okay, Mom?" he asked me.

"Never better," I said.

I drove home and put Savannah to bed and started reading *The Three Little Wolves and the Big Bad Pig*. It's a very funny story, and Savannah could never get enough of it. I had to stop a few pages in, to catch my breath.

"What's wrong, Mom?" she asked.

"Nothing," I said. "I love the way the Big Bad Pig changes."

"That's no reason to cry," she said.

She was wrong. The Big Bad Pig could change, but *I* was never going to fucking change. I pulled myself together and finished the story and turned out the light and tucked her in.

"Good night," I said.

"I love you, Mom," she said.

"I love you, too," I said, and I crept out of the room and down the hall to my own. I lay on the bed, lost in deep, troubling thought, until sleep carried me away.

The next morning, a Saturday, Savannah was back in bed with me, snuggling again. "I want to make my own birthday invitations," she said.

"Okay," I said. And that's what we did. We sat at the table in the den, Savannah and I, making the invitations on the computer. She wanted them to be perfect. She drew a little ticking clock in the upper left-hand corner. "Get it?" she said. "*Time Machine*. A clock. Time."

"Very clever," I said.

We printed out the invitations and she had me hand-address each envelope. "You have beautiful handwriting, Mom," she said. "I hope I have beautiful handwriting when I grow up."

"Of course you will," I said. "They have handwriting classes in Beverly Hills."

"Really?"

"No," I said, smiling down at her. "I'm just kidding."

"You're funny, Mom."

We walked hand in hand to the corner mailbox, with our stack of envelopes. We were inviting every kid in her class, along with assorted hangers-on. She insisted on dropping the envelopes through the slot one by one, counting as she went. "Boy," she said, "I'm really popular, huh?"

"Yes," I said. "A girl can't get more popular than you."

On the way back to the house, I realized we hadn't printed up an invitation for Birnbaum. *Well, fuck him,* I thought. *He knows the truth now. Maybe he'll do the right thing.*

Her birthday fell on a Thursday that year—February 24, 2001—but we were having the party a couple of days later, the following Saturday. Still, I wanted that Thursday to be special, too. I invited Nathan for dinner, along with two of Savannah's best friends, and a good time was had by all. I sang loudly and embarrassed my kids. Everyone was laughing. When Savannah blew out the candles, I felt like I was looking at a Norman Rockwell painting. Or *part* of a painting, anyway. The good part. A bunch of happy kids. And me? I stayed on the fringes, trying not to ruin the picture.

I crawled into bed that night feeling pretty good about myself—better, in fact, than I had in a very long time. For days now, I'd been running around like a typical suburban mother. We weren't going to overdo it, I told Savannah. We weren't trying to compete. But we still needed the expensive caterers for the peanut-butter-and-jelly sandwiches, and the helium balloons with Savannah's name on them, and the Pokemon birthday cake from the best bakery in Los Angeles. As I lay there thinking about what I still needed to do, the phone rang. It was Michael Birnbaum. "We need to talk," he said.

We met for drinks the following night. He picked a nightclub that was loud and dark. I guess he didn't want me to see his face. Maybe he was worried he might start crying. What is it about men and tears? The guy had a right to cry; he *should've* been crying.

I explained again why I'd never told him about Savannah, how afraid I'd been of losing her. And I apologized for the way I'd treated him when we were together. "I'm really ashamed," I said. "I have done a lot of things in my life I'm ashamed of, but this is at the top of the list."

"I can't believe I have a daughter," he said.

"Will you forgive me?" I asked. He didn't answer. "Will you come to her party? It's tomorrow."

Michael took a long time answering. Then he shook his head from side to side. "I don't think so," he said. "I don't think that's the right place for it."

"Please don't abandon her, Michael," I begged. "Please don't punish her for my mistakes."

"What must people think of me?" he said. "That I'm a five-minute dad?"

"Nobody knows, Michael. I'm the only one who knows."

"No," he said. He was angry. "*I* know."

"Why don't you just say 'This is great. I have a lovely young daughter. I'm a lucky man,' and move on?"

But he didn't say it. He signed the bill and left without a good-bye. I didn't know what to do with myself. I ordered a drink. And then another. And then I walked upstairs, to the disco, and sat at the bar and had a drink. I watched the people on the dance floor, kids mostly, and thought of the kid I had been. Christ, I was a middle-aged woman. *Was I ever going to figure any of it out?*

I didn't finish my drink. I went outside and got in my car and drove home.

CLEAN AND SOBER

>>>

The next morning, Savannah woke me up an hour earlier than usual.

"Come on," she said. "Today's my party!"

I only had a trace of a hangover, thanks largely to a megadose of aspirin the night before.

"What party?" I said, but I was smiling. Savannah laughed. She couldn't contain herself. She wanted me up and dressed and ready to rock and roll. We had to make sure we were at The Time Machine early, *real* early. So she dragged me downstairs and I made breakfast—Corn Pops for her, coffee for me—and we were there by eleven o'clock.

The balloons arrived. The caterers arrived. The cake arrived. And then the kids arrived. And for the next four hours everyone had loads of fun. Including me. I looked at all those happy kids and thought, *This is it. This is as good as it gets*.

I bought Savannah a new Barbie doll, along with the huge expensive dollhouse she'd been pining for since Christmas. (So I overdid it; sue me.) I helped her set it up when we got home, but not until after she'd bathed and changed into her pajamas. "I love it," she said, admiring her collection. "That was my best birthday ever, Mom. Honest."

"Guess what?" I said. "They're just going to keep getting better."

"Really!?"

"Yes," I said. I was going to make sure of it.

I tucked her in and kissed her on the forehead and turned out the light. She was asleep before I left her room.

I had saved one present for last, though Savannah didn't know about it, and I wasn't sure she ever would. I got back to my bedroom and picked up the phone and called my friend Tony Peck to make the necessary arrangements.

"It's me," I said. "I'm ready to try again."

On Monday morning, after I'd dropped Savannah at school, I met Tony at the café on Sunset Boulevard. I stayed sober . . . for five miserable days. Then I tried again and failed again and tried again. But the periods between drinks began to get longer and longer, and there were times when I actually felt like a human being. (A frightened one, to be sure, but a human being all the same.)

It was during one of those periods that I invited Simon to lunch. He had remarried, and though I'd never really made peace with the idea that I could be "replaced," in my sobriety I realized it had nothing to do with replacing me— it was about moving on, which is something we all need to do. So we made up. And I asked him if I could see more of Nathan. And he said sure, whatever I wanted, and he smiled at me. It was a nice smile, too. I'd always loved the little gap between his teeth.

"I didn't know it was going to be this easy," I said.

"Life can be remarkably easy," he said. "We're the ones who make it hard."

A week later, still sober, I called Michael. I took him to lunch, too. I wanted to face him in broad daylight, pores and all. We met poolside at the swank Peninsula Hotel, in the heart of Beverly Hills.

"I want you to get to know your daughter," I said. "She's a terrific human being. And you're not so bad yourself. So don't let me down."

He didn't let me down. He agreed to come over the following Sunday, in the early evening. But he asked me to prepare her for his visit.

I kept wondering what I was going to tell Savannah. I practiced in front of the mirror. "Sav—good news! I found your daddy!" Or, "Sav, does the name Michael Birnbaum mean anything to you? Well, don't worry, it will." It all sounded pretty lame.

Finally, Sunday morning rolled around. I could no longer put it off. Savannah and I took the dogs for a long hike, and I told her the whole truth, more or less. I told her that I'd been involved with more than one man when she was conceived, and that I didn't know which one her father was, and that by the time I'd found out it was too late: I was no longer involved with any of them. "But I had you," I said. "And I didn't want to lose you. And I decided I would raise you on my own."

"Wow," she said. "He didn't even want to visit me?"

"Oh, honey—that wasn't it at all," I said. "He didn't even know you existed. That was my fault. I never told him about you."

"But you've told him now?"

"Yes," I said.

She took a beat. It was a lot to handle. "And he wants to visit?"

"He's coming for dinner tonight. But only if it's okay with you."

"Tonight?"

"Tonight. Late this afternoon."

She thought about this some more. "I'm a little nervous," she said finally.

"I can understand that," I said. "But you have nothing to worry about. He's a terrific guy. I think you're going to like him."

"Do you think he's going to like me?"

"I showed him pictures. He said he's never seen a more beautiful little girl. And I'll let you in on a little secret . . . "

"What?"

"He's a little nervous, too. He wants to make sure you like him, too."

She thought about this, then stopped to dig a pebble out of her sneaker. "Do I have to call him 'Daddy'?" she asked.

"No," I said. "You can call him Michael."

"Good," she said.

We made arrangements to meet at the Santa Monica Pier in front of the lemonade stand, and Michael arrived at 5:30 sharp. He was visibly nervous. I loved him for it. He actually reached down and shook Savannah's hand and told her it was nice to meet her.

"I'm not going to call you 'Daddy,' " Savannah said by way of introduction. "Not for right now, anyway."

"Okay," Michael said. He was smiling. He was *grinning*.

"Would you like a glass of lemonade?" she asked, pointing to the drink.

"I think so," Michael said.

"Well," she said, "come with me." She took him by the hand and led him to the counter and started ordering lemonade for Mom and Dad. I watched them from a short distance.

We sat outside, just the three of us. It was a warm, breezy night in Southern California. The three of us sipped lemonade. Savannah talked nonstop. She wanted him to know everything about her life. She told him about every

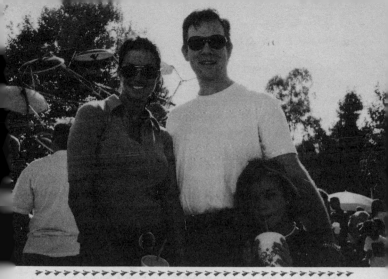

kid in her class. Told him about her birthday party. Described everything in great detail, from the Pokemon cake to her "most favorite" presents.

"I have a brother," she said. "Nathan Fields."

"Do you see a lot of him?"

"He's here all the time!" she said.

"That sounds nice," he said.

"He had two hamsters," she said.

"Oh God!" I said. "Please don't tell him that story."

"My mother was supposed to take care of them one week," she went on, completely ignoring me. "Nathan was away with his dad."

"Savannah—"

"Mom forgot to feed them. So one of them ate the other one. Or part of him, anyway. It was gross."

Michael gave me a look.

"All right," I said, shrugging my shoulders. "I'm not perfect."

"My mother used to be a famous model," Savannah said.

"So I'd heard," Michael said.

"She was the original supermodel," she said.

"That's what I'd been told," Michael said, and he looked at me. He was nice to look at.

"I hope we'll be seeing more of you," I said.

"Me too," he said.

When we walked him back to his Porsche at the end of the evening, he asked Savannah for a little hug. She gave him one—just a little one—and said, "That's enough."

"Thanks for coming," I said.

"You're welcome," he said.

"When will we see you again?" I asked. I had promised myself not to ask, but I couldn't help myself.

"I'm pretty open this week," he said. "Next week, too. I'm sort of, like, you know—available." He smiled that Michael smile again. "At the moment, I'm pretty much open for the rest of my life. For *her*, anyway."

"You bastard," I said. "You're going to make me cry."

He didn't kiss me good-bye. He waved as he drove off, and I closed my eyes, squeezed Savannah's hand, and thanked God for a perfect evening.

FAMILY

❯❯❯❯❯❯❯❯❯❯❯❯❯❯❯❯❯❯❯❯❯❯❯❯❯❯❯❯❯❯❯❯❯❯❯

Every day I am closer to becoming the person I want to be. I am becoming myself. I wake up in the morning and I look forward to the day ahead. I look forward to breakfast. I look forward to the drive to school with Savannah. I look forward to sitting home nights with a good book. I look forward to weekends with both my children. I look forward to Savannah's gymnastics class and Nathan's baseball practice. Sometimes I believe I even look forward to their whining.

At the end of the day, we are a family. Families come in all shapes and sizes. The

LOOKING LIKE THE FLORIDA GIRL I STARTED OUT AS.
❯❯❯❯❯❯❯❯❯❯❯

permutations are endless. And this is my family. It's not a traditional family, no, but it's a real family. And I love my family.

When I was growing up, my parents weren't good to me. There wasn't any love there. I didn't feel good about myself. So I spent the better part of my life looking for reasons to feel good about myself. If a man wanted me, I felt good about myself. If I got the cover of *Vogue,* I felt good about myself. If I made lots of money, I felt good about myself. And, sure, those are wonderful reasons to feel good. But they aren't enough. At the end of the day, life isn't about having other people telling you that you're wonderful. That's too goddamn risky. Because down the line there's always the chance they might *stop* telling you you're wonderful. That they'll stop wanting you for the cover of *Vogue.* That they'll stop loving you. I understood this, sure. But for a long time I couldn't accept it. All I remembered was what that one shrink had told me—that I didn't feel lovable; and it was true. I didn't feel lovable. And it frightened the hell out of me.

It also made me angry. I was angry about what had been done to me as a child, and the more I thought about it the angrier I became.

One afternoon, not all that long ago, feeling particularly angry, and wallowing in self-pity, I broke down and drove to the local liquor store. But I stopped myself at the door and got back in my car and went home. And I dug up an old notebook and began to write.

The words just poured out of me. I wrote about my anger. And about my pain. I wrote about all the things I'd been told but had never truly understood. This whole business about the familiar, for example, how we re-create history because we think we can fix it: I'd been doing that my whole life. I'd been looking for men I could turn into my father; men who wanted me as he had wanted me, for sex; men who treated me as he had treated me—as worthless trash.

And suddenly it struck me: I was still seeing myself through my father's eyes. *I was still letting my father define me.*

Yeah. There it was. My epiphany. One moment—a blinding flash—and you fucking *get it.* Well, no. Not quite. Just because you understand a problem doesn't mean you've conquered it. But it's a great first step.

It had taken me forty years to figure out that I'd spent my entire life seeing myself as my father had seen me. He told me that I was worthless and unlovable, and I believed him. I was a fucking child, for God's sake—of course I believed him. There was one version of Janice—his version—and I'd been clinging to it since the beginning: *I'm worthless. I'm unlovable. I'm only good for sex.*

I thought, *If only I could stop seeing myself through his eyes.* . . . And I wrote that down—words that changed my life: *Stop seeing yourself through his eyes.*

Simple words, yes. But they really, truly changed my life.

In the weeks and months ahead, I kept writing—working, unknowingly, on what would eventually become this book—and learned more about myself than I had in the preceding four decades.

I learned that change is hard, for everyone. And that if I wanted to change, I was going to have to fight like hell. And I did. I fought because I was tired of waking up in the morning and looking in the mirror and seeing the Janice my father had defined for me. It was time to create my own definitions.

I began to *imagine* myself as the person I wanted to be.

I wanted to be *good* and *lovable* and a *great mother* and a whole lot more. And I began to behave as if I were truly good and lovable and a whole lot more. And damn if it didn't begin to work!

Fake it till you make it. That was my new mantra. Act good till you are good. Act confident, and confidence will take you over. "Act out" the person you want to be. Act patient, interested, Zen—and you will become those things, and more.

I began to act as if success were inevitable, as if I was already the person I wanted to be.

And it worked. Sometimes. Sometimes it only worked for a few hours. Sometimes it worked for several days, weeks even. And sometimes—sometimes the past would rear its ugly head. And I would feel terrible about myself all over again. Until I began to see the past for what it was worth. The past had been my education. All those mistakes and heartbreak and failures and humiliations—those experiences had shaped me. The person I was then had turned me into the person I was becoming, and I was beginning to like the new me. Really truly. I would look in the mirror and think, "You're okay, babe. You're better than okay. You *rock.*"

So I began getting over the past. I stopped blaming everything on my father, my childhood, my early experiences, society's "injustices," whatever. *Why dwell on them?* I told myself. *I've learned all I'm going to learn from them, and now it's time to move on.* I didn't need the past anymore. The past explained how I got here. But the future—well, the future was my responsibility.

I had another responsibility, too—far greater even than my responsibility to myself. I was responsible for my two children. I wanted them to be happy, sure. But happiness is elusive. It comes and goes. And what they needed from me was something that went well beyond happiness, something I never got from my own family: a sense of *self-worth*.

And I give it to them every day. I *try*, anyway. I listen when they talk. I validate their feelings. I'm there for them. Most of all, I try to make them feel loved; I try to impress upon them that they really matter, that there's a place for them in the world. I have faith that this will make all the difference in their lives. They will grow up feeling good about themselves. *Worthy*. And people who feel good about themselves are generally good to others. Goodness begets goodness. Love begets love.

Yeah—change is fucking hard. But it's worth it. Here's one small example:

Last year, I took Savannah and Nathan to the annual pre-Halloween fund-raiser at Warner Elementary, in Holmby Hills, where Savannah goes to school. Simon said he'd meet us there. Michael said he'd try to make it, too.

So we get there. It's crowded. There are carnival rides and games and balloons and lots of food, and a band is just warming up on stage. And everyone's coming up to congratulate me, like it was my party or something. And, sure—in some small ways—it *was*. I'm on the goddamn PTA, people. I helped organize it. I'm there taking pictures for the yearbook. And I'm thanking them and grinning my alligator grin and here comes Simon Fields, my ex, with his wife, Melanie, and their adorable little rugrat, Isabel. And we say hello and hug each other—and we fucking *mean* it. I am hugging these people with genuine love. This man is the father of my eldest child, and he is not a bad person. And this is the woman who is making him happy.

And a moment later Michael shows up. And of course everyone knows everyone, because life is full of ironies. And this week both Simon and Michael have movies opening in theaters nationwide: Simon produced *Serendipity*, starring John Cusack. Michael produced *Bandits*, starring Bruce Willis and Billy Bob Thornton. And then Nathan comes up—and he's talking *numbers*, box-office grosses. And I look at him and think, *I swear to God, my little poet is going to be running a Hollywood studio some day.*

And for a moment there I feel like I'm having an out-of-body experience. I see myself literally floating above my little gang. Nathan and Savannah and Michael and Simon and Melanie. And I'm thinking, *These are great people! I am lucky to have these people in my life!*

And it's all so cordial. All of us behaving like regular goddamn people. And it hits me. *I'm an adult, for God's sake. I am an ex-wife and mother. I am all grown up.* I'm not freaking out. I'm not patting my pocket for my vial of cocaine, or looking around for a drink. I'm not jumping out of my skin. I'm just plain fucking happy. And I take a deep breath and find myself smiling like a lunatic.

WITH MY KIDS AND SIMON AT NATHAN'S SEVENTH BIRTHDAY.

Of course, I know: Life has a way of wiping that smile off your face. I'm going about my business and it all comes flooding back, sudden and terrifying. The years of abuse. The torture. The bad marriages. The foolish choices. And suddenly I feel like Alice again, tumbling down the rabbit hole. And I wonder whether I'll ever stop falling, and where I'll land this time. And I'm here to tell you: *It is goddamn terrifying*. Falling, twisting, tumbling—with that evil goddamn demon breathing down my neck.

And just as suddenly, I stop falling. Usually. And I realize I'm okay. No bones broken. Heart's racing a little, sure, but it'll ease up in a few minutes. And I'm here, right? *Alive*. I've fallen into the abyss before and surely I'll fall in again. And I'll be stronger for it. It's not going to kill me. I've survived this fall and I'll make it through the next.

There. See? Heart rate practically normal now. No demons here; just me, good old Janice. And that's my face in the mirror. Not bad. I mean, sure, gravity's done a number on it. And sometimes I think I need a little plastic surgery to go with my Manolo Blahniks. But I'm not there yet, babe. No. I'm fine. I'm holding up fine. I'm holding up almost as well as my tits. I'm a fucking champ.

Okay, you say. *That's all very well and good, Janice. But what about love?*

You're asking me?

Thousands of years of civilization and nobody's figured it out yet. Is it real? An illusion? An illness? Is it a biological imperative? A trick of nature to make us procreate?

I don't know. I'm not sure anyone does. But I'll tell you what it *isn't*. It isn't what Hollywood tells you it is. It isn't that at all, not by a long shot.

I'll give you an example. The other day I was watching *Jerry Maguire*—for the third time. It's a wonderful movie. But there's a scene in it that's all wrong. It's the scene where Tom Cruise breaks down in front of Renee Zellweger, and—his voice cracking with emotion—tells her: "You complete me."

Not to put too fine a point on it, people, but that scene—that scene is complete bullshit. That scene right there—that's what makes it so hard for the rest of us, those of us who have to operate in the Real World.

Hollywood—Jesus. These romantic illusions; that's the *real* violence.

I don't need another person to complete me, *amigo*. I need to complete myself. And I don't need another person to make me happy; I need to make *myself* happy. And not with drink or drugs, but with real homegrown happiness—happiness that comes from within. Happiness that comes from change—changes in me, not in others.

The funny thing is, most people don't even know what makes them happy. I mean, seriously. Think about it. Ask yourself what makes you happy. Friendship? Good sex? A hot car? Health? Money? Freedom? And when something makes you happy, does it really make you happy for any length of time?

Men are okay, yes. But I like being a mother, with all its ups and downs. And I like food; food is no longer the enemy. And I like yoga and taking my dogs for a run in the hills above my house and going to movies on Sunday afternoons.

I like dating, too. Sitting in a nice restaurant with a man who might or might not become a lover. I like knowing that it's my choice; I like knowing that his wanting me isn't really the issue. Of course he wants me. Hell, he's a guy. That's what men *do:* want us.

But things have changed. Big-time. Nowadays, *I* want me, too. And you know what? Sometimes that's plenty.

I called Alexis the other day and said, "We don't talk

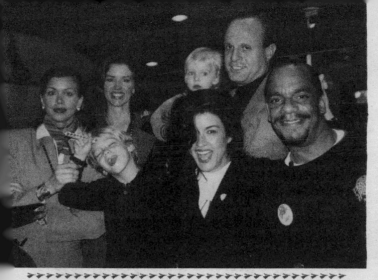

A FAMILY I CAN LOVE. TOP, FROM LEFT: DEBBIE, ALEXIS, ALEXIS'S SON, MORGAN, MITCH. BOTTOM ROW: NATHAN, ME, AND SOME SEXY MAN.

enough." And she said, "You're right, we don't." She has a ten-year-old son now, a husband who adores her, and a real suburban-mom life. "Hold on," she said. She put her son on the speaker-phone and he played his cello for me. He was astonishing.

I called Debbie, too. We don't talk enough, either. She's the mother of a wonderful six-year-old son and she's doing all kinds of things—acting, modeling, public relations, teaching kids, and being actively happy. We talked about our aches and pains. And she said, "I love my life."

God, she's changed. And Alexis has changed. And *I've* changed!

The thing is, life is *dynamic;* it's *about* change. And when we change, as we must, inevitably, the things that make us happy tend to lose their hold. So the hot car doesn't make us as happy as it used to. And the good sex isn't all that good anymore. And that friendship has lost its allure. And our love? Where did it go? When did we stop loving each other?

At the end of the day, I've learned to stop looking for The Answer. Because there isn't *one* answer. There are many answers. Love is not the answer. It's *part* of the answer. And money's nice, too. As is sex and good health and flirting at the mall.

And passion's nice, too. Remember passion?

But passion can be many things. Passion can be gardening. Hiking. Passion can be salsa dancing. Or writing a book like this book. Passion can be big and unwieldy and mind-bending, or it can be many small passions that add up to—well, a life, a real life.

This is what my life is now. Friendships. Health. Sobriety. Good works. Photography. And motherhood. Yes, motherhood most of all. Don't tell me there's nothing heroic about being a mother; it doesn't get more heroic. The notion of taking a child, shaping him, helping him grow—of guiding him along in this uncertain world—does it really get any better than that, people?

Okay. Sure. I've made my share of mistakes. Maybe more than my share. And I'm not proud of everything I've done. But I'm proud of who I am today and proud of the woman I hope to become. As I said, I was shaped by my mistakes and disappointments just as I was shaped by my successes. But I'm done with history. The past explains how I got here, but the future is up to me.

And what a future!

I'm Janice, babe. I broke the mold. I lived life at full throttle.

Vroom.

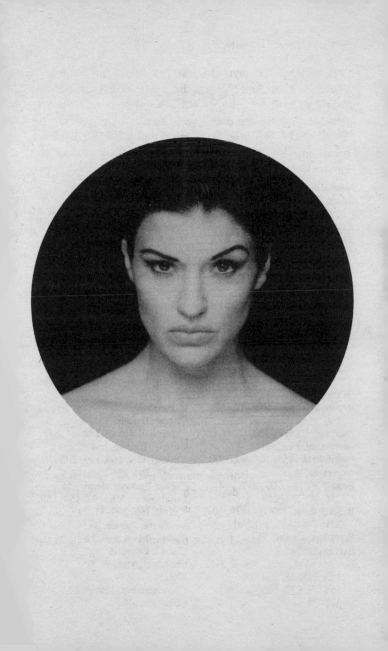

INDEX

Bestselling intimate portraits
of the people behind the personalities

NO LIFEGUARD ON DUTY
The Accidental Life of the World's First Supermodel
by Janice Dickinson
> 0-06-056617-5/$7.99 US/$10.99 Can

GEORGE AND LAURA
Portrait of an American Marriage
by Christopher Andersen
> 0-06-103224-7/$7.99 US/$10.99 Can

HAVE A NICE DAY!
A Tale of Blood and Sweatsocks
by Mankind
> 0-06-103101-1/$7.99 US/$10.99 Can

THE ROCK SAYS
The Most Electrifying Man in Sports-Entertainment
by The Rock, with Joe Layden
> 0-06-103116-X/$7.99 US/$10.99 Can

CELINE DION
My Story, My Dream
by Celine Dion
> 0-380-81905-8/ $7.99 US

WALK THIS WAY:
The Autobiography of Aerosmith
by Aerosmith, with Stephen Davis
> 0-380-79531-0/ $7.99 US/ $10.99 Can

EINSTEIN: THE LIFE AND TIMES
by Ronald W. Clark
> 0-380-01159-X/$7.99 US/$10.99 Can

....